Unconscious for Sale

Theory and History of Literature
Edited by Wlad Godzich and Jochen Schulte-Sasse

For other books in the series, see p. 215.

Unconscious for Sale
Advertising, Psychoanalysis, and the Public

Doris-Louise Haineault and Jean-Yves Roy

Foreword by Wlad Godzich

Translated by Kimball Lockhart
with Barbara Kerslake

Theory and History of Literature, Volume 86

University of Minnesota Press
Minneapolis
London

Originally published as *L'Inconscient qu'on affiche*. Copyright 1984 by Editions Aubier
Montaigne, Paris.

Published by the University of Minnesota Press
2037 University Avenue Southeast, Minneapolis, MN 55455-3092
Printed in the United States of America on acid-free paper

Library of Congress Cataloging-in-Publication Data

Haineault, Doris-Louis.
  [Inconscient qu'on affiche.   English]
  Unconscious for sale : advertising, psychoanalysis, and public
life / Doris-Louise Haineault and Jean-Yves Roy : translated by
Kimball Lockhart with Barbara Kerslake.
      p.   cm. — (Theory and history of literature : v. 86)
  Includes bibliographical references and index.
  ISBN 0-8166-2185-3 (hard). — ISBN 0-8166-2186-1 (pbk.)
  1. Advertising—Psychological aspects.   I. Roy, Jean-Yves, 1942-
II. Title.   III. Series.
HF5822.H26713   1993
659.1'01'9—dc20   92-32340
                                                                   CIP

This book is dedicated to Roland Barthes,
Michel Serres, and Julia Kristeva, as well
as to those preoccupied by the necessary
unblocking of basic knowledge.

Contents

Foreword
Subjects without Society

Wlad Godzich

Billboards around Geneva and newspaper inserts throughout Switzerland have been waging a campaign in defense of advertising for several months now. Without advertising, they proclaim, concerts, sports events, newspapers and magazines, and indeed many other things, would be so expensive as to be out of the reach of most consumers. This campaign comes in response to increasing questioning of the role of advertising in contemporary society, and especially to calls for its limitation. France, in an abrupt break with a cultural icon that defined its identity, has launched a strong antismoking campaign that eliminates all tobacco advertising, including the so-called secondary advertising that takes the form of brand logos or names on sportswear or racing cars, thus forcing the cancellation of Grand Prix racing from French television. The efforts to limit advertising are a testimony to the persuasive power of the advertising industry: they grant advertising the power to affect consumers, especially young ones, but they seek to affirm a societal interest in curtailing this power. The proadvertising campaign in Switzerland seeks, by contrast, to bring out the beneficent aspects of advertising. The issue is far from being decided, and it is likely to be discussed for a long time. The discussion would profit immensely from the reading of the present book. *Unconscious for Sale* stands out in the abundant literature on advertising, for it represents a principled theoretical and methodological approach to the question of the effects of advertising from the perspective of psychoanalysis. It is an exploration of the sort of society advertising fosters, and of the type of subject it summons into existence. It contributes to our understanding of contemporary society and of the forces that shape it, and it offers an object lesson in the way in which psychoanalysis can help in this understanding.

It is not by chance that Haineault and Roy's first example is the now legendary banner of Solidarity, the Polish social movement, and though they fail to appreciate that the colors of the banner are Poland's national colors, they bring out quite well the fact that the calligraphy of the banner projects both the mutual solidarity of the letters upon each other and their manifest urge to dance to individual rhythms. There is no need to recall that Aristotle saw such individual rhythm as the very basis of individual character (nor indeed that in Haineault and Roy's French, *caractère* refers to both character and font) to realize that the graphics of the banner made manifest the deepest urge of the social movement of which it was the emblem: the constitution of a civil society that would not be under the aegis of the state but represent the harmonization, however awkward or provisional, of individual aspirations. If this banner achieved emblematic status while so many others did not survive a single use, it is because it expressed this urge in an instantly recognizable form and summoned it forth in those who had not yet felt it. It made manifest that which was inchoate and not conscious and permitted those who chose to march under it to recognize themselves in the image it was projecting. It would be easy to argue that the banner played no such role, that the Polish workers, peasants, and intellectuals who adopted it did so as an afterthought to a more reasoned and deliberate determination of their political stance. It is one of the signal merits of this book to suggest that this is not the case, and that political stances, just as much as consumer behavior, have a great deal to do with processes of self-constitution that involve the hijacking or redirecting of psychic forces. The nature of these processes warrants closer examination from both historical and theoretical perspectives.

The application of psychoanalysis to the study of social phenomena, though a common enough occurrence, has always given rise to a malaise. Psychoanalysis, after all, takes the individual psyche and its formative unconscious processes as its object, whereas the study of collective behavior has focused on conscious, and even willful, actions. In addition, psychoanalysis is primarily a form of therapeutic intervention; its extension to the sphere of the social thus can proceed only by means of analogy, with all the risks this entails. But there is no denying that psychoanalysts, starting with Freud himself, have always had a strong interest in the exploration of the social, and the resistance has come mostly from the social scientists. They have argued, quite persuasively, that the psychoanalyst is a practitioner who combines theoretical knowledge with a therapeutic know-how in a form of intervention that requires the active participation of the analysand. No society has ever come forward with such a request, nor is this likely, although some societal subgroups (institutions, corporations, schools) on occasion have done so. And even then, these subgroups have tended to turn to psychologists or psychiatrists rather than to psychoanalysts. This is due in large measure to the ambiguous position of the psychoanalyst: in a therapeutic context, a specific analyst is selected by the analysand because the latter perceives him or her as the best person with whom to embark on the process of self-exploration. This choice is dictated by personal, and largely unconscious, considerations, for the analysand knows that the cure is not a matter of having an expert apply specialized knowledge to a specific case but the development of a complex personal relationship (of transference) that depends on the analyst's skill in interpreting not only what the analysand relates but also the interaction between them. Thus whereas a psychologist or a psychiatrist comes armed with scientific credentials, a psychoanalyst can at best be invested with a murky authority only by the person he or she is going to help. This authority vanishes altogether when social problems become the object of inquiry.

In addition, a cure is an exercise in attentiveness to the singularity of the individual who undergoes it. Psychoanalysts may speak of neurotics or psychotics, but no two neurotics are alike and they certainly cannot be treated alike. One of the reasons why psychoanalytic literature is so heavily narrative is precisely because cures do not lend themselves to generalization. Yet, as soon as the psychoanalyst turns to social phenomena, generalization prevails. In a cure, the psychoanalyst is engaged in processes of understanding and interpretation, whereas the study of the social calls for explanations. Everything in the cure is ambiguous and ambivalent, and the road toward the elucidation of meaning is tortuous, full of reversals and cul-de-sacs, whereas explanations require clarity of exposition and a testable set of propositions.

For all of these reasons, the adoption of a rigorous psychoanalytical perspective for the study of social phenomena has met with resistance and, in fact, has been rarely carried out or, when it has, it has relied on analogy and has produced at best interesting *aperçus* on the social. Yet it need not be so, as the very example of Freud demonstrates. Freud realizes, of course, that he is not in a therapeutic relationship to the social, and that he has to function as an observer rather than as a participant or an intervenor, but he does not take this to mean that he has to adopt the research style of positivistic social science. He does not proceed by formulating a research protocol in which he would first examine the state of the literature; identify the weak points of prevalent theories; formulate hypotheses; circumscribe and carefully weigh the composition of representative populations on which to test the hypotheses; and develop instruments for carrying out the tests. He adopts a more speculative style that proceeds by bits and pieces, fragments of analysis, reversals, and abrupt turns. More than one reader has observed that books such as *Totem and Taboo* and *Group Psychology and the Analysis of the Ego* have complex presentational structures that have nothing to do with the unfolding of ordinary arguments.

Because Freud was trained in research biology, and wrote a significant number of papers in this field, it is not through lack of knowledge of inductive and deductive methods that he writes the way he does in his studies of the social. Freud rejects the style of objective distantiation as well as the position of external observer that it presupposes in relation to social phenomena, for he does not believe that such a position is possible. To study the social is to study ourselves, to see ourselves as we are and as we have been shaped by the larger forces around us. It is precisely not to have distance and not to have objectivity but rather to track the constitution of our subjectivity. Our vision of such things is always going to be partial and provisional. It is only through the illusion of scientism fostered by those who call themselves social scientists that one can imagine that a totalized and external view of these phenomena can be achieved. Instead, one can only construct usable fictions of this totality. This is why Freud's writings on the social always turn to myth and proclaim myth: the primitive horde or the murder of the father by the sons.

Haineault and Roy follow in Freud's footsteps. Steeped in the linguistic and semiotic analytical procedures of French structuralism, they do not succumb to the latter's claim of scientific authority; they restore to the flat and well-defined objects of this structuralism the rich depth and ambiguity they possess by interrogating their meaning and not merely describing the conditions of its constitution, for the constitution that interests them is that of the contemporary subject.

Two overriding concerns govern the present-day use of the term "subject": the search for the "most effective focus for descriptions that would deal with the ways in which cultures most radically differ from one another" (Marcus and Fischer: 45) on the one hand, and the need to produce a notion of a human being that will satisfy the demands of available theories without surrendering the exigencies of a practice of resistance within the present social order. These two concerns literally come to terms around the word "subject" as a result of their perception that the institutional forms of contemporary social life are increasingly homogenized and deprive individual agents of their agency. Inquiries into the "subject" are expected to yield a better way of "capturing the distinctiveness of a culture" (Marcus and Fischer) and of preventing a foreclosing of resistance. But whereas one side reexamines the "grounds of human capabilities and actions, ideas about the self, and the expression of emotions" (Marcus and Fischer), the other argues that "the human agent *exceeds* the 'subject' as it is constructed" (Smith: xxx) in recent theory as well as the discourses against which this theory is reacting. I shall begin by describing how this sense of self and of agency is constituted in an oral culture. I resort to a narrative of communication technology not because I wish to endow it with explanatory power but because it possesses great heuristic expository value.

The point has been made repeatedly that in an oral culture narratives are collective property, yet the consequences of this statement are rarely drawn out. To begin with, such a statement means that a storyteller presents himself or herself not as the originator of a story but rather as a relay in a long chain of tellers, the earliest of whom, if they are known at all, are either mythical ancestors or divine emissaries. It means, further, that no new stories are elaborated, except at most as variants of older stories. We should expect, then, a waning of interest in stories that are fundamentally repetitive and rehashed over and over again, yet paradoxically all such human societies lay a great deal of stock in storytelling, so much so that we tend to think of them as narrative bound. To tell a story under such circumstances entails a different attitude toward narrative from the one moderns bring to the same experience. The performance or the telling of stories in oral societies is essentially *commemorative*.

This term refers to the peculiar function of memory in oral societies. On the basis of empirical evidence, members of a literate culture have a far more limited mnemonic capability than their counterparts in an oral culture; after all, far less is at stake in a literate society than in an oral one as far as memory is concerned. It would not be an exaggeration to say that oral societies experience a particular form of anxiety linked to the fear of losing their memory that literate societies cannot even begin to imagine. For it is in this vast *memoria* that are contained all the sacred texts, all the foundational myths, all the explanatory regresses that provide the members of a particular collectivity with a hold on their lived experience and distinguish them from their neighbors. In this type of mind-set, a story told is not cognitively processed for the information it contains—there are other ways of accomplishing such a utilitarian task; it is told in order to animate as many of the constitutive elements of memoria as possible. Because the audience is familiar with the narrative, be it an epic or a myth, it is not interested in its thread, structure, or even its thrust, as much as in the way in which the performance of the storyteller can achieve this function of animation in which large numbers of dormant memorial strands can be set into motion and vibrate together, thereby giving its meaning to the term commemorate. Commemoration in such a context does not have the modern meaning of an action whereby a number of individuals come together in order to recall some event or figure; it designates the process through which the latent powers of memoria are brought to life. There are no individuals here, for those who are gathered at such a storytelling do not conceive of themselves as autonomous entities that have the power or the right to associate freely among themselves. They are there as the necessary material correlatives of the memoria from which they derive their sense of identity and purpose. Rather than being individuals with inherently endowed rights and privileges, they are *persons* in the etymological sense of the term—that is, material purports of roles they do not write but accept, in the form of fate, from the power that resides in memoria, a power that is beyond human ken or control.

To be a person in this sense is to accept that one's life does not obey a discernible order of coherence while maintaining a belief in the ultimate existence of such a coherence. In other words, if I perceive myself as playing roles that are handed down to me, I am aware of the fact that I am generally called on to play more than one role and that there is no inherent link between two or more of the successive roles I play. At the same time, I believe firmly that all the roles being played simultaneously somehow make sense, but not necessarily to me who am but one player among many. Sense, in the form of the coherence of the global play, resides at a higher level, that of the memoria no longer conceived as a pure repository but as an animating force itself. By contrast, persons are largely heterogeneous, since they do not necessarly achieve any coherence in the roles they play. Yet this heterogeneity does not give rise to any anxiety, quite the contrary: it reinforces the belief that one's sense transcends oneself and that such a sense resides in a transcendental dimension that is at the same time immanent.

To be a person in this sense, to see oneself as assuming roles that are cast upon one, requires a conception of language and of the larger semiotic system as a set of parts available to oneself. A part is a limited ordering of verbal and nonverbal behavior, endowed with internal coherence and designed to achieve specifiable effects. In contemporary semiolinguistic terms, it is a discourse. Each discourse is organized in such a way as to place its utterer in the position of the subject of that discourse, which is what we call role playing. Persons are heterogeneous insofar as they are called on to play different roles; we can thus define a person as someone with the ability to assume different subject positions. Such a definition is excessively voluntaristic, however, and presumes that one chooses, or has the right and the ability to choose, the roles one will play. It is, in other words, a definition of an individual assuming the function of a person. We have seen earlier that persons do not choose their roles but have them thrust on them, and that they experience them as fate. It is more accurate, then, to define persons as the loci in which discourses intersect and produce subject positions. Persons are thus defined not ontologically but discursively, and their aggregate, the community of persons, is equally derived from memoria as the treasure trove of discourses.

The notion of "subject position" invoked in relation to this discursive definition of person will gain great philosophical significance with the historical passage from "person" to "individual," for it is going to account for the latter's putative stability in a world of change as we witness an evolution from "subject position" of a specific discourse to that of "subject" of discursivity and thought, best exemplified in Descartes's "Cogito ergo sum." Let us examine this historical transformation, albeit very sketchily.

The passage from traditional societies to modernity involves a reversal of ontological priority, since it is effected around the newly defined primacy of the individual over the group. In current theoretical and descriptive discourse this passage is increasingly described in cultural terms: it involves two broad collective structures of representation, one centered on the collective and the other on the individual. The difference would thus lie between two cultures, with the culture of individualism being typical of Western Europe. (This mode of conceiving of the passage is of considerable interest, since it is a good instance of the post-modern tendency to characterize every type of variation as "cultural," something I will return to later.) The problem is that this passage is not a cultural but a political phenomenon. In fact, the advent of modernity, as a general project of rationalizing social practices and emancipating the individual, takes place explicitly against a world in which traditional culture reigns supreme. The passage to modernity has to do with the fact that the modes of social regulation are no longer vested in the cultural but in the political. This is the major reason why so much of modernity has presented itself, and continues to present itself, in the discourses of modernization used in Third World settings, as a sort of "meta culture" vested in the apparatuses of the state and aimed at the traditionally transmitted cultures (cf., for example, the imposition of national languages on local dialects). Modernity presents itself as the project of building a society on a universalizing basis (which is why we speak of modernity in the singular and of traditional societies in the plural). From the point of view of this project, cultural and geographical particularisms are shortcomings and hindrances, and the traditional model of conceptualizing the relationship of the individual to the collective, which is rooted in the notion that everyone occupies a definite place within a pregiven natural order endowed a priori with meaning and relevance, is rejected. Modernity never succeeds in defining and enshrining one model of this articulation of the individual and the collective, and its specificity cannot be described in terms of this one model, but it confines its search for such a model to the possibilities that revolve around the idea that a rationalization of the social sphere based on individualism is not only possible but is the only desirable one. It revolves, in other words, around the notion that the individual is a member both of civil society and of political society, that he (and it is no accident that the masculine form is the historically correct one here) is both Man and Citizen. The regulation of social relations is ensured by institutions guaranteed by the state; and the individual, taken as an abstract and universal being, is their normative subject.

This is of some importance because it means that this individual, far from being another "value" forged in the crucible of culture, is actually the definition of an ideal subject placed at the very foundation of the political constitution of the modern state (the citizen) and, at the same time, an a priori defined bearer of formal and universal principles of institutional regulation of social relations and practices (Man endowed with inalienable rights). It is only on this basis, which is political in nature, that further definitions of the cultural values of individualism will take place.

I have said several times that this is the way modernity has presented itself, and it is important to stress this fact, for it is rather clear that modernity has not fulfilled this program. We had already noted in passing that its commitment to universalizing rationality could not overcome the deep-seated gender prejudice that favored men over women, and it would stumble just as much over issues of race or indeed many other principles of differentiation, thereby convincing many scholars and observers that a return to a cultural explanation for social regulation is warranted. I have no problem with such a conclusion provided we understand that a postmodern culture has very little to do indeed with a premodern one. Let me try to characterize this passage from modernity to postmodernity, which has as one of its stakes the redefinition of social regulation by cultural means as opposed to political ones.

If we take the dialectic between civil society and the sphere of the state as our point of departure, the history of modernity can be described in terms of an increasing encroachment of the state and its apparatuses on the civil sphere: the state takes over the production of the social bond and empties of any political content former mediating instances such as families, churches, and professional bodies, or, even better, appropriates them to its own ends as is readily visible in the reliance on the medicalization and juridicalization of an increasing number of personal, interpersonal, and intergroup conflicts (henceforth described as "dysfunctions"). It is generally not appreciated that this encroachment of the state can be, and is, depicted as an increase in the autonomy of individuals who are told that they are now "freer" to pursue their own needs, desires, and inclinations. This accounts, by the way, for the success of conservative politicians who, in recent years, have all maintained or even increased the power of the state while ostensibly denouncing it. In any case, the equation of modernity is being rewritten in such a way that we have an ever more sovereign state on the one hand and ever more autonomous individuals on the other. The principled individualism of modernity, which was rational and universal in its aspiration, and implied the submission of individuals to specifiable social regulations as well as the existence of important processes of socialization, is now being replaced with a form of total individualism that invades areas heretofore immune to individualist ideology.

The result is postmodernity, wherein the forms of social regulation are no longer mediated through the figure of the ideal individual but rather involve concrete persons in the contemporary sense of the term—that is, empirical individuals and groups and their mode of conceiving of their self or selves. We should observe that this result leads to a situation in which new modalities of social integration have to appear. These modalities do not provide a collective identity since they treat individuals through technocratic and consumer-society mechanisms, so that postmodern individuals are constantly referred back to themselves at the very moment when they lose the symbolic signposts constitutive of their identity. The so-called me-generation or the revival of narcissism or the decline of public man all bear witness to this process. And it is this process that ultimately leads to the progressive abandonment of the notion of the individual and the adoption of that of the "subject." In part, this notion marks a desire to assume the philosophical burden placed on the term "subject" in modernity: at a

time of growing disorientation and tearing between competing and frequently in-
compatible demands, the "subject" is to be the unified and coherent bearer of
consciousness. But, alongside this wistful reaffirmation of modernity's foundational belief in individual agency, there is a recognition that we are all "subject"
to the new modalities of social integration and that we have precious little knowledge of what they are and how they function. It is on this basis that we concep-
tualize our present subjection as being cultural, thereby vesting "culture" and its
components with an agency we feel deprived of. And we turn to the study of
other "cultures," mostly premodern, in the hope that an elucidation of their
modes of subjectivation will shed light on ours. Such a hope rests wholly, in my
view, on a misprision between premodern and postmodern modes of social regulation.

In summary, I have attempted to trace the current fascination with the "subject"
in various regions of the Western organization of knowledge to the emergence of
a new mode of social regulation that abandons the political ground of such regulation characteristic of modernity in favor of new modalities that deal with concrete individuals and groups in terms of their differentiated needs and desires. In
this respect they appear to resemble the modalities of premodern societies, which
eschewed political means in favor of so-called cultural ones. But whereas in the
latter, the determinant level was that of what I have called memoria (i.e., a collective imaginary that embraces the historical past of the society), the postmodern one takes hold of individual imaginations and exploits them for private rather
than collective ends. In other words, if the passage from traditional societies to
modernity involved a change from a cultural to a political paradigm, then the
passage from modernity to postmodernity is being effected through the change-
over from a political to an economic paradigm, in which we are the subjects of
the new machines of production and consumption.

In this all-too-brief account, it should be apparent that modernity represents
the tendency to think of society as an entity that is coextensive with its political
organization. One would certainly need to nuance this proposition, since it is
generally held that the very notion of civil society is a hallmark of modernity, but
one should be careful to distinguish between concepts and notions advanced by
thinkers working within the orbit of modernity and the historical forces that
shaped it. The latter, especially in the absolutist phase of its development, certainly favored the identification of society with the political order, thereby giving
the latter the right and latitude to intervene in the social and to shape it according
to its needs. The central conflict of modern societies, over the ownership of
modes of production, and beyond that, over the status of private property, reveals
the limitations of this political action. Present-day, postcommunist public opinion
is not wrong in equating civil society with the economic sphere, for it is this
sphere that has resisted most strongly political control, to the point of collapsing

where this control has asserted itself too forcefully. Today "society" is routinely equated with processes of production, exchange, and consumption, and there is widespread belief that these processes possess an inner dynamic that does not admit of external tampering (except for the massive intervention of those forces, such as the International Monetary Fund in its campaign of structural adjustment, that claim to be acting on behalf of the unshackling of this dynamic).

This notion of society as an autonomous economy working itself out is thoroughly alienating: it is based on the very notion that there are no capable agents of intervention at the level of its totality. Agents, or rather actors, since they should confine themselves to their own role, should play their part and leave it to the mysterious inner dynamic to produce the adjustments necessary to prevent the whole from crashing. There is a considerable shortfall of meaningfulness in this view of society: its most important processes are, almost by definition, removed from view or declared to be unknowable. Nietzsche was quite right in describing the contemporary order as based on a form of belief far stronger than the faith of our premodern ancestors.

This shortfall of meaning has summoned into existence a compensatory mechanism, the so-called public sphere, in which the problem of meaning is addressed and the production of meanings for consumption is undertaken. The function of the public sphere is to neutralize or to compensate the alienating conception of society as autonomous economy. The public sphere is supposed to be a site of deliberation and discussion in which what is felt to be in common is defined and where a nonalienated form of society comes into being and delineates its own courses of action. The history of the eighteenth century is crucial here, for it was in this century that, first, the autonomy of the economy was asserted and, second, a compensatory public sphere, equally independent of political power, was brought into existence through the processes rendered familiar by Jürgen Habermas. Intellectuals tend to value this sphere because it is the space in which they operate. They also believe that it is in the public sphere that political options and projects can be elaborated, and capable agents summoned into existence so that the autonomy of the economic sphere can be breached. One can readily see that this hope is an instance of wishful thinking, because the very genealogy of the public sphere shows clearly that it exists for the purpose of compensating for the deficit of meaning produced by the autonomization of the economy and the identification of the latter with society. The existence of the public sphere is a symptom of the alienation produced by this autonomization and a site for neutralizing rejectionary forces.

Advertising, by contrast, is fully at home in this sphere. It does not forget that the public sphere exists solely in reference to the economic one. In fact, it plugs it directly into it. This is the source of its power. Whereas the intellectual conception of the public sphere searches for a form of political power that could intervene into the economic process, advertising connects individuals to the power that animates this process. It provides an experience of power by simultaneously offering access to the sole form of meaning that is accessible under market rules, a meaning for and through consumption, and to the power inherent in any capable agency, that of defining a subject, a subject of and for consumption. Haineault and Roy analyze this process precisely, showing in particular that advertising taps into the inherent power of desire to subvert any existing order, for desire is a life-affirming force and order is always a form of death, in order to divert it ''pervert'' it is their word) toward a death-affirming act of order sustenance, an act of consumption.

This process is particularly acute in a globalized economy, for it turns out that the eighteenth-century conception of an autonomous economic sphere as a definition of a society independent of political power is not tenable on a global scale. The earlier version of economy as society can be seen in retrospect as nothing more than a ruse to homogenize a territory for market operations. The collapse of the communist order that sought to equate society with the political order and to make the economic sphere subservient to the political one has freed the economic sphere from the pretense that it needs society. The hegemony of liberalism today masks the fact that we no longer have a usable theory of society and that, more important, the very operations of the economic order, far from defining a form of society, specify only forms of subjection. The rapid rise of global media accompanies this shedding of its societal envelope by the economy and seeks to compensate the enormous shortfall of meaning that has been thus created by bombarding us with trivial information that suggests that meanings proliferate and that it is only our inability to grasp them that is the cause of the alienation we feel. Advertising, as analyzed by Haineault and Roy, reveals, however, that in a global economy there can only be subjects and no society, that is, subjects permanently confined to their subjection, robbed of their subjectivity, and deprived of any access to potentially subversive subject positions.

References

Godzich, Wlad. "*In Memoriam*." In E. Vance, *From Topic to Tale*. Minneapolis: University of Minnesota Press, 1987, x-xix.

Marcus, George E., and Michael M. J. Fischer. *Anthropology as Cultural Critique*. Chicago: University of Chicago Press, 1986.

Smith, Paul. *Discerning the Subject*. Minneapolis: University of Minnesota Press, 1988.

Taylor, Charles. "Modes of Civil Society," with a response by Partha Chatterjee. *Public Culture* 3, 1 (Fall 1990): 95-132.

Introduction

In its first meaning, the term *publicity* designates the state of what is public. Only by extension does this term take on the connotation of the promotional or incitive function of a discourse. This terminological heritage is more telling than is generally acknowledged.

Of course such a slippage of meaning is essentially justified by the very intent of advertisers who aim to make awareness of their products public. But there is more: as much in the case of all public discourse as in the case of promotional campaigns, such a shift from secret to known, from private to public, from the intimate to that which is on display by definition entails rhetorical strategies worthy of consideration.

In order to become public, a discourse must in effect gradually get beyond its specificity and win the approval of a broad majority. As a consequence, it can count only on the least emotional or intellectual common denominator of its intended audience. As a result, it will deny itself the human wealth of our profound diversity, all the more so since it will target a wider audience.

The advertiser's form of address, like the art of ideologists, thus consists, essentially, in having us forget our situation as subjects in order to rally us around the common traits of a defined group. As singular as each of us is, the magic of advertising consists in making us become, for a few seconds, *public beings*. In such a situation it is obvious that we have to get over certain trivialities, in the way that pettiness or fragility wear off. For thirty or sixty seconds we are heroes, famous or renowned, magically able to resolve conflicts that, just a moment before, were driving us crazy.

This is fascinating and, what is more, we readily become passionately enamored of these little moments of *publicity* we are granted. We enjoy these moments because they transform what is everyday into majestic feats. We adulate them because, through them, the child-magician beats all odds.

Over the years, as this work developed, we have both had to rediscover this child, delighted by sleights of hand, who prefers naïveté to troubling questions and simplicity to complexity. At times, we were disappointed to have to acknowledge the hoaxes we were able, one or the other of us, to fall for; but, by and large, the experience has been more than enriching.

The psychoanalytic experience is an intimate place, a mode of speech woven and spun antithetically to advertising. Child-magicians, to be sure, preside over this speech, but it also suits them to make just the right moves. In advertising, to the contrary, they triumph in secret, hiding beneath a jumble of verbiage; far from giving themselves away, they cheerfully consume. From the couch to the screen, sometimes their divergence seemed insoluble. But, as we all know, this wise child, aware of its own banality, shares daily life with the magical, triumphant child. They both fight to be front and center on the human stage. By turns they both lay claim to truth.

Writing—an eminently public act—over the years required that we reconcile these two opposing worlds of denial and awareness, like two sides of the same human coin. The result is surely more modest than we had wished—magically so, perhaps—but all the same we hope, in certain cases, to have restored a potential intimacy to a discourse that exults in remaining public.

Chapter 1
The Poster: Desire, Defense

From the printed page of any ordinary periodical to the most ubiquitous subway walls or city streets, the advertising image never stops assaulting us. And yet, even when we are forewarned, it is not certain that this overload will satiate us. No matter how fast we read or how quick our gait, our look pauses on these signs that call out to us. Despite clear warnings from countless consumers' associations, these images touch us and get through to us. Advertising designers do their best to stand out in this mass, trying to surprise or be different. But to some degree we too go along with this attraction. And if it needs to deal with the rhetoric of the other, analysis still has to come back to us, since we too are party to this business of lies and deceit. We shall therefore examine the rhetoric of advertising signs in the first section of this chapter, but in the second part we shall turn our attention to our psychological defenses.

The Poster: General Considerations

Advertising posters as such first appeared around 1880. This was the era of Chéret, Toulouse-Lautrec, Walker. All of them used their own style, their own ideas, and their own intuition to bring about the evolution of this art of persuasion. In this way the art of creating atmosphere and suggestion, in other words, the art of plastically communicating an aspect of the product, was developed. At the very beginning, advertising was more a matter of educating than of selling:

designers were concerned above all with making the product fit the style of the painting or lithograph of a given artist.

Around 1950, however, poster advertising takes on an important new direction. The war has just ended, and large-scale manufacturing is beginning. Radio commercials engender fierce competition, forcing advertising posters to capitalize on what sets them apart: visual illustration. In addition, Americans begin to give over to photography representations that until now were persistently considered the domain of the artist. And so designers start to put away their brushes, pencils, and paints to put an eye behind the camera. Europeans do not immediately follow suit; there is still time for artists like Savignac to emerge. But, ineluctably, the movement leading from canvas to emulsion draws them away, too—to the extent that, henceforth, photography will inexorably dominate the world of advertising.

Just as progressively, thanks to the increasing rigor of competition, either the subtlety or the audacity of the message is asserted. In order to continue to astonish and surprise, the poster has to suggest new and unexpected connections between the product and its sign-image. It is precisely these connections that we have been engaged in examining over the past few years.

In order to shed more light on these connections between product and poster, we collected more than 25,000 posters produced since the 1950s, compiling what seems to us a fairly representative sampling of contemporary advertising.

In order to understand the process that takes artists from product to poster, by way of this notion of *concept* that to them seems fundamental, we interviewed a number of advertisers. In general, they told us very little, saying almost without exception that they were simply following their "intuitions." As a result, we had to rely on the detailed study of these thousands of posters in order to elucidate the potential elements of a structure of advertising representation.

Study of the advertising poster per se—or of its rhetoric, as we would prefer to call it—in turn raised certain questions. This "rhetoric," in fact, is far from univocal. Sometimes the methods used belong to the rhetoric of language while at other times the connection that is suggested is entirely plastic. Usually, however, art directors use a mixture of strategies pertaining to both of these fields. We were therefore forced to sift through this mass of information to make certain choices that led us to a preliminary study of the advertising *signifier* before we dealt with the dimension of the *signified*. An initial dusting away of debris helped us identify the *elementary processes* before we could study the strategies of *composition*. Finally, an initial staking out, by way of an analysis of the *plastic relationships* enunciated around a product, as a result allowed us to construe a subsequent analysis of the *logical relationships* (causality, isomorphism, and so on) advertising employed, depending on the product to be sold.

If one accepts that any too-rigid distinction between signifier and signified is necessarily arbitrary and that one level inevitably recalls the other, one could suggest that the first part of the following text is particularly concerned with the register of the *signifier*. Initially, this analysis identifies the *elementary processes of plastic figuration* (calligraphy, drawing, photography, and graphic design in general) and then considers how they are joined together, and consequently deals with the *processes of composition* of plastic representation. In the second section we take up the register of the *signified* and also the *logical bonds* the advertising designer proposes between a product and an image. But, far from being exclusively "logical" or "objective," this study of the signified is itself what introduces us to a reconsideration of our psychic defenses. Since advertising argumentation specifically addresses this defense mechanism, it would be presumptuous to examine them separately. Thus in this study of the signified one will find a structure that is intimately connected with phenomena that are more psychological than semiological—a structure linked to denial, projection, repression, and identification. This is why metonymical and metaphorical processes are not hidden: they are simply incorporated into this other reading that we thought preferable.

Advertising Posters: Their Elementary Processes

Calligraphy

The word *calligraphy,* used here as a title or to designate a process, does not necessarily refer to the primary meaning of this word, which is that of beautiful handwriting. Instead we refer the reader to the Oriental use of material, one that consists in a minimum of strokes, each highly symbolic, in representing the real as completely as possible. Writing, if it can still be called by this name in such circumstances, no longer strives to make itself merely readable; first and foremost it means to signify as much as possible, to convey the greatest possible amount of information, or, better still, the greatest number of allusive evocations.

To study this process from—it must be stressed—a methodological point of view, we concentrated our attention on advertising illustrations in which calligraphic operations served an important function. In certain cases this calligraphy even takes up the entire space of the advertisement; in others, it hoards a major part of the surface area.

In such advertisements, the *shape* of the writing—its calligraphy—assumes great importance. The choice of a thick character, for example, is not merely a matter of chance. Thickness means to signify a certain density, body, solidity, or potential durability of the product. The lines themselves support words or take on certain dimensions. Depending on the aim of the advertisement, they will be arranged within a triangular, rectangular, or circular area whose signifying value will always have a potential connection with the aspect of the advertised product that is being accentuated.

The now famous banner of the Polish labor union Solidarity provides an eloquent example—proof indeed, were any needed, that Western capitalism has no monopoly on clever design or creativity in representation.

The letters of the single word *Solidarność* painted in red against a white background are linked together part-way up, like an army of marching workers with hands joined. An impertinence regarding an even more legendary Red Army? It is difficult to say. But what is certain, on the other hand, is that these letters have so much *solidarity* with one another that they form a marching unit ready to raise its own banner (creating an infinite number of banners within banners) behind the *N,* giving the effect of relative disorder suggestive of the right to assembly rather than restrictive militarism. A result of this clever design is that the spacing is somewhat irregular at the base of the letters, so they look as if they were dancing. Or perhaps, in the designer's mind, this represents a respect for the individual rhythm (and step) of each of these united marchers.

From quite a different point of view, one could also see the multiple vertical lines of the letters *O, L, I,* and *D* as symbolizing in a certain way the factory gates in Gdansk closed to the workers who demand a relative freedom.

Without joining Solidarity directly, people are willing to wear the button with the logo of this union to show their concern over injustice or even their indignation against totalitarianism, whether it be ours, theirs, or perhaps even that of our leaders. Partly because of its lettering, the Solidarity logo has become part of our culture.

Some will here counter that events are what make history and that in any event the struggles of the Gdansk labor union would eventually have found a place in our preoccupations. From the outset it is important to make clear that we are not denying the factual nature of history, but we maintain on the other hand that if the Solidarity banner has acquired this function of quasi-universal representation such that today we still recognize it, it is because it contained elements favorable to our projections. Otherwise we would have chosen some other object as a symbol—a logo, a tune, or, as in the case of the Ayatollah Khomeini, a photograph. This is one of the primary observations: advertisements that work or that we remember are rarely ordinary. They have to stand out and stand on their own; otherwise we abandon them.

The simple curves and almost childish purity of line in the Club Med posters is in obvious contrast to the very carefully worked out script of Solidarność. Here the single words *eat, sleep, cry, drink,* and *love* are placed side by side with images of the good life in an exotic setting. Nothing in particular should seem complicated. The thickness of the lettering and its clear legibility, the classical style of the characters and their clarity, the minimal prose of the one-word expressions send the viewer back to the idea of simplicity: the kind of simplicity we want when we are on vacation. On the other hand, this very purity leads to an impression of strength, completeness, and even stability. Club Med is an institution that is going to last, capable of exotic settings but also of durability, capable of craziness but also of good sense; our minds are put at ease. Idealization becomes possible. If the exotic setting were transcribed here in voluptuous or unbridled typography, who knows if we would not get scared away, or if we would consume with as much confidence? At any rate, the advertiser did not take the risk.

In its series of small, witty posters (1978), MacKeen (a brand of French jeans) makes use of the way we read in a different way. We have chosen two examples for analysis.

In the first of these pictures, we are confronted with various possible spellings of the brand name: MacKeel, MatKing, MacInn. All of the names in this panel are declared *fakes*. A second, contrasting panel explains "How to use fakes." The back pockets of eight pairs of jeans show the fake, quasi-homonymic labels. Each time the typography and the spelling vary slightly. The eight pairs of jeans are identical. Naturally no one wants to admit to preferring the fake to the real thing, the copy to the original. Each one, of course, claims first of all to be authentic. All the more in that jeans that everyone wants to "copy" must, we would hope, be profoundly original!

Here uniformity and divergence express our need to be different. It becomes all the more apparent that since jeans are subject to certain relatively specific premises, they cannot offer us infinite variety.

The second example is more abstract. The classic optician's eye chart in which the letters become progressively smaller is the "measure" of the acuity of the consumer's eyesight. Spread over six lines, first one by one, then two by two, then more and more letters as the "test" becomes clearer, we have the letters of an artificially disjointed message: "MacKeen's jeans: that's some skin off your back(side)."[1] Further down, the message is repeated in smaller characters. The sentence may be seen as provocative. "Les fesses" (butt, buttocks, buns) here evoke the scatology of our infancy; "the skin off your back(side)" promises to exact an exorbitant price. So, in theory, we ought to keep our distance from a product such as this one.

If we do not do so, it is because the miniposter operates on another level. The skin of the buttocks is here the center of interest. Some will test their eyesight by detecting skin under tight-fitting jeans. In this sense, for anyone wearing MacKeens, the jeans may cost them the skin off their butt. MacKeens: they hide the butt's skin; they charge the skin to the look, since the jeans steal and hide the skin from it.

The fictitious optician is not very demanding, since no one fails the test. We all have "the eyes to see" that are needed to read the "fine print," that is, to see as far as decency permits. Honor is safe.

Euphorisant!

Figure 1-1

On the level of the typography, it may also be noted that the letters at the top of the poster suggest the breadth of a pelvis, while the letters at the bottom become slender and more tapered, like perfect legs. Would MacKeens give us all beautiful legs? It is worth looking into.

Generally speaking, there is an almost absolute code that governs jeans advertisements: men are shown from the front, whereas women are seen from behind. Women's butts and men's crotches. Making a trip to the optician, MacKeens *shoves them into our face* without resorting to this cliché. This is an achievement in and of itself. No doubt it would not have been possible without resorting to typography.

Following this relationship, New Man (1980) uses another stratagem. The words *New Man* are written out in brightly colored pharmaceutical pills (fig. 1-1). The inscription comes fairly close to the trademark of the clothing company, leaving some room for imagination. One wonders a little what this pill writing is supposed to mean; it takes us somewhat by surprise. Do they want to signify to us that the modern man needs vitamins, or tranquilizers? Then a word occurs to us — capsule. In the world of fashion, there is heated competition between two ready-to-wear clothing stores, Capsule and New Man. New Man, *written* this way, contains Capsule. New Man has just swallowed up the competition.

Everyone knows the trademark that for a good many years has stood for products made of "virgin wool": a skein of wool symbolized by intertwining arcs.

This mark can be used by manufacturers whose product meets the standards set by the International Woolmark Institute.

In a valley, in Brittany or in Australia—there is no way of telling—an ingenious shepherd has herded sheep in intertwining arcs in the exact shape of the Woolmark. This is complex and extremely subtle calligraphy: the advertisement is composed by the photographer. Perfect adequation is clearly established between product and its origin. Its integration is remarkable. The raw and the cooked, the natural and the civilized, the ground and the figure here blend together magically. In a blink of the eye, we are supersaturated with information. Woolmark has put to its service a classical but effective strategy. Moreover, is not one of the brand's strategies to give us tradition within modernism? It achieves this objective.

Still other visuals emphasize instead the link between product and consumer. For example, Vittel (1978) incorporates into its *Light* calligraphy men and women obviously in good physical health who make the *V* in Vittel with two fingers (fig. 1-2). Might this be an example of "sound body, sound mind" advertising? There is, however, one detail that cannot be missed: this *V* evokes victory and political struggle. Or is it the victory of gaining control over one's body and winning athletic competitions? The message is utterly double. We are glad to allow this duplicity.

In certain car advertisements, the typography itself is not suggestive; inversely, very plain type is used in a suggestive way. The words stop, in effect, according to certain precise rules, at certain points on the poster. From a distance we can see that the black lettering against the white background forms the shape of the car in question. Viewers are thus informed from the first glance about the nature of the message being transmitted. The surprise effect created by the unusual arrangement of the letters will have caught their attention; in most cases that is all that is needed. At any rate, this is the function of the billboard; detailed information will be supplied in television commercials or elsewhere depending on the advertiser's strategy.

In the same vein, but this time on a bit more symbolic level, the Tigra cigarettes firm offers an advertisement where the printed characters borrow the shape of a tiger (fig. 1-3). The contour of the letters manages, under the artist's hand, to wed, or rather reproduce, the contours of the back and snout of this dangerous feline. Once again, our attention is held captive for at least a few seconds. And this is all the advertiser needs, especially since, for a cigarette, there is really no need to provide a great deal of information.

There is, finally, another level of the use of writing that seems to us important to consider before devoting ourselves to the study of the use of drawing in advertising: the symbolic value of the writing itself.

Figure 1-2

The use of graffiti clearly evokes the history of rebellions or of political and social struggles. In some cases this is to show that the company making the product is avant-garde; in other cases the intent is to stress that the company withstands the most extreme of pressures, and is ready for anything.

Inscriptions carved in stone, on the other hand, evoke permanence or durabil-

Figure 1-3

ity. One will see them used to advertise products that are supposed to last or products one wants to imply are "as old as the hills" — as old, at least, as ancient Hebrew or Egyptian writings.

From this vantage, in the final analysis writing itself assumes a sacred aspect. An everyday gesture, if such a thing exists, it is at the same time a sign of a certain form of inscription of the human gesture in time. "Words last" (*verba manent*), as the proverb says. If it is not certain that all words will last, it must at least be acknowledged that the graphic trace of the human act represents, for this gesture, the only hope of participating in the collective memory. History that is not written, in other words, has every likelihood of dying out.

Perceived in this way, words take on highly symbolic value. Not only do they have specific meaning, but their graphic expression itself has meaning. The material inscription of a thought in any kind of printing makes the word a signifier, but also a signified, or a referent. Because it is a word, the word takes on the consistency of an icon. It is, from the outset, a polysemic image, connotative on several levels. Like a dream image, it is in a way sacred, to the extent that it touches within us a whole range of repressed feelings and emotions. Mythic violences or primal tendernesses, there is, buried deep within us, a series of experiences whose mnesic traces search for a foothold. Around this foothold is woven the dialectic of transgression, desire, and the forbidden — levels that advertising, without a doubt, intends to bring together in each of us.

Drawing

We already pointed out in the introduction to this chapter that photography has very clearly replaced drawing in the advertising apparatus since the 1950s. Photography, in effect, seems to reproduce reality with a high degree of precision. It provides access to a kind of truth, since it presents itself as an authentic document. Finally, it implies or connotes a certain idea of reproducibility that drawing

Figure 1-4. " 'Mommy, what do they put in Fruki to make it smell like strawberries?' Fruki: a yogurt for the ones you love."

does not have. It follows that drawing will be used in circumstances where to some extent one wants to get away from rigorous accuracy, where there is less need for an absolutely realistic document in support of a proposition.

The Comic Strip. Comic strips are an excellent example of this use of drawing. A kind of imitation of the classic comic strip, advertising comics present a series of images one after the other, complete with balloons or captions, linked together by a brief story line. A number of Fruki advertisements follow this model (fig. 1-4). They tell the story of a boy and his mother, who wants to convince him of the benefits of eating yogurt. If he follows her advice, he may later grow up to become a fireman. The admiring mother looks on with delight and pride.

It is clear in this last example that the comic strip image has the advantage of making a young audience feel they are in a world familiar to them, the world of the comic strip; thus from the start the advertisement is geared to the level of its readers. The fact remains that the comic strip has another advantage here: it allows a sort of phantasmagoria or allegory that coincides very well with the paradigm of the comic strip, but clearly runs counter to the effect of reality photography tries to produce. By its appeal to the imagination, by its noncrystallization

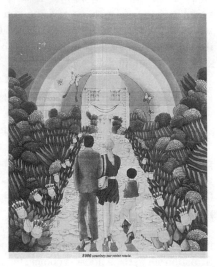

Figure 1-5

of the real, the sketched image allows fantasies to roam more freely than those summoned forth by the factual world of photography.

Once again we find this appeal to fantasy, and more particularly to *legend,* in the 1973 advertisements of Crédit Agricole (fig. 1-5). Here an adult audience is addressed, but the advertisement tries to convey a kind of dreamlike, unreal atmosphere. It goes beyond the anecdotal (more properly the realm of photography) to reach a kind of world where everything runs like clockwork.

Obviously the question needs to be turned around, to ask why contemporary advertising makes relatively little use of drawing. The first thought that comes to mind has to do with the nature of the world in which we live. In a highly technological civilization, recourse to proof (photography) now seems almost a requirement; without it, ''you can't be serious . . . '' When you want to tell the truth, you have to be able to back it up with documentation. And advertising has acquired such a reputation for being "deceptive" that it cannot afford a faux pas in this regard.

On the contrary, taking recourse in a somewhat naive form of pressure, Crédit Agricole communicates an impression of benevolence, giving its own image a halo of simplicity, and does not interpose overly technological machinery between the customer and the local bank branch—which, in the final analysis, is not bad for a bank, where, in general, we feel cornered by numerical, cold, and technological relations.

The Line Drawing. Drawings have the advantage of presenting the essential shape while suggesting to the viewer the whole. Because of its inherent lack of precision, this form of expression can represent only well-known realities for which the viewer can fill in the blanks. Conversely, the use of the line reinforces the impression that the form in question is plausibly familiar enough that the absent details might be grasped.

Volkswagen wagered on this form of drawing, reducing its "beetle" to a clean shape bereft of details. The famous little car, as expected, took on a legendary dimension when it was thus reduced to its essentials.

El Al Airlines used similar tactics to suggest an atmosphere of fairy tale or legend. "No goose, no gander" is the slogan of an advertisement showing drawings of two geese, one over the word *gander* and the other over the word *goose*. On a more subtle level, this is a reply to the advertisements of North African airline companies (Royal Air Maroc, in particular), in which large birds like geese serve as a symbol of prestige. The expression "no goose, no gander" also means, on the idiomatic level, "not the one without the other." This vernacular use of the expression seems to direct us back to an atmosphere of peace and benevolent neutrality. The subliminal affirmation suggests, a priori, a choice; the manifest expression assures us there will be no dishonest or disreputable dealings.

Obviously, looking down on the words that today might prove provocative, the implicit allusion to universal figures, a sign of what one understands well in order to define its content, names a climate of durability. It evokes the fantasy of an Israeli nation having, so to speak, almost always existed; of a kind of permanence, or, at the very least, an attitude of defiance and confidence in survival that could not be expressed except in a symbolic mode. It is very unlikely that a photograph of birds could have as great an effect as these drawings.

Another use of drawing consists in representing an object or an animal with symbolic value more or less directly related to the publicized product. In this way a stylized pig will stand for a piggy bank, for the idea of saving money, or for economy (fig. 1-6). The tiger will often represent power (in advertisements for gasoline); the cat will suggest grip (of certain tires), or long-wearing shoe soles (Cat's Paw), since cats are supposed to have nine lives. Cats are also associated

Figure 1-6. ''The more you earn . . . the more it is difficult to save.''

Figure 1-7

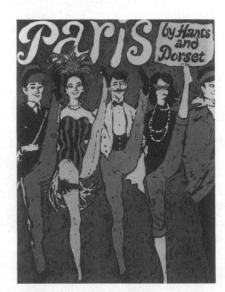

Figure 1-8

with savings, coffee, electricity, gas, the sophisticated charm of a high-fashion designer or a hat shop.

In other words, in each case there is an appeal to the symbolic or suggestive value of the trait. There is no need for precision in any of these examples; on the contrary, the evocative, or polysemic, atmosphere is intended and sought after.

Certain drawings employed with the aim of suggesting a particular atmosphere work in exactly the same way. The French underwear manufacturer Eminence, for example, in 1972 presented its new collection of men's underwear by having T-shirts and underpants stand out in attractive colors against a dark background (fig. 1-7). The dark portion of the picture was cleverly chosen: it suggests, with no possible confusion, the tall silhouettes in long coats and broad-brimmed hats made popular at the time by the films of Sergio Leone. Leone's talent for producing striking images, which our subconscious almost instantly accepts on an archetypal level, is quite remarkable. The drawing suggests legendary images that hark back to the Western folklore tradition and return the spectator to the days of epic deeds and bravado of the last century. Undoubtedly, the men of "the golden age" were supposed to be "supermales" of unfailing virility. An important part of the advertising message lies, precisely, in this supermale legend skillfully transmitted to viewers who cherish this fantasy. In fact, the viewers are persuaded to identify with these strong figures, all the more mysterious and fascinating because they are unknown and suggested by a drawing rather than faithfully reproduced with the antimythological precision of the camera.

The proposed identification is not always of the same type. In certain cases one may want to suggest the atmosphere of a particular period. It is upon this phenomenon of identification with a historical period that certain advertisements wager, advertisements that in their style imitate pictorial productions of thirty or forty years ago. A drawing of a man or woman posing self-consciously, a badly printed drawing of a product, reminiscent of the days before the development of sophisticated printing techniques, are used to compose the poster. The overall picture recalls the advertising placards of the forties, and from the combined anachronisms emerges an impression of permanence. It would seem as though the product had weathered over years of use. Furthermore, the company that manufactures this product seemingly does not even need to update its advertising techniques, since the product sells so well; this company apparently can afford to economize on advertising. Simmenthal, an Italian company specializing in canned and processed foods, often uses this old-fashioned style of advertising, despite the preponderant tendency in Italy for very modern forms of aesthetic expression in advertising.

Following the pursued intention, by one detail or another one either will or will not indicate the temporal time frame of the poster. Thus, in some of Simmenthal's posters that use drawing, a very contemporary photo of a celebrity serves to date the message to some degree. In other cases this dating is com-

Grand Prix VR 70 parce qu'à plus de 210 km/h un pneu ordinaire ne suffit pas.

Figure 1-9

pletely omitted. To lure tourists to visit Paris (1971), a line of figures was shown in the classical pose of the dancers of the Folies Bergères; they included a typical Parisian *gendarme,* an existentialist young girl, an artist in a beret, and, of course, the obligatory dancer doing the cancan (fig. 1-8). Here the date would have confused the message. The impression sought is that of an eternal, timeless Paris, a city where everything is pleasure, dance, or fantasy. This is not a real policeman they want us to meet, but a sort of legendary, mythical policeman; the young existentialist is the eternal bohemian student whose praise they want to sing, and who will bring greater enjoyment to your visit to the City of Light. And, without a doubt, the concrete realism of photography would have created a barrier to this imagery of fable and illusion.

Does this mean that photography must always function as a reminder of reality? Advertising production assuredly is subject to very complex laws that we are barely beginning to discern, and in considering this subject many subtle distinctions must be made. This is what we shall try to do now by studying the use of advertising photography.

Photography

Supporting Evidence. The typically *documentary* function of photography can most clearly be seen in those cases where this medium of expression is used in conjunction with another, such as drawing. For example, Goodyear (1970–1971, 1972, 1973), presents us with billboards where we see photographs of tires placed at strategic points on drawings whose function is to evoke for us *the* road, in a few essential strokes (fig. 1-9). And, as we have already mentioned in our discussion of drawing, this road is to some extent timeless, and does not correspond to any specific place. This road is all the roads we can imagine. Contrasting with this vague and illusory background, highly detailed inset photographs allow us to examine closely the tire's tread and its inner construction. Each of the photographs illustrates a particular angle of the object. Even before printing a

Figure 1-10

single word of text, the billboard has already spoken: the road is yours to imagine, any way you like; we leave that up to you. There is, however, one thing about which we cannot allow ourselves to be vague and imprecise, and that is tires. Tires are a technical reality (requiring infinite precision), and this reality must be seen in contrast to the dream aspect of travel, with the adventure of the road, and so on.

Volkswagen (1972) superimposes the photograph of the latest model of its Beetle on the photo of a previous model. Arrows or indications point out the very minor changes made to the body. ''They can't be seen by the naked eye,'' one can almost hear. But the photograph, by providing invaluable supporting evidence, helps to identify the real subtleties of the transformation.

In an advertisement for a turntable (Philips, 1975), a close-up illustrates the machine's interior (fig. 1-10). In a triangular cutout, like an epigraph to the image, the turntable is shown in all the technical complexity and intricacy of its components; through modern technology, the feature the advertiser particularly wants to emphasize is enlarged. It is, in a way, microscopic proof. Truth, thanks to these demonstrations, should become, one might say, irrefutable.

But Technique Knows How to Dream, Too . . . If there has been a revolution in print advertising art, however, if photography has finally almost totally displaced sketches and drawings, it is less by representing the real in its exact and technological dimensions than by learning how to dream, to suggest. In effect, the formula we proposed earlier (drawing = imagination; photography = documentary precision) may be very interesting, but it has one major drawback. Ultimately, following this line of reasoning, it is impossible to escape from the confines of everyday life or concrete reality except by artificial means (represented here by drawing, for example). Therefore, still following the same argument, material reality is an impediment to freedom of expression, of movement or of invention, and so on.

As one might guess, this logic is extremely limiting. It hinders, so to speak, freedom of contact between buyer and seller, especially since consumers are all too familiar with the restrictions of everyday reality.

The ultimate trick, therefore, starting in fact precisely from the documentary aspect of photography, is to give dreams and illusions a semblance of reality. With all of the paradox it entails, this means providing proof for the fantastic. Dreams exist; they are not simply in a painter's palette or in the mind of an artist. "We have managed to photograph the unreal, the dream, the bizarre, the imaginary," these advertisers are saying. "We have even achieved absolute technical control over this imaginary universe." We will cite a number of advertisements of this type. The Myriam billboards (1981; fig. 1-11) have already caused more ink to be spilled than one might have wished. Nevertheless, we shall use this advertisement to undertake an analysis of this method of work that unites dreams to reality, to the conditions of an absolute mastery of the technical apparatus.

It should perhaps be made clear before we discuss this spectacular advertisement that roadside signs and outdoor billboard advertising sometimes pose a problem in France. On the one hand, since the advent of television, sponsors do not use this medium as much; on the other hand, as a result of cost cutting, the sign companies themselves sometimes neglect this type of advertising. Therefore, a billboard scheduled to appear on June 3, for example, may appear on the 15th; advertisements for a sale may be left up for two weeks after the sale is over. Under this haphazard system, some sponsors may either gain or lose two or more weeks of public exposure, with no way of knowing in advance which it will be. In other words, billboards are not always properly monitored.

The advertising agency Avenir-Publicité, which is known for its effective billboards, wanted to show its clients that it could overcome these habitual drawbacks and exercise complete control over the technological parameters of the medium.

Objective: to show that all of the billboards for a given advertising campaign throughout France could be replaced by a specified date, even within deadlines almost impossible to meet.

Such was the agency's initial mandate.

The next phase in designing the campaign was perfectly straightforward. The first sign promised that on a given date I will put up a given advertisement, and on that date the advertisement would appear. Up to that point there was nothing unusual about this campaign. The trick was to take it even further. This adver-

Figure 1-11

tisement of "something" had to show and the deadlines had to be spectacularly tight.

What happened next is now well known. In the first advertisement, Myriam, a French model who became famous overnight, wears a navy blue bikini. She (having become a billboard) promises: "September 2, I take off the top." September 2, breasts bare, she declares: "September 4, I take off the bottom." On September 4, we see her from behind, completely nude: she has kept her promise.

If we take a closer look at the way this campaign was organized, we can locate numerous levels of signification. The first level is already explicit: this advertiser keeps its promises and has smoothly running technology at its disposal.

On a second level, however, the advertisers are also telling us that women, in this case Myriam, are under their control. She obeys, we could almost say, their every wish. They have her undress on a specific and predetermined date. Therefore these advertisers know exactly how to seduce and dominate the female of the species.

Yet another level: these advertisers are capable of a relative imprudence and know how to defy the law. It would have been against French law to show pubic hair and full frontal nudity in this kind of advertising, and quite a few people wondered how the advertisers would extricate themselves from the hornet's nest into which they had apparently blundered. But they can handle it: they know their limits and exactly how far they can go. We can trust them.

Myriam, who is both the promise and the product, therefore becomes the guarantee of these advertisers' mastery over both technology and fantasy.

These effective advertisers never take no for an answer. For them, people are ready to do anything, including flirting with illegality. Interest is huge. And if you are a sponsor, if you wish to buy advertising space, you will be very tempted to trust your design ideas to such an agency. The implication is that other agencies let themselves be weighed down by reality, that they come too late or ejaculate prematurely. They are bogged down, clumsy and ineffectual, they do not keep their promises, or they never rise above mediocrity, and, above all, they have no imagination. Is not real technology the one that gives pleasure?

This advertising campaign has since often been plagiarized. But the initial effect could never be duplicated. Thus was an advertising classic born.

A 1974 poster for J. B. Martin shows five legs wearing different colored pantyhose (orange, brown, red, navy, and rust) sticking out of the back of the trunk of a Mercedes (fig. 1-12). How did those legs get there? Whose are they, and why are there five of them? The odd number adds to the mystery. What is more, each leg is wearing a different colored hose. What are five different people doing in the trunk of a car, and were they locked in? Whatever the answers to these questions may be, one fact remains: the legs are there, they exist, and there

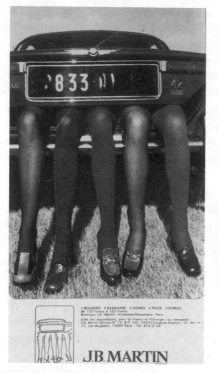

Figure 1-12

Figure 1-16

Figure 1-13

Figure 1-14

Figure 1-15

is tangible proof of their existence. The fantasy has been recorded on film. In legal parlance, the illusion has basis in fact. In the same vein, Levi's used Ingres's painting *The Water Carrier* (fig. 1-13), Michelangelo's *David* (fig. 1-15), and, with incredible irreverence, Michelangelo's *Creation of Adam* (fig. 1-14). God the Father is handing Adam a pair of bell-bottom jeans. The water carrier is dressed in matching jeans and jacket. David sports a pair of denim cutoffs. Fantasy suddenly assumes the value of reality, and photography, which is supposed to be an accurate means of documentation, guarantees the authenticity of this reality.

When the musical *Hair* was still very popular, Levi's borrowed typical attitudes and gestures from this rock musical. The advertisement (fig. 1-16) shows a group of young people exulting in the love and togetherness typical of the sixties, and raising their arms to the sky in an ecstatic gesture of freedom, recalling the finale of the musical.

Another advertising campaign that mixed fantasy and reality was the ''Dutch Masters'' campaign of the Stella Artois beer company (fig. 1-17). It made references to the rich tradition of Dutch painting (including works by Rembrandt) using the modern medium of photography. No doubt with a wink in the direction of respect for historical continuity, this is also a prelude to putting the viewer in the mood for drinking beer. In any case, the pictures evoke both the subjects and the lighting of the great masters. Here we see familiar objects, a knowing look. We are on *home turf*. Does this mean we will buy more beer? This is not immediately obvious, but Europeans seem to appreciate this type of cultural reference. Aphrodis Wines uses similar allusions to mythology and classical art. Hermès, on the other hand, contrasts a palace garden and a very modern woman within the same small advertisement (fig. 1-18). Perhaps this opposition expresses the real question: how can we achieve this marriage between our cultural heritage and its contemporary transformation? Products that promise to help resolve such a problematic are apparently more likely to sell better than others.

In a 1983 campaign, Pall Mall takes full advantage of this surrealistic blend of art and concrete reality. In the foreground of photographs of magnificent, dreamlike scenery (the Grand Canyon or a beautiful beach, for example) there appears an unlikely object (fig. 1-19). A rectangular container, the same size and almost the exact replica of the Pall Mall cigarette pack, this object is sometimes a soft drink can (a rectangular one, naturally), sometimes a car battery (terminals added). The effect is somewhat startling, like a painting by Magritte or De Chirico.

There is, however, one detail missing in this description. The ''Pall Mall'' object is a box of matches, or at least that is what is *written* on the package. If we saw cigarettes, it was because *we* added them. This is more than a clever trick. Thanks to our own projection, we ourselves become designers.

What is more, the metaphoric redundance of the repudiated object is not accidental. The pack of cigarettes that was first rejected, then transformed into a

Figure 1-17

Figure 1-18

Figure 1-19

box of matches, and later turned into a can of soda pop, conjures up an extremely complex series of associations. From the taboo against smoking, we are led to the idea of ''playing with fire,'' and from there to ''refreshment,'' to ''recharging'' or to ''relaxation,'' with no time to pay attention to the thought process. The photographic image is extremely sharp and the beads of moisture on the soft drink can, for example, indicate the use of top-quality film. The appeal of this hyper-realism cancels out the guilt-producing presence of tobacco and makes the paradox of smoking/not smoking possible, at least on the visual level. The technique here is ultraconcrete, but it makes full use of fantasy.

But photography is not satisfied merely to merge with art, stealing, so to speak, its effects and its classic canvases. It also wants to create its very own effects, in other words, to create an illusory and real world relying only on its own resources.

If several photos are cut up and then put together haphazardly on a piece of cardboard, they create the definite impression of a hodgepodge of images. When the pictures are of cars, it is impossible to tell how they fit together. The body of one car can just as easily match up with the rear or front section of a completely different make of car. The relative position of these parts becomes completely random, and if, in addition, they are vehicles that have been damaged in a collision, they are simply no longer recognizable as cars. Everything seems to become mangled, tangled and piled up into the most indescribably mixed-up mess. This is the image the Swiss government decided to use in a campaign for accident prevention. The visual shock came from the way the components of the image were arranged, rather than from the individual fragmentary pictures. But once again, photography, by "guaranteeing" the veracity of this document, made it far more powerful and convincing than a drawing.

In an advertisement for the Mexican Tourist Office, the technique used to appeal to the viewer's fantasies is extremely simple, if not downright elementary. Quite simply, two photographs are superimposed. One shows a young European woman on vacation, with a broad smile on her face, completely relaxed, enjoying her freedom (fig. 1-20). Her skirt fades into and merges with the underlying photo of a typically Mexican landscape of sun-parched mountains and an Aztec temple, the classical setting. Obviously, this woman is "part of" the mountain. Her happiness is photographically linked with the scenery, merging and mingling with this innocuous pleasure. She is the happiness that is Mexico, and the dream-like impression works very well, particularly since the diaphanous outlines of this picture recall the transparency, the veiled insubstantiality of certain dream images. The blurred effect, achieved here technically by superimposing the two photographs and necessarily affecting the definition of some details, is reminiscent of the vague, hazy quality of dreams. But at the same time, photography, which allows us to master reality, makes this dream appear real and concrete — which goes to show that it is not always the most complicated techniques that are most effective.

The Plureal. As we have said, photography is both persuasive "proof" of reality, which must exist since it can leave an impression on film, and at the same time supporting evidence for unreality and fantasy, a testimony to the enchanting, spellbinding translucence of certain dreams. Following this logic, has there

Figure 1-20

ever been an advertising poster that tried to render a reality more real than the real? In other words, a poster that showed that illusion can absolutely take on flesh and blood existence? That advertisement was for the Brandt company, to promote television sets. A cowboy is on the screen; on the floor, in front of the set, as if it were an extension of the screen, we see the very distinct shadow of this same cowboy, right out of a Leone film (fig. 1-21). The character on the screen is so real that he even casts a shadow on the floor.

This advertisement, along with some others we have looked at since, confirmed our initial intuition that if photography has managed to supplant drawing in advertising over the past few years, it was possible only on one condition: photography, like drawing, had to find out how to figure the unfigurable. As the medium became more refined, it mastered this art. It therefore becomes usable as a "purveyor of illusions," illusions for which it has the immense advantage of being able to confer a character of absolute reality.

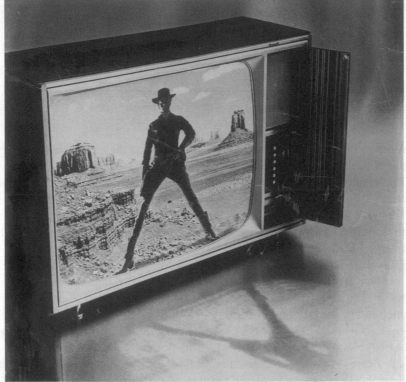

Figure 1-21. "Brandt talks to you straight."

Design

As we said at the beginning of this chapter, walls, streets, and cities are over-run with posters. And yet these messages have to get through to the already over-whelmed, harried spectator. As we continue to peel away the outer layers of advertising techniques, we begin to understand the complex process of capturing the viewer's attention. We already suspect that by contrasting with the gray sameness of everyday life, advertisements offer themselves as an invitation to dream. To stand out sharply against a background of reality, they become unreal, surprising, unusual, precisely because they slip away from ordinary, everyday life.

Figure 1-22

They fill a kind of void, a need we have to transcend the predictable, flat regularity of commute, job, bedtime.

With this in mind, the graphic design element of the poster takes on great importance. What we call *design* or *graphics* here is nothing other than those curved or straight, regular or irregular lines borrowed from op or pop art that adorn many advertisements, just as they appear elsewhere on walls or in images with a more specifically aesthetic intention.

This *design* is not meant to be a specific representation of the real. In contrast to line drawing, it does not seek to represent the essential outline of an object. Its purpose is quite different: to reflect a mood or an atmosphere. Because it is not limited to the representation of reality, it can distance itself from what is real, suggest futuristic visions, and deal with an unexpected dimension of the object — its speed or its lightness, for example (see the poster for *Easy Rider* in chapter 2). In other cases it will evoke celebration or fanfare, as in certain posters for international fairs or circuses. It is to be found in advertising for athletic events and in publicity for museums and art galleries, where it represents the impact of ideas. Since it is an extremely fluid and flexible means of expression, design could, if necessary, express everything. Recall the advertisement for electricity in France in 1973: concentric circles recalling the spirals of a snail's shell, simultaneously turning in on itself and radiating outward. How could photography or writing have been conducive to such an atmosphere? This could only be achieved by a graphic technique. What is more, this drawing must try to represent not the real, but something else, which is entirely appropriate for this means of expression we are calling design.

In a Roche-Bobois advertisement we are not shown a single piece of furniture (fig. 1-22). Presumably the public is sufficiently aware of this company's reputation for manufacturing furniture. But the luxury and originality of an ultramod-

Figure 1-23

ern decor are suggested by curved lines whose sensuality, gratuitousness, and freedom express the very elements the advertiser wishes to accentuate in the promotion of the product.

Modernism, if not futurism, is in itself a subject worthy of study in great depth. In fact, the message contained in many advertisements hinges on the idea of escape from reality. In contrast with the attachment to the past mentioned earlier (in the Simmenthal advertisements, among others), the use of *design* suggests escape not backward, but forward. The escape hatch leads to the future. Tomorrow will bring better days and nobler deeds, and although we cannot picture it today, we can at least suggest a vague, allusive outline, a hint of what is yet to come. This hint of tomorrow, this blueprint for a time when everything will be pure and simple, finds its natural expression in pure and simple lines, in aerodynamic curves freed from all restraint—that is, in design. It is appropriate to mention here that Roche-Bobois specializes in ultramodern furniture, and on the level of style it is always striving for purity of curve and line. In this particular case, there is an almost perfect isomorphism between the medium (design) and the product (ultramodern furniture).

In other cases, the liberating and symbolic intent of design does not necessarily have the futuristic overtones we have just described. A 1970 advertisement for Hamol, for example, shows a woman sitting with her back to us, wearing a swimsuit (fig. 1-23). Her back is bare and she wears a hat to protect her from the

Figure 1-24

Figure 1-25. ''The biggest shiver since *Jaws*.''

sun. We can easily imagine her on a beach getting a suntan. But the focus of interest in this poster is the woman's swimsuit. It is made up of colored bands. To put it more precisely, it is an exact replica of the colors of the visual spectrum. To be less technical, we could say that it shows all the colors of the rainbow. On this level, we see a representation in design of the warmth of the sun's rays, or of optimism, or of the promise of good weather, all of which are usually suggested by rainbows. On another level, however, it must be made clear that these colored stripes are typically found on the packaging of Hamol products, especially their suntan cream. The rainbow colors are a direct reference both to the product and to the situation in which it is used. The simplicity of this message allows the advertiser to reduce the text to, simply, "Hamol ultra." The rest is *said* elsewhere. The message is suggested, and for the purpose at hand, the suggestion is more than enough.

In a very similar way, advertisements for Seitanes and Gallia rely on nothing more than a very clever interplay of colors and shapes to express their message. Curving, branchlike shapes are barely visible against the velvety sheen of a deep-blue background in harmony with the packaging of the product: this is the advertising formula used to promote Seitanes. Design without artifice. Free-flowing creativity. The artistic effect is the one major consideration. The same is true of the Gallia advertisement where the sky becomes a strip of blue between two strips of white (fig. 1-24). Here again the setting is marked by a highly stylized white tree. We are definitely in the realm of the imagination. And if it were not for the product, which is seen in profile as a sort of label for the picture, we would think we were in a museum. The poster for Pernod, which works along the same lines, is somewhat more complex (fig. 1-25). The illustration is not quite as pure, and even though on the whole it deserves to be called design, it already introduces us to complex processes and to the more sophisticated compositions of visual advertisements.

With these remarks on design, we complete our commentary on the elementary processes used in print advertising. The next step is to examine the way in which these elements are combined. Writing, the eternal medium, is used mostly in combination with other media. Drawing rarely appears by itself. Its imaginary aspect is often supplemented by the documentary evidence of photography or the evocative power of design. Most effective advertising is the result of a skillful blend of these various elements. We shall now concentrate more specifically on the issue of advertising composition.

Advertising Posters: Their Composition

A 1971 print advertisement shows a typical French street scene: a no parking sign signals as much (fig. 1-26). It is in fact a street corner in a large city. A building site surrounded by a rough plywood fence shows that construction or renovation is in progress: we are in a city where construction is booming or in a neighbor-

Figure 1-26

hood where buildings are either being demolished or under construction. The boarding around the construction site appears to be covered with wire mesh, perforated panels, or some unusual kind of barrier. Our attention is drawn by the words on these see-through boards: "Urgo is full of holes." Is this graffiti, some kind of revolutionary slogan, or just antiestablishment grumblings? Could this be a slur aimed at some politician whose name is Urgo? These conjectures seem unlikely, given the typography of this brief message. The letters are too regular, too perfectly made, too well-balanced to fit in with the rest of the picture. They are completely at odds with the overall impression (and here we should consider everything the word *impression* evokes — impression, printing, imprint). We were anticipating a protest against the monstrous growth of the megalopolis, or an accusation against a politician responsible for flagrant or indiscriminate development of an urban neighborhood. But we are taken aback when this expectation is thwarted by an advertising message. Urgo is in fact the brand name of a bandage. Naturally it is full of holes, as it should be, and what we mistook at first glance for a mesh fence is just a reproduction of how this bandage looks. The urban wound it covers is simply meant to suggest all of those other minor wounds for which Urgo might be used. From the gaping atrocity of urban wounds, we have come down to harmless individual cuts and scrapes. Dissident graffiti have become an advertising message. If we wanted to examine this image from a political point of view, there would certainly be no lack of details to support such an interpretation. But at this point it is not our intention to stress the ideological value of the advertisement; to begin with we are merely trying to analyze the rules of its composition.

With this in mind, the Urgo advertisement allows us to identify several basic elements. Indeed, as rudimentary as this may appear, every print advertisement consists of an image, a direct reference to the product, and, finally, a text. This last element, the text, should in turn be subdivided; in fact we make a distinction between the *slogan* and the more strictly *informative* text. In the Urgo advertisement this element of information is lacking. It is not there because the viewer is presumably already familiar with the product. The name Larousse [Webster or Oxford for anglophones] needs no further explanation; everyone knows that this word is synonymous with dictionary. Similarly, Urgo denotes bandage [as "Band-Aid" does in the United States]. In this case, the direct reference to the product is included in the slogan: "Urgo is full of holes." We have already described the indirect reference to the product, in other words the image. This is a bandage designed to protect wounds of varying degrees of seriousness.

In many situations, however, the advertiser cannot afford to use such a concise message. Each of the components will therefore take on a different value, depending on the intention of the advertiser.

Nice 'n Easy advertisements are an excellent illustration of this point. Two thirds of the advertising space is occupied by a photograph of a woman with dark brown hair (fig. 1-27). The text beside it is a slogan: "Free to be me." In one corner of the advertisements the words "Nice 'n Easy" and an illustration of the packaging of these hair-color products provide a direct reference to the product. Once again informational text is lacking. In fact, the product is very well known to the public, or at least can claim as much. In 1950, however, when it was relatively new, a long explanatory text was included in these advertisements.

Generally speaking, we find explanatory texts with products that are new, not well known, or technically complex. Volkswagen, for instance, could justifiably claim to be sufficiently well known to do without explanatory comments. It does not do so, because its product, an automobile, requires the inclusion of technical information. Moreover, the text in Volkswagen advertisements systematically describes the car's unseen advantages, such as technical performance, gas mileage, and passenger capacity, or relates anecdotes about the difference it makes in one's daily life. The typography of this text, which has not changed in several years, is purposely spare and unadorned. Its lack of artifice conveys the impression of a discreet technical document. The slogan is usually placed with the photography in these advertisements, whereas the logo, a circle containing a *V* over a *W*, appears at the end of the written text as a final period. Unlike Urgo's, Volkswagen advertisements are models of flawless classicism.

The fashion house Rodier added a certain classical touch to its 1970–1971 advertising (fig. 1-28). And as in the case of Volkswagen, the classicism in the advertise-

Figure 1-27. "Free to be me."

ment refers directly to the classical lines of its product. In the three Rodier advertisements we are examining here, the arrangement of compositional elements is
perfectly balanced. The text takes up one page and the image fills the other in a two-
page spread. The slogan serves as a title for the explanatory text; it is therefore
printed in large, bold type. The Rodier logo, the only direct reference to the product,
appears at the bottom of the text, like a signature. Another important feature is the
reappearance of the large image on the left side of the advertisement in miniature at
the end of the printed text, as though to underline the fact that this text was referring
to the image and also to make the image part of the text.

There is nothing really surprising, then, in the composition of these three advertisements. But, as we said before, modern advertising must be unusual, provocative, and compelling. This is not a problem, since the unusual element here
is in the slogan:

"How to look like an intellectual without getting a headache."

Figure 1-28

"How to look athletic without getting muscle-bound."

"How to look like an artist without the angst."

Aren't these, finally, the kinds of questions many women ask themselves?— along with how to give birth without pain, how to learn German without difficulty, how to lose weight without sacrifice, and so on.

The level of humor found in these advertisements is likely to provoke a chuckle from a certain class of consumers, exactly the kind of people at whom Rodier's advertisements are aimed. Their clothes are well made, fairly expensive, and intended for a reasonably sophisticated clientele. The explanatory text carries on in the same comic vein: "If you really *are* an intellectual . . . ," "If you really *are* an athlete . . . "

If a classical layout brings out, or in any case accentuates, the classical nature of a product, it does not seem aberrant to maintain that compositions that are irregular, incongruous, or unexpected also aim at underlining the eccentric, whimsical, unpredictable, or exotic dimensions of a product. Its extraordinary aspect is thus conveyed pictorially.

We are all voyeurs to some extent, although generally we do not easily dare admit it to ourselves. This tendency might conceivably lead us to, for example, stare at the buttocks of persons of either sex who happen to be standing in front of us. Through their clothing we might try to imagine the shape of their bodies. But at the same time, the unavowability of this urge would lead us to turn our look, out of modesty, to other, less overtly sexual parts of the body.

In one of its advertisements, Camel offers us this kind of spectacle (fig. 1-29). The entire page is taken up by the buttocks and thighs of a person of undetermined sex. So as not to shock or offend our voyeurism, this rear end is clothed in denim jeans. But the photography is done with such precision that we can see every fiber of the denim, every thread of the orange stitching (at the top of the pocket, for example). No pun intended, our nose is glued to this pair of buns, and the whole thing would be almost obscene if there were nowhere else to direct our look. By skillful effects of lighting, the crotch, potentially too provocative, has been left in shadow. The only thing left to look at is the decorative stitching on the back pocket of these fashionable jeans. And this is where shrewdness comes in: the camel on the famous cigarette pack is embroidered on the pocket. The direct reference to the product, its name, and the specifics are also found in this place at which we can look without embarrassment. The slogan is at the top of the page where the prurient sharpness of the photograph has no interest; the product is also presented in a "neutral zone" of the page, on the leg of the person we are looking at. The slogan says simply: "Now everyone loves camels." Does this mean that, faced with such a feast for the eyes, we begin to love (to desire) camels (the behind) in front of us? Does "now" mean now that we have seen that?

One thing is certain: our attention has been attracted by an erotic come-on, and by trying not to appear immodest, our eye is trapped into absorbing infor-

Figure 1-29. "Now everyone loves camels."

mation. Since Camel is a well-known brand, any informative text would be superfluous, especially when we consider that technical information is hardly necessary for a cigarette.

The documentary aspect the text usually adds to an advertisement is here largely supplied by the documentary precision of the photograph, which was almost certainly taken with a large-format camera. And as a result, the layout of the poster is magnificently balanced.

When we say that the essential balance of the advertisement is achieved by means of the documentary photograph, it is certainly not to construct a metaphor. It seems to us, on the contrary, that the myriad dimensions of the advertising act are generally deliberately conceived according to a design governed by certain specific laws.

The frequency with which fantasy and reality, the imaginary and the informative, are contrasted is by no means the result of chance. On the contrary, the sacred and the profane, the desired and the unobtainable and the forbidden, are all so omnipresent in advertising rhetoric that it must be concluded that this polarity is a desired effect.

In this advertisement for Camel cigarettes, the buttocks represent, to some extent, the element of the profane; on the other hand, this concept of the profane is counterbalanced by a notion of the sacred, the methodical and scientific precision with which the denim fabric is represented. The casualness that is suggested finds its counterpart in the effort of representation. The obsession with sexual parts of the body and voyeurism are contradicted by the obsession with accurate reproduction and the painstaking work of the photographer.

The camel embroidered on denim may seem eccentric; the words "Camel Filters" appear to remind us of the sacred character of print. The allusive slogan suggests that the person wearing these jeans adores Camels to the point of embroidering the brand image on his or her pants pocket. That is undoubtedly a sensitive area (are the buttocks not a sensitive, erogenous zone?). So that now (in other words, now that we know this person has such a soft spot for Camels), everyone loves camels. This person is, of course, none other than the personified object of desire, an object that is both forbidden and attainable (by purchasing the product), an object we are at once tempted to hold sacred and to profane.

We said earlier, in our discussion of the various elements, or, more precisely, the elementary processes of advertising composition, that some of these processes were more conducive to the expression of fantasy or the fantastic (comics, for example), of unreality juxtaposed with reality (out-of-focus or abstract photography), and so on. It should be pointed out here that very few advertisements convey their messages using only one of these elementary processes. In most cases we find instead a skillful blend of techniques, where reality verges on fantasy, where the sacred refers to the profane (Rodier used humor to lighten or "demystify" a page that otherwise would have been too austere).

The function of writing in this delicate balance is to accentuate the sacred, except in cases where type is deliberately distorted to the point where it becomes profane. Usually, moreover, the profane or whimsical aspect is better served by an unorthodox image or else by a sharp, witty (and hence irrational) slogan. The factual aspect will be brought out by the information supplied in the text, or by an image that is technically hyperaccurate.

Even in the poster promoting the attractions of Paris, in which a group of typical Parisians dance an improbable and completely fanciful cancan, the word *Paris* alone supplies what is needed for a sacred element.

Obviously, the relationship between sacred and profane, between fantastic and factual, will vary from one advertisement to another, but we have yet to find one without at least some indication that these barriers have been crossed.

When all is said and done, are these remarks really so surprising? Surely we all know, at least intuitively, that the true function of advertising is none other than to suggest, without drawing undue attention to the fact, the possibility of escape from reality and factuality, by opening the door to fantasy and by offering the product as a means of escape.[2]

Appeal to Defense

Psychoanalytic practice often leads, sometimes even imperceptibly, to a denunciation of defense mechanisms in order to help the individual find healthier and more flexible ways of adjusting to reality. We are too prone to forget the equally important positive aspects of these mechanisms—at least in terms of adaptivity—and the extreme frequency with which they are used by the psychic apparatus. It is clear, for example, that in day-to-day existence the individual would find the exemplary lucidity of perpetual self-criticism unbearable and prefers to rely on processes of displacement and projection. These processes of course do not lead to an accurate assessment of a situation. But is it psychologically possible to maintain constant and scrupulous awareness of all factors in any situation?

Advertising, in any case, is based on a negative response to this question. Far from encouraging human beings to engage in constant reflection on the extent of their freedom of action and the importance of their personal role in the sequence of events, it encourages them to make use of their most common psychological defenses. Instead of calling them to order with self-awareness, it offers them a message whose structure is modeled on such mental habits as projection, displacement, identification, or repression, if not denial or condensation. An impression of ease finally authorized, or at least one of "unconscious permitted," emerges. It is possibly for this reason that some advertisements seem to elicit a feeling of well-being.

In the following section, therefore, it is not the effects of discursive rhetoric that we are going to examine, but rather the defenses to which advertising appeals. Nevertheless, rhetorical discourse will be studied as part of this operation, since it inevitably contributes to this appeal to unconscious defenses.

Displacement: A Basic Objective of Advertising

The psychoanalytic theory of displacement is closely linked with the economic hypothesis that states that the quanta of psychic energy connected with a representation can eventually become separated from it, travel along associative pathways toward another representation, and then become attached to this second representation in an equivalent, or rather a substitutive, manner. This phenomenon, as can be demonstrated, frequently occurs in the case of dreams, where the object vested with power is seen to be represented by one of its associative representations, or one of its symbols. Similarly, in everyday life, we often attribute to representations a quantum of energy that does not actually belong to them, representations that are really only substitutes for profoundly vested objects.

Obviously, the expression "along associative pathways" leaves room for more than one hypothesis, and it is clear that we have not finished exploring all of these subtle connections linking together signs or representations—whether visual or aural—of the psychic apparatus. To put it briefly, we could even say that this task constitutes the essential part of the practical and theoretical work of psychoanalysis. Our aim is not, however, to engage in further psychoanalysis, but merely to see how the advertising message uses and capitalizes on this phenomenon of displacement to constantly direct the eye as it reads the message intended to capture its attention.

If, for example, we think back to Freud's famous case of Little Hans, we will recall the logic of association that leads the child from the image of the potentially castrating father to the representative horse. Between these two images— the father and the horse—the semantic identity is obviously not maintained, but the psychic apparatus still tries to find a relative equivalence. The horse, it will be recalled, helps to conceal the sexual and oedipal aspects of the conflict, and in this sense is more economically convenient.

Indisputably, the advertising sign will try to take advantage of this phenomenon of representations traveling along associative pathways. Thus, in place of images that might cause anxiety, it will try to substitute representations that are more acceptable, more in tune with psychological defenses. This is obviously where its primary interest lies.

In 1955, Marlboro introduced into its advertising the very appealing figure of a cowboy, who eventually became known as "the Marlboro man."

This man is tall, lean, and virile; his outfit includes all the requisite accessories—leather chaps, spurs, a wide belt complete with a Colt .45, and a broad-brimmed Stetson. A tall man on a tall horse, he is, in short, the classic image of the handsome cowboy.

There is no doubt that the aim of the advertiser here is to force home the association between cowboy and cigarette and to produce in each of us a displacement along this chain of associations. But what is much less explicit is the latent axis of this displacement: its point of origin and its ultimate outcome. The advertisement is merely a trace or a fraction of the distance covered. The rest is hidden.

Therefore, in order to understand the entire process, we must break it down. Initially we must draw attention to trivial details. Given its different variations, the advertisement generally includes the following elements:

1. A vast, untamed landscape, which is also, in the sense of the classic image of the Wild West, legendary.
2. A cowboy and his horse: usually at rest, although in more recent advertisements this element of repose is no longer a constant.
3. A reference to the product.
4. An ambiguous slogan linking cigarette and country.

Another thing we know is that this associative chain works, since for twenty-five years it has done a great job of selling one of the world's most popular cigarettes.

The connection between the cowboy and the scene is fairly banal. The man in question is master of the country, a pioneer, who takes the law into his own hands and must fight to protect his livestock. In return, the endless horizon belongs to him and he enjoys possession of the land he calls his own. In one sense he is the American conqueror of the Wild West, but in another sense he is also the European looking for a world where history is still to be made. He is the kind of outlaw each of us secretly carries within.

Curiously enough, what he is "publicizing" is also a product that is to some extent outside the law. Smoking is well known to be dangerous to health. Indeed, in 1955, cigarette manufacturers and advertisers were perfectly well aware of this aspect of nicotine addiction, even though it was not as well documented as it is now.

The cowboy also risks his life. He lives in a lawless country. From him the image can easily shift toward the cigarette.

The daredevil aspect of the Marlboro cowboy becomes even clearer since this company has invested large sums of money in the endorsement of Formula One race car drivers.

In the wake of recent antismoking campaigns, many companies have focused their advertising on the low tar and nicotine content of their product, using comparative figures, and so on. Marlboro, like a few other tobacco manufacturers, has not changed its tactics one bit. It knows full well it is outside the law, and the cowboy who has been its symbol for more than twenty years is still perfectly in keeping with the company's advertising objectives.

The inscription at the top of the advertisement is nothing other than the suggested route for achieving the desired displacement: "Come to Marlboro Country."

"Come." Come! Join this cowboy! Come: this vast, rugged country, this virgin land belongs to you. Come! *Come* obviously includes all of the sexual connotations the word implies, which are also evoked by the strong masculine appeal of the man and his thoroughbred horse.

"To Marlboro Country" suggests a free country, one free of laws. This is danger country, where every day brings total freedom and a brush with death. This cowboy really does face death, bedding down in the desert and in the snow. He travels light, and he is entitled to smoke, since he is already risking his life anyway. You can get away to this country, too, by smoking these cigarettes. You are basically powerless, castrated people, not daring enough to invent such a country. Your humdrum everyday experience never puts your life immediately in danger. But we can offer you a chance to live dangerously. Go ahead and smoke! Your adventures begin in Marlboro Country.

Figure 1-30

It will no doubt be objected that this allusion to death is probably going too far, except in particular cases. By way of an answer it must be stated that while the figure of the cowboy is primarily an American myth, it nevertheless constitutes one of the archetypes of contemporary imagery. This free and unfettered man of adventure, in complete contrast to the standard bureaucrat, in fact corresponds to a desire deep within every one of us to live life as we please without having to answer to anyone. At the same time, we are fully aware of the constraints of reality on such an existence. And this image is as appealing in Europe as anywhere else. It is found, for example, in the advertising for Brandt (television sets), which is aimed at a strictly European audience. Therefore, in our view, the first objection simply does not hold water.

As for the allusion to death and the death wish, it is easy to find in a more or less explicit form in various advertisements. Canadian Club, a brand of Canadian rye whiskey, for example, for several years (1975–1982) offered its readers a series of death-defying adventures. More recently, Real cigarettes adopted this theme of the daredevil-adventurer, shown in the desert or elsewhere (fig. 1-30). Camel (1981) uses the same theme, with African jungle settings, and Peter Stuyvesant (1983) shows people traveling in hot-air balloons (fig. 1-31). Death is again in evidence in an advertisement for watches in the January 1979 issue of *Vogue* in which the watch is simply shown beside a marble tomb effigy

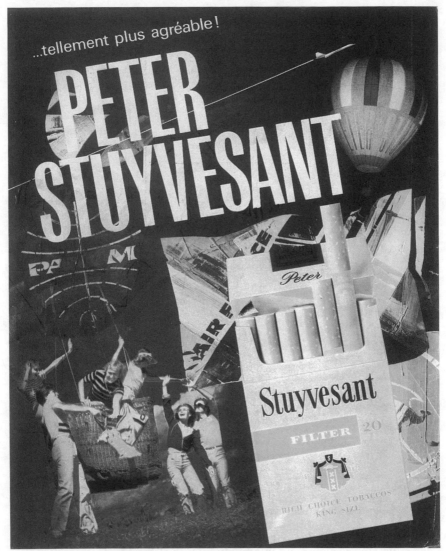

Figure 1-31. "So much milder!"

(fig. 1-32), no doubt indicating that with this watch you are able to disregard the time that leads you to your death. Therefore, on this point also, the objection does not stand up to analysis.

With some degree of certainty, therefore, we can now trace the route suggested for our possible defensive displacement in this type of advertising, as synthesized in the accompanying arrangement.

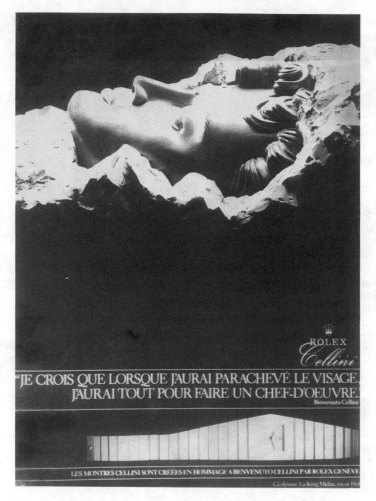

Figure 1-32. "I think that once I've finished the face, I will have done everything to create a masterpiece."

Path of displacement in advertisements of the Marlboro type

Logic
The product to be advertised has a close connection with death and the dread of death.

Typical examples
Cigarettes are a threat to health; consumption of alcohol is linked to a dread of existential void.

To hide this connection, the strategy consists in showing a character in a relation with death . . .	Marlboro and Winston cowboys, Real and Parliament pilots, Marlboro Formula 1 race car drivers, Canadian Club mountain climber, Camel safari hunter, Peter Stuyvesant adventurer
. . . but one that stresses healthy, attractive, positive dimensions.	The freedom of the great outdoors for the cowboy, the adulation of the crowd for the race car driver, the warmth of friendship in Canadian Club, photographic substitution in Pall Mall
In order to associate it with the product for sale,	Pictorial proximity of the logo and the protagonist
the association is summed up by a simple slogan.	Come to Marlboro Country, Peter Stuyvesant Mildness

It is fairly obvious that this displacement moves from the death wish to desire to overcome death and attain freedom; as in the case of Little Hans and his horse, it is self-evident that the second proposition (freedom) produces far less anxiety than the first. Thus it offers a much more plausible focus for energy than the image of castration or death. There is probably no real choice, and we are therefore more or less forced to invest energy in the cowboy if we do not want to think about our castration or our death.

Obviously, all advertising does not always have such a tragic underlying meaning. Displacement is often directed more toward the libido. On the other hand, it can be said that there is no advertising without displacement and that, in most instances, it offers us a more or less conscious choice between two pictorial propositions, of which one, defensive but pleasant, will be markedly preferable to the other, which is castrating or anxiety-producing.

Denial, Denegation

The tactic of displacing libidinal energy from an unpleasant or unacceptable representation to one that is pleasant and acceptable can sometimes, because of the extreme polarity of the contrasted objects, be tantamount to denying a certain reality, to negating a drive to which one appeals, or inversion of this drive to its opposite.

Reference was made earlier to the advertisement for Cellini watches. In a more detailed analysis here we will point out that the two values shown together are extremely contradictory. The representation "watch" refers to the measurement of time, to limitation, and to noneternity, in other words, to the mortality, corporeality, and narcissistic castration of the subject. Conversely, the carved marble bust recalls the timelessness of great works of art and of stone.

On the other hand, and this is where the two propositions come together, the bust is shown here lying or having fallen down. It reminds us of the effigy on a tomb and, very clearly, of death itself. At the same time, the watch as measurement of time and narcissistic castration is encased in gold and described by the text as eternal: "From this object we have created a work of art." It has therefore been transformed into its opposite and associated with the search for eternity.

Very clearly, we are witnessing a double propositional mutation:

What you see is an instrument for keeping time.
denial
What you see *is not* an instrument for keeping time.
reversal into its opposite
What you see is a token of eternity.

The viewer is invited into a displacement. But this particular displacement is characterized by the fact that the final proposition is the symmetrical inversion of the original proposition, which has in the meantime been denied.

In our analysis of the Marlboro advertisements, we noted that the death wish was not referred to in and of itself, but instead was redirected to the cigarette under the guise of exploring boundaries.

Other cigarette manufacturers (Salem and Gallia) did not dare to take such a risk. Their advertisements tend instead to deny the death drive. The images suggest a rural setting: a little brook or clear spring water serve as supporting decor. The text evokes freshness, a taste for life, the purity of nature. This is more than mere displacement; in fact we are witnessing a denial of the death urge, a denial of the toxic effects of smoking, and a reversal to the opposite qualities of freshness, life, and purity.

In another example of this phenomenon, the text reads: "They see your hair. Not the hair spray." Indeed, standing out against the black background of the poster, we see a close-up of a head of blond hair. The outstretched hand in front of the hair seems to be holding an object, but the hand is actually empty. We do not see the hair spray because it is invisible, so invisible in fact that we cannot even see its container.

It is clear that from a logical point of view, the operation suggested here is one of denial.

"If you want to be beautiful, you need a hair spray."
(Denial of castration)

"If you want to be beautiful, you don't need a hair spray."
(Since this hair spray is an absence of hair spray)

The rhetoric of advertising, which we attempted to decode and classify at the beginning of this work, does not strictly serve, as we have seen, to bring out any particular detail or to direct attention to any particular aspect of the product; it aims primarily at encouraging or appealing to the customary defense mechanisms that allow us to gain in apparent ease what we lose in worrisome lucidity.

Invitation to Repression

It is fairly well known that a drive that is too shameful to be admitted will very often be repressed, but will also subsequently resurface in the consciousness in a disguised form that represents both the drive and the taboo attached to it. This explains, in psychoanalysis, the formation of the symptom. This also explains, on the more general level of defense mechanisms, "compromise formation." A good many advertising structures appeal to this process.

One example is a perfume advertisement that proclaims that its fragrance is both untamed (a reference to drive) and civilized (drive brought under control).

But there are even more subtle ones. Recently, for example, there has been a tendency in advertising for women's underwear to use images of two pretty women standing close together (fig. 1-33). Obviously, this is a subtle way of suggesting closeness, innocent homosexuality, the particular kind of friendship women share. It is also a way of flattering the women's movement. In advertisements for bras made by the French firm Barbara, two tanned women are shown touching each other, one facing front, the other with her back to the camera; both of their faces are left discreetly in shadow. The curves of one body actually fill the hollows of the other. Even Yashica cameras have focused on this lesbian theme. We might almost conclude that following the masculine myth, the feminine myth came into its own, since products like Kim cigarettes claim that they are "too elegant for a man's hand" (fig. 1-34). (There are many examples of this phenomenon, although sometimes it is dealt with more subtly.) Three women are shown sharing a pack of Kim cigarettes in a safari-type vehicle: capable of adventure, without men.

On the level of the propositions, the underlying logic in these advertisements reproduces exactly, point by point, the psyche's process of repression and subsequent creation of compromise:

You have lesbian tendencies (men even seem to you a bit thick-headed). (Kim)
↓
These drives can be partially repressed . . .
↓
. . . but can be experienced on the level of affectionate friendship (Barbara), by

pour celles qui aiment... *le naturel la douceur le confo*

Pony
de **Barbara**
17 rue Vergniaud, 75640 PARIS Cedex 13 - tél. 589.40.60

LA MODE EST AU NU...

Suivez-la
en soutien-gorge AUBADE

Elles ont choisi les ensembles "invisibles" Warner...

Figure 1-33

Une cigarette
longue, fine, racée,
un peu précieuse.
Un mélange raffiné
de tabacs blonds.
kim, une cigarette
vraiment différente.

Figure 1-34

sharing a certain togetherness (Kim) or the same attitude of aloofness toward men (Kim).

The advertising for Yashica cameras appeals to a somewhat more complex set of drives. Voyeuristic tendencies are certainly acknowledged, since the camera allows access to the private places where women come close together. But homosexual tendencies are also at play here, since this image is suggestive for men and women alike. Finally, it is an aesthetic compromise that is suggested to us: use these drives to take beautiful, artistic pictures.

The proven effectiveness of these advertisements shows that by allowing our defenses to be gratified, we easily consume compromises that are part of our everyday life.

Normative or Ideal Identification

In the analytic hypothesis, the child has a tendency to appropriate the object-other by cannibalistic interjection; this tendency, particularly during the oedipal phase, gradually becomes fragmented and transformed into a desire for a part or a particular property of the other. The original aggressiveness thus serves to appropriate a desirable fragment that has been abstracted from the other in the hope that one will thus no longer feel the lack within oneself. Relying on this process,

Figure 1-35. "A famous singer tells us: 'In this business, a pair of Jil's is a necessity.' "

advertising often creates a desire in the viewer for a part of a person or for a quality by focusing on that fragment. Because the process is so familiar, it does not create the barrier of censorship.

Thus, to show a man wearing Jil underwear in a Rolls Royce (fig. 1-35), or at a seaside resort, is tantamount to presenting the image of a man who has attained social success. He is to be envied. He is a model to be emulated. The object thus integrated into an atmosphere of the materialistic dream—apparently the only ideal that exists in advertising—then becomes desirable as a partial object. All energy, desire, and ambition are channeled into wealth. According to the same logic, cigarettes, automobiles, alcohol, and even food seem more desirable in luxurious rooms or aesthetically appealing outdoor settings. Each of these objects is connected with a woman, rather than a man, or with a couple actually shown or indirectly suggested by a piece of feminine jewelry, a pair of women's gloves, or a woman's hand. The viewer is being offered, very ostentatiously, a little of what he longs for most. And advertisers know exactly what people want because this question has been thoroughly studied in marketing surveys.

In certain circumstances, the identification takes subtle detours. In fact, the Jil underwear advertisements are too blatant and obvious. But plenty of other advertising relies only on a few understated but "perfect" forms to achieve a deliberately aesthetic effect. This applies particularly to luxury items such as elegant bathroom fixtures, expensive perfumes, exclusive lighters in Chinese lacquer (made by Dupont or Dunhill), as well as certain kinds of jewelry, including watches. In many advertisements of this type, all the viewer sees is a form—naturally a perfectly exquisite form—that occasionally approaches abstract art (as in the Rochas perfume advertisements). The text is kept to a minimum. Chanel and Dupont posters contain no text (fig. 1-36), and in other cases only one word—the manufacturer's name—appears: in advertisements for Caron, Jacomo, and Saint Laurent (fig. 1-37).

What these posters express visually is clearly a form of identification:

"You would like to devour or interject one or more characters from your own personal story whose elegance or sophistication used to make you feel insignificant."

"Control this drive; transform it into a partial drive; take away their sophistication" (the extreme elegance of the image).

"The elegance of the product is an acceptable object for your need for identification."

The denunciation of this formula of identification, that is, the redirection of desire toward a portion of the object, will probably be seen as an abuse of language. Let it suffice to recall the three Rodier advertisements analyzed earlier ("How to look like an artist without the angst," etc.) from a rhetorical point of view to show that the process can sometimes even be made explicit without embarrassing the viewer.

The practice of using photographs of certain film or television stars in direct association with a product is sufficiently well known and widespread that there is no need to recall it here.

"Ultra-aestheticism," which we have been discussing, clearly involves an appeal to superior values, indeed even to highly refined taste and an appreciation for the sublime.

For more everyday products, the suggested identification has to be more down to earth, reassuring viewers that their actions conform to normal use. For example, in introducing products such as instant foods, soups requiring no preparation, or dishwashers that eliminate the usual drudgery of doing dishes, in order to change people's habits it is important to assure them that they are not the only ones making such changes, that in fact they are part of a trend that is fast becoming widespread.

Thus certain archetypal images gradually become more clearly defined. The figure of the typical housewife has been rejected. This was confirmed in Quebec following a survey done by an advertising agency. A similar trend is evident in

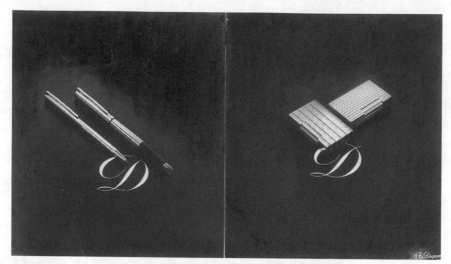

Figure 1-36

Figure 1-37

Figure 1-38. "Chesterfield presents super hose that won't slip. A crazy comfort!"

France, where a picture of a woman on her hands and knees scrubbing a floor is seen in the background, in black and white like an old-fashioned photograph, hardly visible, hidden by three colored panels covered with type.

The popular image of woman is now someone who takes care of herself, who smiles and delights people with her practical sense (like the blonde who promotes Philips color television sets in four well-phrased sentences), her radiant physical glow (for example, the nimble girl in the advertisements for Chesterfield Lance, fig. 1-38), or her elegant and romantic good looks (the blonde model with the old-fashioned hairdo in the advertisements for Elidanse hair spray).

Rationalization

As a defense mechanism of the psychic apparatus, rationalization allows drive and its inhibition to be expressed simultaneously within a compromise in which wish is camouflaged by intellectual arguments that appear to have motivated a specific action, whereas desire does not have to be acknowledged.

It is abundantly clear that the acquisition of certain goods above all does not depend on intellectual arguments; it is motivated instead by power or by narcissistic or phallic libido. In some cases the advertising message offers a range of intellectual arguments that can be used as camouflage or rationalizations. This is particularly true in the case of some expensive consumer items whose usefulness is not immediately self-evident.

Perhaps the classic example of this type of rationalization is the Volkswagen advertisement we analyzed earlier. The image, which occupies three-quarters of the page, can be seen as an appeal to drive; the remaining quarter page, containing the text, corresponds to the rationalization/intellectualization for buying the product.

This formula worked so well that it was later copied in a great many other automobile advertisements. An image, taking up three-quarters to four-fifths of a page, illustrating the luxury, comfort, or sporty lines of a car, is accompanied by its underlying text, at the bottom of the page, which is both serious and informative. Here the reader finds a series of extremely rational arguments, sometimes including graphs, detailed drawings of the engine, and impressive performance charts that are largely incomprehensible to most readers. But reason is there, with no lack of supporting arguments. In fact, all of this intellectualization serves as a pretext for yielding to a completely different drive: the drive to impress our neighbors, for example, or to display our social status, or to conform to certain class standards, or even simply the urge to take out our aggressions on a vehicle that cannot get back at us.

Volvo uses the rational approach by announcing simply that "X% of Volvo owners are academics."

But rationalization does not always work.

In 1971 the BNP (National Bank of Paris) wanted to align its advertising according to such a mechanism. As its central figure, it used the supposedly appealing image of a friendly, reliable, and honest banker (fig. 1-39). With disarming candor he declared that he had an interest in your money. According to a survey done by the firm Publicis, the man's face evoked quite different connotations: he seemed deceitful, dishonest. Some even went so far as to say that he looked Jewish, that he looked like the French actor Michel Piccoli. Somehow the creative directors must have made a mistake. Nevertheless, the bank persisted in thinking that the public had to get used to the idea of identifying the bank with a person with whom they could freely communicate. The BNP continued its campaign, using the same face, with the explanation that the complaints had come from people who generally did not use banks and that they were the ones who had to be educated.

Everything ended in failure.

Prospective customers apparently were not ready to acknowledge that one banking service was as good as another and that, after all, as long as this bank is honest, why not go there?

One does not rationalize (here, more specifically, one does not fool around)

Figure 1-39. "You trust your money with me. I let
you make use of my bank. Give and take."

with money; one needs *good reasons,* and the distance-intellectualization proposed here asked too much of its viewers.

A rival bank adopted a reverse strategy, showing a smiling bank customer
rather than a banker. This advertisement, based on denial of the reality of banking
or dread of financial transactions as well as on simple identification with the satisfied customer, was much more successful.

It should perhaps be pointed out, however, that the BNP advertisement required a rationalization but, unlike the Volkswagen advertisements, did not actually provide one, did not make one explicit.

Following this logic, it is not by appealing to defense mechanisms that advertising works, but rather by reproducing them, imitating them, and, thereby, per-
petuating them mimetically.

The Advertising Hand

A whole book could be written just on the use of hands in advertising imagery.
Our aim here is rather more modest. We merely wish to point out the frequently
clever use of a metonymic or deictic device whose impact is not usually understood by the viewer.

Masculine or feminine, with or without gloves, work worn or well manicured, hands do in fact have the power to suggest human contact—the relationship between mother and child, between man and woman—and also connection with the product in question. The masculine hand that holds a Black & Decker sander is not the same hand that Lux or Palmolive has made beautiful. The gloved hand of a race car driver is not the velvet-gloved hand of the woman who selects her diamond necklace from a world-renowned jeweler. Hands that are protective or arrogant, hands symbolizing victory (Vittel) or defeat, hands adorned with engagement rings or pale hands wearing expensive watches, the chubby hands of children calling for their mothers or the outstretched hands of disabled or undernourished children: hands are the epitome of the person and tell more about the whole body than we realize.

A focus for sexuality and emotion, hands are an indication of social class or intention, of charity or criminality, of everyday occurrences or of extraordinary events. Nail polish makes a woman catty. Dirty hands indicate a laborer. Placed on a partner's knee or arm, a hand indicates impending intimacy. Authoritarian or imperious, hands command respect. Held partly open, they are a sign of submission.

Almost all advertisements could be analyzed just in the way they use hands. They are among the most fascinating components of any advertisement, one of the more or less conscious hiding places for the essential part of the message to be conveyed.

But there is so much to be said, and it would be presumptuous to think that we have exhausted all the possibilities in a domain where everything works to turn us into accomplices.

The New Sandwich-Board Man

The most obvious aspect of advertising rhetoric is that it pours in from all sides so that we never know where it will stop, since, on the one hand, it has developed so surreptitiously, and on the other, it has become so much a part of us that it is like a second skin. Here is the last frontier for advertising: our skin, our clothing, our pens, our lighters, our luggage, our towels, and our belts—turning us into volunteer sandwich-board men, sponsors for the very advertisements meant for us. To be convinced of this, all you have to do is to go to any big shopping mall. The best advertising is advertising we ourselves display: clothes with Cardin or Saint Laurent labels, Mickey Mouse sweaters, Adidas sports bags, caps and lighters imprinted with famous brand names. I Love the Bahamas. Paris Is Eternal. Such phrases are now emblazoned on expensive T-shirts. What exactly do we say when we wear them? Surely we are expressing our desires. But at the same time, we are obviously exhibiting the defense mechanisms we all need, the projections to which we consent, and the compromises that keep our fears at bay—in other words, the numerous shortcuts with which we have chosen to live.

Strolling through the crowds at Disney World, one sees millions of Mickeys and Plutos bought a minute ago at an authentic "period" store. It is as if the decor the advertisers have set up were in no way enough to recreate the comic strip fantasy world, so that every visitor, whether adult or child, has to join in the game, has to contribute to the great conspiracy of representations, adds character to the general masquerade, and lofts a balloon into the hurly-burly of false self-images that dance by, swaying and nodding knowingly to one another.

There is no end to the charade. To become part of the cheery atmosphere, all add their ambiguity to the scenario; everybody rewrites the story.

Perhaps the world of Disney is not quite so fake and artificial after all. What about all the other places in the world, such as the fashionable sixteenth *arrondissement* in Paris, where one likes to show a desire to take part in the action? Can we condemn nonstop without, one way or the other, taking part ourselves in the deception that seems to us to be so crucial?

Sometimes advertisers seem to be the only ones who pay attention to this need—and that may be the source of the problem. They fulfill our desires aesthetically, and, delighted, we compensate them handsomely.

Chapter 2
History of a Passage into Sameness

Acknowledgment of a certain symmetry between psychological defenses and the rhetoric of advertising obviously does not exhaust all of the possibilities of the advertising phenomenon.

What this parallel does make clear, however, is that, in the case of defense mechanisms as in that of advertisements, we witness the formation of a compromise, in other words, the elaboration of a proposition where desire and censure will always remain half satisfied. In this process, once desire has been used as a source of energy, it will see itself transformed into need and be diverted onto a partial object following the bias of a specific action. Censure, for its part, will to a degree become overwhelmed by an appeal to the familial or predominant ethic, which clearly permits itself the more selfish desire for fundamental originality.

From there we would seem to be just one step away from saying that the advertising proposition is of a symptomatic order. By jumping too quickly to this conclusion, we would undoubtedly forget a number of real theoretical problems that we must, at least in part, resolve. Nevertheless, there is still the question of what becomes of desire in the formulation of advertising, and it is to the attempt at responding appropriately to this question that we devote the following pages.

Let us recall, with Laplanche and Pontalis, that desire belongs to this group of psychic entities so basic that, ultimately, they remain indefinable. In spite of the impossibility of definition concerning this concept, however, these authors stress certain essential traits.

Desire differs from need in that it is a psychic and unconscious phenomenon, whereas need is an organic reality. As a psychic entity, desire is related to the infant's first experiences of satisfaction. Indissolubly linked with certain mnesic traces that accompanied these first experiences of satisfaction, it seeks to reproduce this original experience by means of hallucinations.

Desire originates from the gap between need (biology) and demand (specific action of a search for love). While drive, which originates from need, relies on memories to undertake a specific action (demand or other action) likely to reduce tension in the body, desire, on the other hand, seeks its fulfillment in an object *A* organizes signs in the form of phantasms, and finds its fulfillment in a hallucinatory representation of an originary experience of satisfaction.

Further, desire seems to be linked to more than just a single tension; it seems to stem from a state of anguish, the probable result of a disappointment relative to *object a* compared to *Object A*.

In other words, in most cases the need experienced is psychically represented by a drive that seeks to reduce tension by a specific action triggered by detailed memories. However, if the action that is undertaken and, more precisely, the demand, far from coinciding with need, underscores the gap between them, then need will be psychically represented by desire, which will seek fulfillment in a hallucinatory reproduction of the perceptual context of the originary experience of satisfaction.

As succinct as it is—and we admit as much—this formulation hardly comes close to accounting for the totality of human actions. If we took this formulation literally, we would undertake only those specific actions that aimed at relieving internal tension, in which we would spend all of our time fantasizing the experience that brought satisfaction. This does not happen.

Certain of our gestures are not motivated merely by immediate pleasure; on the contrary, some of our actions and attitudes, so it would seem, aim at keeping the state of tension open, which is, after all, what keeps us alive. The situation of students or researchers who keep an open mind in the pursuit of knowledge whose end result will be achieved much later is a good example of this phenomenon.

Psychoanalytical formulations, in this regard, follow the hypothesis of a subjugation of the psychic processes, that is, the ability to introduce, when satisfaction is at stake, a temporal or spatial delay, justified by hope for "greater pleasure." This process of subjugation in turn is justified by a secondary type of narcissism in which the ideal of the ego and the ideal ego "agree" on goals to be attained by the subject in order to remain consistent with a self-image that is not just acceptable, but in the long run flattering. Actions taken in accordance with this secondarization are also motivated by desire: a secondary desire, but a desire all the same.

It is not our intention to bring up the psychoanalytic formulation of metapsychology again, and, to this end, we will abandon our incursions into Freudian and post-Freudian statements. What we do consider essential is to focus on what happens to Freudian and post-Freudian metapsychological desire in the advertising message, and this just as much for primary desire as for more secondary desire. Our initial general hypothesis is that advertising, by calling for a specific action (consumption), is psychically represented by a drive and carefully avoids letting desire take hold, which would be more basic and especially, it seems to us, more subversive.

The Place of Desire in the Work of Art

Works of art supposedly fulfill desire. No doubt this is an elegant and even seductive formula, but, on examination, what exactly does it hold? Clearly, the question merits pause, and in this sense we will begin with the works of Jean-François Lyotard and Jacques Lacan.

To the degree that we schematize the work of these authors, we are drawn to conclude that the work of art is a locus where, on the one hand, certain conditions essential for engaging desire and, on the other hand, certain mainstreams, which without confining the imagery free it precisely by way of paths favorable to the phantasmatic fulfillment of desire, are put into place.

Consequently, holes, voids, hollows, and absence from now on become central.

As we pointed out earlier, desire does not stem from just one tension. This tension can in fact easily take on the form of a drive and be reabsorbed through specific action. Desire originates from the gap between need and demand, but also from the gap called the state of distress between the immediacy of satisfaction and initial want.

Desire originates from an incommensurable yawning gap,[1] the sure sign of a narcissistic castration, through which the world does not bring us the love we have dreamed of, but through which, at the same time, we are also never equal in power to the imaginary being living in us. (See as well Kohut's concept of the grandiose self.)

If we follow this line of argument, the work of art ought to represent this *gap,* and, by virtue of this fact, in a way it does. Lacan demonstrated this rigorously concerning Hans Holbein's painting. His demonstration could just as easily be applied to contemporary works: we will restrict our discussion to one example only, a painting by Mark Rothko entitled *Orange and Yellow* (fig. 2-1).

At first glance, nothing could be more simple or childish than these two rectangles, one yellow and the other salmon, against a pinkish background. ''My two-year-old could have painted that,'' one might be tempted to say.

But upon closer examination the outlines of the rectangles are much less clearly defined than was evident at first glance. The yellow and salmon fields have many more levels of meaning than was initially apparent. Little by little, a

Figure 2-1

transparent area becomes visible in both swaths of color, which tempts us to imagine, beyond the foreground, a kind of *elsewhere, an other Place*. The wavering of the outlines of color masses produces the illusion of a form becoming apparent, in the process of taking shape.

A void is created and becomes manifest. The picture perceived is double. It is the one we are looking at, but it is nevertheless the one we can imagine. The gap between these two paintings draws us in and possesses us. The eye finds itself caught. The other image needs to be perceived as imaginary to fill this gap. The only thing we can do is fantasize.

The support Rothko provides for this phantasmization is sufficiently vague or neutral to leave room for the wildest flights of imagination. We all get something out of it; above all, we all find our own picture, using the emptiness to reinvent perceptions reminiscent of the experience of satisfaction. Every viewer makes up a different story.

But on a secondary narcissistic level, everyone also projects a symbolic system, a supposedly personal manner of organizing universe and self. In short, given this blank space and this extremely generous support, the spectator takes back the power of autosymbolization.

This *possibility of autosymbolization* in itself constitutes what we call the *subversive value* of the work of art.[2] This subversive value appears to us, among others, as the antithesis to the engagement of drive and its result: specific action. The possibility and the freedom of autosymbolization, if they have to go the way of the avenues of the abyss and despair, nonetheless lead to the only possible opening to an existence of the subjects as authors of their own lives. In the final analysis, this may be the most brutal lesson of Rothko the painter.

Obviously, our argument could be extended to include literary work and we could postulate that books like *Finnegans Wake* (James Joyce) and *Le Camion* [*The Truck*] (Marguerite Duras) ultimately lead us to become the authors of our own lives. As fascinating as this generalization might be, it is clearly beyond the scope of this book, which seeks to specify the place of advertising.

An Ambiguous Poster: *Easy Rider,* 1970

From the preceding remarks one might conclude that we did not consider advertising to have artistic or creative merit of any sort. Far from it. We are only too well aware that this would be to diminish the talent of artists such as Lautrec or Savignac. It would also mean denying the obvious talent, sometimes even the genius, of certain photographers and writers who work in this field.

Our question is more complex: it concerns the passage of desire in the direction of drive. From another point of view, the question also involves the transformation of the subversive into direct solicitation. Artistic merit is not denied, but we are concerned with its use in the service of specific action.

A 1970 poster inspired by the American film *Easy Rider* will clarify our discussion.

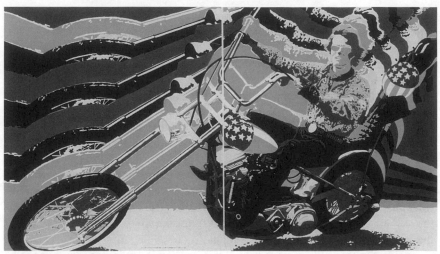

Figure 2-2

In its own way, *Easy Rider* certainly marked, or reflected, for the entire world, the character of an important period in the history of the United States. It was the end of the sixties, a decade of unprecedented liberalism, and also the end of the greatest excesses of the hippie movement. In California, the use of cannabis had reached a peak and was beginning to level off. Ecological groups were calling for environmental responsibility. The formerly naive and idealistic hippie attitude threatened to become a much more coherent and articulate protest movement. "Peace and Love" had made way for a new slogan of freedom within restraint.

This freedom within restraint is clearly the theme of the film *Easy Rider*. Two motorcyclists set out to travel across the United States. They are young, good-looking, and unattached. Their needs are few; they have no driving ambition for anything more. Simple meals, friendly discussions: this is the material of the film, which takes place in plain, rural settings. This freedom is subversive; it is in fact intolerable to the affluent. Their journey ends with a murder.

Inspired by this film, or at least by this theme, Théobald designed a poster that is part of the series of Personality Posters of 1970. In it Peter Fonda sits on a motorcycle, like those in the film, with extra high handlebars and a disproportionately long fork supporting the front wheel.

Technically, the poster is achieved by rhythmically superimposing three independent photographic prints resulting from a process known as "color separation." The total image gives the impression of multiplying the number of motorbikes and riders: eight of them are clearly discernible. Since none of the photographic prints is complete in itself as far as color is concerned, each one being of only one color—red, yellow, or green—we are equally fascinated by the unreality of the image. But there is more. Where exactly is the eye supposed to look? What is represented is far from the static stillness frequently found in photographs. The eye is enticed in different directions. The biker's face is confused with the background. The foreground seems to disappear into the image, or, depending on what one chooses to perceive, the background is projected onto the foreground. Something about this poster makes us uncomfortable. Its perspective — and this may be the source of our discomfort — is far from classical. The absence of depth is particularly blatant: there is no vanishing point at the back of the picture; at the most there is a point of convergence to the right, indicating a focal point, a center of gravity. The construction is kinetic, and the spectator is plunged more into a world of movement than into any attempt to define space. The overlapping lines from the bottom to the top of the poster reinforce this impression of a two-dimensional world. But at the same time, this stabilized image functions as a "hiding place" for certain elements. At the left of the image, for example, the wheel of the motorcycle, in stylized repetitions, gives us a clue to another image behind this one, a hidden image, an image to be seen but that must not be seen. And this sets in motion manifold evocations, leading us, as we try to grasp the meaning of the lines, to get lost in conjecture. The universe is polysemic. These allusive, accumulated curves could just as easily remind us of the light rays of pop or op art as of ski hills. Unless of course they refer to energy zones?

We are no longer sure of anything; just as in images chosen by dreams, we are faced with a condensation — that is, we are in the presence of a representation that invites us to follow several associative pathways. In fact, these lines have an infinite number of meanings, and the space is completely invaded by the forms to the point of being completely saturated by them, to the point of overload.

On the right side of the poster, a man in a diagonal position, parallel to the contrasting lines of the motorcycle, occupies a conical portion of the space. Only his arms, shoulders, and hair are repeated one after the other in the same proportions all the way to the top of the poster. This repetition directs us to the designer's purpose, which is to have the spectator identify with this multiple man, to magnify the power and potential strength of the hero, and to make room for a choice of different interpretations of the same character.

This man is easily recognizable as the hero of a film, but also as a champion motorcyclist. He is a man of youthful and contemporary tastes, and the formal presentation, in overlapping images, merely reflects the multiplicity of the character he portrays, whose different aspects can be seen in several details. Leather boots, belt, gloves, goggles, and jeans are all part of the uniform of the experienced motorcyclist. Here is the modern man with his technological gadgets, his practical sense, and his trend-setting attitudes. Patterned shirts in psychedelic colors and long, artificially colored hair presuppose a refusal to conform coupled with a desire to live a life of dreams and poetry. One element of the image has multiple connotations. As in dreams, the elements of the representation have been chosen for their many layers of meaning. This is total and unabashed condensation, which is also obvious on the level of color. Let us itemize, for example, the cool colors (blue and green), the warm colors (red and yellow), and the contrasting colors (black and white). If we examine the sleeves of the shirt, we find:

blue, yellow	cool, warm
red, yellow	warm, warm
black, white	contrasting/achromatic
blue, green	cool
black, white	contrasting
blue	cool

The color mentioned second is the color of the shoulder; this line continues the parallel lines of the outstretched arm. From bottom to top, starting from the ''design'' aspect, we see the following pattern:

red	warm
black (spotted white)	contrasting
blue (flecked green)	cool
black (flecked white)	contrasting
blue (flecked green)	cool
black (flecked white)	contrasting
red (flecked yellow)	warm
blue	cool

The first six colors could be said to correspond with one another, except for the side with the lines: the red and the blue are in stark contrast, with no other color in between. This color coding also helps to condense the emotions. To begin with, each primary color is paired with another that makes it more vivid, except for the red in the center, the zone of concentration. To temper this red, which is splashed lavishly from the center to the left side, it seems necessary to duplicate the receding colors juxtaposed with black—black, blue, black, blue. The viewer is being conditioned to the calculated emotion, despite what appears to be a chaotic tumult of color. With blue and yellow rays radiating from the red at the center, what emerges is the symbol of fire. This is the fire of youth, in hot pursuit of speed, burning up the road. There is an association to be made with violent emotions, the display of life, of power, of explosive energy.

This force, blocked on the right by a mass, supported by a black form, crossed by tangled lines, associates directly in our minds with death. Eternity transcends all constraints in the form of this marvelous curved line with dips and hollows in red over black, blue, and green. These colors, of course, suggest earth, water, and air. Their positions and their ''patterns'' in relation to the red offset the intensity of the red and are associated with more neutral feelings and calmer, perhaps more introspective, moments. One thinks of everyday life, waiting for things to happen, boredom, hope—in short, of slow and sinuous inner processes.

Shapes, lines, and colors are organized to form a living mathematics releasing a shower of impressions and emotions. Superimposed, interpenetrating, one calling forth another or canceling one another out, they produce an impression of excess, ambiguity, and multiplicity of possible interpretations. Any single form contains a whole underlying network of other forms, and all of them combined, with their myriad associations, dazzle viewers who are trying to get their bearings. This feeling of being invaded comes no doubt from visual overload, superimposed images, and condensation. One conviction gradually becomes clear: it is difficult to make an absolute distinction here between art and advertising. Precisely because of its polysemic nature, this work belongs in a museum. And where are we with respect to our desires?

On this point, we have to return to our discussion of desire and drives at the beginning of this chapter and attempt to look at the poster in relation to its appeal to desiring forces.

For desire to be fulfilled, as we suggested in our preliminary theoretical remarks, there must be some kind of void, a place of important "distress," which, following the suggestions of an appropriate imagistic medium, will lead to the development not of a real but of a phantasmatic construction. Dreams are one way in which these various conditions are brought together.

The void, the yawning gap, the lack, the distance, and the point of entry to the work are indisputably present in this poster. We must not underestimate the fact that this illustration upsets the value system of a certain portion of the public. Calling for freedom in a world of constraint, this poster is suggestive on several levels of the possibility of taking to the road (the motorcycle) and of creating one's own image (the remarkable mastery of photographic techniques); the human drama is amply evoked, and there is abundant appeal to dreams.

The message of this poster is ultimately revolutionary. The road belongs to you; take back the freedom that is your own. The iconic support system allows for dreams. Its structure, based on condensation similar to the condensation in dreams, engages the imagination. We dream of getting away. In fact, we are already gone.

Thus, in a certain sense, this poster fulfills desire. The void, the gap, and the gulf are represented here. The phantasmatic support system intervenes as well. This material has been used, however, in an advertising formula. When this design is put on a larger panel with promotional material for a movie theater where the film is playing, it instantly becomes an advertisement. All that is required is a brief text—a film schedule, for example, a list of actors, or a similar message—for the poster to take on a new meaning.

From that moment the frame becomes visible, our eye meets the promotional text, the real is introduced to obstruct the flow of dreams and the hallucinatory fulfillment of desire. When it is constructed in this way, the space recalls the back and forth movement between dreams and reality, between positive and negative, between true and false. The desire set into motion now finds itself caught in the trap of the real. For the possibility of phantasm is substituted concrete action. The advertising place exists, and by virtue of its existence dreams are eliminated as an infringement on reality. The advertising place exists because there is action, that is, in current sociological terms, there is a *directed act,* setting desire into motion, putting drive into gear, so that finally the main thrust of the advertising message will start to work—so that it will turn into action.

The poster itself, furthermore, thus put back into a promotional context, offers several features favorable to this action. The repetition of the central figure reassures the viewer that there are many such motorcyclists, and by a shrewd twist of logic, provides proof of the acceptability of such behavior. The motorcycle, at one time scorned, is thus raised to the rank of an example to be followed. This seems to be one of the fundamental characteristics of advertising. Desire is not fulfilled by advertising, but a drive that serves as a substitute is, in its place, promised a conditional pleasure. Such a pleasure is set in place; the pleasure of the motorcycle, for example, is understood through the medium of the shapes and colors, *but, to experience it, to have more than just an idea of it, you have to act.*[3] The advertising poster supposedly gives a taste of the real experience. It is supposed that you have to put yourself into a situation similar to the one in the advertisement. The first condition to be fulfilled is in fact to bond with the product. This is the assumption that counts. Everything else follows as a bonus. The physical appearance of the characters, the settings, their connotations are presented on the same level as the product. While the advertised merchandise is for sale, the moral, social, and human values conveyed by text and image cannot be bought. This is the basic ambiguity behind all publicity: everything is advertised all at once; a quality product is promised, but to enjoy it, you have to buy it. More is promised in a show and tell focused on certain themes. Desire is not fulfilled since these images, these texts do not exist for their own sake: they exist via an intermediary. These images refer us back to ourselves, to the world of consumption. The *Easy Rider* poster, for example, is so loaded from the plastic point of view that it projects the viewer into the world of aesthetics, of reverie, of sensations. But, at the same time, it is impossible to find artistic gratification in this pictorial (iconic) space, since everything is directed toward a single aspect of the image—the actor on the motorcycle. Taking off and grinding to a halt. It is no longer possible to push any further. The real impinges on us very sharply because of the commercial context that comes into play, impeding any quest for the aesthetic (if there is one). Condensation on the formal level leads into the world of connotations. We set out in search of pleasure. The outlines are sketched; they seduce and excite.

The world of forms is homogenized around one motif, one icon so pregnant that all imagination is stopped dead in its tracks. The motorcycle rider directs us back to the real, to the film, and calls for identification. Therefore fulfillment of desire does not happen. Desire was born, was barely formulated before it had to acknowledge its unreality. The frame and the reference to everyday life were imposed. The whole process of condensation served to create expectation and hope. To come up against the poster's support is to agree or refuse to transpose the feeling of desire into everyday life. Saying yes sometimes leads to a purchase. Saying no means making do with what is at hand.

Provisional Comments on the Specificity of Advertising

There are several reasons why this poster inspired by the film *Easy Rider* raises questions. Artistic in its own right, this poster, which is just waiting for the fulfillment of desire, becomes, so to speak, advertising fodder. Is this a special case, an exception to the rule? Or does this example bring us face to face with a mechanism essential to the advertising process? On analysis, we will indeed have to agree that the latter hypothesis is more plausible.

In fact, the thought that this is an exceptional case in no way holds up. Most art galleries announce a forthcoming exhibition by reproducing one of the works in the form of a poster. A large number of images that serve as a basis for advertising messages for luxury items—perfumes, silks, jewelry—clearly have an aesthetic quality reminiscent of works of art. Most "promotional" photographs that accompany or serve as a background to all kinds of advertisements, for everything from cars and record players to cigarettes, are flawless from a representational point of view, and many of them, in a different context or simply taken by themselves, would be worthy of the title of works of art. Moreover, we spent several pages in the previous chapter describing advertisements of undeniable artistic quality. The advertising element of a poster, it seems to us, originates elsewhere.

Unlike those who consider that the work of art occupies a very marginal place in advertising, we are inclined to believe that the pictorial part of an advertisement can easily be a work of art and therefore provide a means of fulfillment for desire.[4] On the other hand, what seems to us to be specifically promotional is what subsequently happens to this engaged desire and how it is transformed into a drive toward specific action. Here, whatever the preferred process of representation, without exception there is no advertising without a *rerouting of desire toward specific action*.

The *Easy Rider* poster becomes an advertisement from the moment we as viewers are denied the privilege of musing on it and are urged instead to take action, in other words, to go see the film. Without this roadblock, without this return to the real, there is no *advertising*. It is in the way this barrier to dreams is introduced, with more or less effectiveness and subtlety, where the real cleverness of a good advertiser shows through. The best antidote to dreams, advertisers seem to think, is nothing other than the real; the best antidote to hope is satiation by the product.

Consequently, and on various levels of the advertising representation, this real will have to show itself. In opposition to the singular nature of dreams, it will have to set forth its ''consensual'' idiolect. As a kind of counterpoint to the difference of dreams, the advertiser's utterance will will have to set forth an equanimical resemblance. This may be the origin, finally, of reference, in advertising discourse, to consensus and ideology.[5] It is certainly in this *passage into sameness* where, finally, the suggestion of this gesture is articulated: the recuperation of the subversive.

Somewhere along the road to becoming an advertisement, the *Easy Rider* poster is naturalized—becomes too accessible to retain its power to disturb. In the same vein, an 1880 poster for Howe bicycles and tricycles elicits no stronger feeling than a nostalgia for the similar and sameness. We are squarely in the middle of an advertising campaign.

The 1880 Tricycle Poster and Its Relation to the Real

There is, of course, more than one possible reading of the Howe tricycle poster of 1880 (fig. 2-3). The interpretation upon which we have chosen to focus involves a particular reading of the real that this poster proposes: an explanation of the world around it that, far from being anodyne or neutral, suggests the passage into sameness we have evoked.

Around 1880 the tricycle was considered to be a sophisticted means of transportation, particularly suited to city life: it was also seen as a testimony to human ingenuity, a sign of modern technical progress.

The Howe poster shows us this tricycle in the midst of a remote rural landscape, which is painted a washed-out monochrome green—in other words, one might think, utterly out of context. A train is visible in the middle distance. Another means of transportation, the train could be interpreted as merely redundant to the paradigm of methods of transportation. But we also know that trains were frequently used during that period to transport people from the countryside into the cities and were therefore a form of public transport, as opposed to the resolutely individual tricycle. Finally, a village is suggested, rather than clearly delineated, in the background. Its blurred shapes, along with the harmonious

Figure 2-3

vagueness of the whole rural background, provides a definite contrast with the precise and detailed lines of the tricycle.

The triple opposition employed here (city/country, crowd/solitude, blur/ definition) creates a kind of rupture. This illogic shocks, seduces, disturbs, and, above all, troubles the viewer's usual orientation with respect to this modern innovation.

Whereas the development of industry was bringing about massive urbanization leading to overpopulation and fundamental changes in the human relationship to nature, this development is here depicted as beneficial, because of the tricycle. The countryside can be rediscovered. The crowded train fades into the distance. The dream of a bucolic existence is once again within reach. Now, this poster is doubly shrewd: on the one hand, the contradiction of the period is presented as an established, inevitable fact; on the other hand, the solution to this contradiction lies in the tricycle. This is undoubtedly a falsehood, but it is even more than that. It is a particular interpretation of the world that raises real questions only to deny them and to claim with more insistence to have found a solution, so that as viewers read the poster they gain access to their anxiety and, by this very fact, to their desire. But on the other hand they run out of energy, run up against the image's frame and its formal treatment. Like the label on a product, the product on the poster shows the price to be paid in order to get rid of anxiety and the action to be taken to be free of desire. A specific action is engaged.

At first glance, what captures attention in this image is its iconic nature: we have seen these patterns many times before, and the shapes are already known to us. This representation is in some way familiar. Here, an enormous tricycle in the foreground of an outdoor setting engages desire. The prototype of the heroic man dominates the middle distance and the background, creating a sort of envy and wish for identification. As a result of seeing the image frequently repeated, or of looking at it for a long time, however, the "voyeurs" no longer see what they would like to see. They cannot reach the aesthetic, imaginary, or mystical "nirvana" because too many things bring them back to everyday life or to the promotional context. Then, as if this iconic reference to a social reality were not enough to block a more authentic desire, written words complete the product's identification. We are informed of the manufacturer's name and the address where the "solution" can be purchased. We are urged not into contemplation but into acquisition; not to desire, but to action.

In *Le Séminaire XI,* Jacques Lacan stresses that spectators of the work of art necessarily find themselves in the position of voyeurs but also, by a subtle reversal, in the position of being seen. It seems to us that the tricycle poster obeys a slightly different logic.

In the final analysis, the voyeur cannot be the man in the poster, since that man is too specific, too present: he is statuesque, has a frozen demeanor, a chiseled profile. The person in the drawing is artificial, over-"mechanized" by his creator. The symbols of the man portrayed here are rather too obvious (although rightly so, given that this is a commercial advertisement). He represents the conquering hero, which is indicated by his headgear, and the tricycle takes the place of a horse. The strength and power of a god are suggested by the position of his body, in three-quarters view, with his arms slightly apart and his large hands closed, reminiscent of Greek and Roman statues. He is a free man, scarf flowing in the wind, his suit in the latest style, master of a means of locomotion—all elements that still connote freedom today. On the other hand, the whole of the background is nonrealistic. Because of its blurring of details, unrealistic proportions, and monochromatic treatment, it is obviously a drawing and is therefore unbelievable. Curiously enough, this means that viewers are no longer in the position of voyeurs. Quite quickly they become aware that the purpose of this rather fanciful background is to show off the tricycle, which is portrayed with great precision. This is therefore not a work of art, in which any departure from reality finds justification only within the image itself. Clearly the background, the man, and their forms exist only in relation to an object that was part of everyday life in 1880. Consequently, the poster ultimately projects outwardly, and desire cannot be fulfilled within it, since it is in fact directed back to the surrounding reality. Because of the unreality suggested in the background graphics, and the single-minded commercialism of the structure, in which the central object is framed by writing above and below it, the poster works directly on the subconscious, without gratifying it. The displacement in the poster probably causes a craving on the level of the imagination that is only satisfied in tangible reality. *Expectation begins as soon as imagination is blocked by the image and cannot lose itself in the enjoyment of pleasure.* It is this subtle interplay between unreality and pregnant, insurmountable reality that gives birth to a desire that cannot be realized and that is ultimately *perverse,* since it is the desire for desire.

At this point, all that is left is to channel this powerful energy in some direction; hence need, hence a claim of satisfaction to be had from an object of any kind. Since the whole "desiring machine" is working, the level of operations is turned around: desire in reserve remains in reserve but continues to pursue satisfaction, and therefore eternal desire, from object to object. As we have seen, this poster evokes victory, liberty, power, peace of mind, and well-being. But unlike a painting, a film, or a sculpture, it does not allow us to experience these feelings, even for a moment. We remain at the level of tantalizing flavor, of foretaste, of the merest outline, as with all advertising. Displacement and condensation cloud the issue, as often occurs in dreams. But there the analogy ends. The *superego* intervenes, the social contract speaks; the real weighs heavily, and dreams, so to speak, never get out of the starting block. Desire willingly steps aside, need takes the spotlight; the only way out is specific action.

Obviously, if we pursue the comparison of the drawing and construction of the advertisement to the process of the elaboration of dreams, yet again we will have to take note of a certain parallelism. In both cases, the images are chosen for their figurative power. Very discreetly, always to flirt with the spectator's desire, blotches of yellowish gold stand out, for example here at the bottom of the image, where it means looking for fortune, leaving the countryside, stressed by the swath of green in the distance. Does not this heroic man on his tricycle remind us that, as the saying goes, "everything runs like clockwork" when you are en route to the city? The three wheels above the gold, turned toward a golden future, symbolize on some level the "wheels of fortune," wheels of chance, and sometimes of reward. On the other hand, the static position of dominance and self-assurance of the male figure sitting securely on his vehicle, which seems to be moving along at a regular speed, cannot but remind us of the maxim "Haste makes waste, best leave early." Everything floats in ambiguity here, since these last connections with the verbal barely show through on the level of the signification of the image.

If we consider the *Easy Rider* poster, we can discern in it the mind-set of today's youth. The poster seems to say that speed equals living life to the fullest. At the same time, we cannot help but remember the well-known slogan "Speed kills." Risk is present in the image in the juxtaposition of red and black at the central point and the diagonal, unbalanced line of the figure. Thus, the image represents the love of danger and the passion for life lived to the limit in the face of physical or moral death. The colors, lines, and shapes have combined to form a language to convey to us an entire philosophy.

At the same time, however, death and its undeniably subversive potential become naturalized: they are multiplied infinitely, disarmed of all singularity — in other words, turned into an ideology. Even without the text, the *Easy Rider* poster already contains elements of "consensual" rhetoric that turn it into a plausible piece of advertising.

Visually, the 1880 poster is characterized by its monochromatics. An interesting parallel might be drawn with the earliest known pictorial works (such as paintings by the Phoenicians or the Egyptians), in which the extension of the same color indicated depth and the space occupied in relation to objects of different colors and the relative size of the colored surfaces indicated the hierarchical order of the different elements, according to power, strength, or importance. Thus, far from achieving spatial perspective, the paintings never represented more than a single order of value.

From a certain perspective, the artist who designed the 1880 poster worked precisely according to this established code. Everything that is not the central figure is cast in the same moss green. Therefore the same importance and the same value are accorded to these objects, despite their differences. Train, hill, houses, meadows all come down to the same thing. Standing out against this monotone background, the main character takes up the central space, from top to bottom. His clothing differs from the rest of the painted area in that it is of a much darker green. He is clearly seen as the most important part of the picture. Even the tricycle, which in a sense is disproportionately large, attracts less attention because of its almost indefinable half green, half gold. The tricycle is an accessory to the person, even on a visual level, and although in itself it leads the eye to another formal representation, we have to look at the bottom of the picture to find the gold, the only real interruption in this monochrome world of green. There is no doubt that the gold is there for a reason; this was the time of the gold rush, the opening up of the Klondike goldfields. This tricycle *runs on gold*. Signifier and signified correspond perfectly. Primitive art reappears in a modern pictorial technique. The countryside can be found in the city; solitude lives in harmony with the crowd; the Middle Ages and modern industrial society exist in perfect continuity; disparity no longer exists: nothing precludes anything else. So where is the cause for concern?

From the point of view of its perspective, the 1880 poster situates itself in a curious position—which is to say, finally, that it situates itself utterly ambiguously. On the one hand it borrows from primitive art; on the other, it heralds the twentieth century.

The first paintings, we will remember, faced with the problem of the relative placement of an icon within the picture, often resolved it by the establishment of a vertical structure. The center and lower portions of the painting were interpreted in this context as the favored position for the most important figure; as figures approached the top and sides of the picture, they diminished progressively in importance.

If we rely on this code, we find that the 1880 poster can easily be interpreted. The name of the bicycle manufacturer immediately catches our eye. Next comes the promised gold, closely followed by the tricycle, drawn in the minutest detail. There is no doubt that on a formal level the promotional message here is in the foreground. The hero comes next, since there could conceivably be no hero without this machine. Then we see the train that is left far behind, the faraway village, and the landscape fading into the distance.

In this strict hierarchy, the logic of the advertiser becomes clear: purchasing the product makes the buyer into a hero who can forget the contradictions of the time.

Obviously, from a twentieth-century vantage point, this argument appears somewhat simplistic, if not naive; it does not seem aggressive enough. For the nineteenth-century viewer still accustomed to this representational code, however, it was probably quite simple to interpret.

From a completely different point of view, the extreme precision in the drawing of the tricycle and its invasive presence in the foreground space seem to us to foreshadow a representational school that was still to come.

While the background does allow us to forget the context, it highlights in a particular way the tricycle on which attention is to be focused. The drawing necessarily gives excessive importance to a completely exceptional object. The drawing of the tricycle also provides a sneak preview of the photographic techniques employed by certain posters that were to follow. Although the Middle Ages are still present in the Howe tricycle poster, it must be admitted that the twentieth century is clearly being advertised almost as much as the product itself. After all, is it not the function of all advertising to promote both current ideas and the product for sale?

The Passage into Sameness Requires Recourse to Ideology

The use of ancient codes of both color and perspective in the Howe tricycle poster cannot be considered the product of chance. On the contrary, here it is, for us, a matter of a primordial effect. Many authors have demonstrated or established the close relationship existing between the general characteristics of various forms of artistic expression (paintings, novels, plays) of a given period and the period's social norms, customs, and attitudes — in other words, its ideology. We certainly endorse this assertion. There are, however, some important distinctions to be made in describing or analyzing the connection between certain artistic works or certain media and this same ideology. It seems to us absurd to assert, for example, that Einstein's theories or the films of Marguerite Duras are the place of an ideological relationship, almost like the kind of story that appears in tabloids. From this viewpoint, it seems clear to us that advertising is infinitely more directly linked to ideology than is, for example, a novel by Joyce.

A work of public expression of any kind always endeavors, it seems to us, to achieve an effect that lies somewhere between creating sameness and creating difference. Even when it is seen to depict social values, art attempts to create difference. Advertising is one of those forms of expression that constantly strive to produce sameness, if not the identical, and from this point of view, it shares many traits with propaganda and with all attempts to promote consensus.

This question could be considered differently by imagining, at a given time in history, or better still in a particular social and economic climate, some kind of anxiety. In the case of the Howe poster, this anxiety stems explicitly from two factors — urbanization and industrialization — but obviously it could be quite different in other places or under different circumstances.

This anxiety, which is possibly linked, in this case at least, to a new collective experience, requires some examination.

It is as if the following question were collectively being asked: In all of the confusion of cities, factories, commuter trains, and disappearing small towns, how can we cope and find our way?

Inevitably, when they are confronted with this kind of anxiety or partially formulated question, different types of discourse will try to provide an answer. Political analysts, for example, will use the opportunity to show how accurate their charts are and to point out middle-class forces at work in the process of grinding down the proletariat, or the novelist will bring together various characters involved in a conflict of this kind.

What is interesting here is that advertising discourse, far from being free from the issue at hand, focuses on it and then immediately reappropriates it on the level of a *passage into sameness*. All lucid examination of a highly relevant question is short-circuited in this process; the question is merely raised, without any intention of looking at it more closely, so that the dramatic depths of the conflict are hidden, and the product is used to deny them.

Cities, factories, commuter trains, workers, the disappearance of small towns, all of these problems have a *solution;* there is a way of *getting around* all of this: Howe cycles. From this point on, no real desire is possible; the only way out is the act of buying. There is no longer any question of expressing one's individuality, since all you have to do to be free of anxiety is draw on the reservoir of ideologically determined answers to a question that is instantly nullified.

In opposition to this process we find creative, scientific, literary, or pictorial works, in other words, those forms of discourse that, when they are confronted with an anxiety-laden question, produce an elucidating statement but first of all *stimulate imagination* and *prompt creativity*. The place of desire and the ensuing phantasmatic development are respected in this kind of work. We are given no fixed answer to the question, but rather an alternate route for releasing tension: a matrix of associations through which the phantasm can be worked out and desire can therefore be fulfilled. This freedom provided by a creative work can, of course, lead to more personal, more "extra-ideological" representations. In advertising, this must be avoided at all costs.

In a single stroke, the problem strangely brings up that of psychoanalytical interpretation since we know that faced with an anxiety-laden question, the analyst can produce either a revealing interpretation, leading to the exploration of fears, or a restrictive interpretation that shuts the lid on discourse and returns it to silence. Advertising, in terms of this analogy, is in the realm of interpretations that stifle. Nothing more to be said: we consume meaning. Nothing more to be thought: we contemplate the solution. The creative work, on the other hand, with its appeal to desire and the phantasmization response of the interlocutor, would be on the order of an interpretation that opens. Since this desire-phantasmization apparatus in itself constitutes the essence of the creative act, it seems logical to say that the creative work is one that forces us to create, at least on the level of phantasmatic elaboration. Because the author of the work assumes the right to create, the creative work calls forth in the viewer the possibility of creation. Clearly, advertising has to guard against this tendency. Sameness here offers itself as a means of avoiding the dissimilar.

It is clear that, in order to remain consistent on the very narrow ledge of a perfectly maintained sameness, advertisers must make sure, as they evoke the important issues of the day, never to overstep the bounds of current discourse, never, in some sense, to be ahead of ideology.

In the Howe poster, for example, we notice the rigidly upright posture and overly formal clothing of this noble figure. Here we have the statement of a problem. At the very least, this figure is far from an evocation of a champion cyclist. This is a man of the city; his posture and appearance show that he leads a sedentary existence, that he is not used to physical exercise. And the question is obvious: one begins to wonder what happens to the human body in an urban environment. Calisthenics, for instance, which promote "strength, health, and courage,"[6] become popular precisely because people are cut off from physical exertion.

The advertiser, however, cannot violate certain standards. To feature an athlete would be out of the ordinary and would go against convention. Similarly, to point out too explicitly this cyclist's poor physical condition would be in bad taste. The man pictured here is deliberately made to look like an ordinary, respectable middle-class man whose attitude toward his body is still somewhat inhibited.

The same argument is used in evoking the need to get away from the multiple demands and almost inhuman pressures of the city. Once again, the tricycle is forced on us as the *solution,* in other words, it gets in the way of clarity, which, were it not blocked, would probably provoke desire and its development.

We might still imagine that the analysis of the "oppressive" situation here takes the form of a critique of the industrial and industrializing system. Not at all. The cure, it would appear, lies in the disease. The tricycle is a remarkable industrial product, a complex mechanism made with great precision, but at the same time a marvel of simplicity. The beginning of industrialization creates an enigma, but the tricycle provides an answer. The complexity of the social situation, new levels of unemployment, alarming fluctuations in the economy, and redefinitions of land use all seem to point to social upheaval. The remarkable balance and even stability of the image, the unity expressed in color and line miraculously erase these troubling symptoms. Progress is on the march; civilization easily solves whatever problem it creates.

The connection between the *Easy Rider* poster and the sameness of ideology is also explicit, even though the context has changed in nearly a century. Industry has given way to technology; urban stress has become an almost inevitable reality. Continual movement and high-speed travel have been factored into the conditions prevailing in 1880. Getting away, if such a thing is possible, has become almost essential. Instead of concealing this dimension, the poster provides quite an original interpretation of it. It has created its own unique lighting. The clash of opposing colors creates a harsh, glaring, artificial, and unmodulated brightness. Glare is associated in our minds (through visual memory) with various sensations such as speed, danger, fear, and so on. As in real situations of this kind, the eye here has no resting point, no point of focus. It constantly scans, from right to left, drawn back to the center, and then immediately sent out toward the periphery of the picture. Continually changing space in time, the eye thus reconstitutes the experience of movement. This sensation is further reinforced by the repetition, in ''detached forms,'' of different aspects of the same pattern at different levels of the image.

To be sure, we are furnished with a reading of a universe where the values of mobility, movement, and speed occupy a central position. Our modern perception, for example — the way objects appear as we pass quickly by in cars, the blaze of neon signs that can turn a city street into a veritable kaleidoscope, the shimmering, multiple images in store windows — could hardly have been imagined in the nineteenth century. Given this new perception, it is no longer enough to provide an accurate illustration of a static object (for example, ''the Howe tricycle''). The modern eye needs to see the particularly dynamic qualities of an object to appreciate it and give it value. Artificial lighting, the various gadgets that can produce varied and diffuse light effects, give us a kinetic sensation of color, which is a completely new experience. Moreover, viewers themselves are more mobile than before. They travel from place to place by plane, car, or bus, and all of this movement gives them a perception of the world and of objects that is far from static. Objects are presented to our eyes now in a scanning that is very different from that of people in previous centuries, who used to walk through the streets and had time to look at things in detail. Besides, architecture itself has completely changed in the sense that detail matters less than the whole, less than the overall impression (compare, for example, a modern building and a Gothic cathedral). The first thing the modern eye sees is movement. In order to understand how any piece of machinery works, more than knowing about the individual parts, we have to grasp all of the processes that make the machine operate. Thus, films, radio, and television require us to think and see in such a way as to be carried along in perpetual motion.

The modern mind naturally compensates for changes of every sort, for interpretation, ellipsis, simultaneity. To follow the action of a film, one has to notice changes in details and actions, understand that one scene takes place at the same time as another, and know that something that happens as a result of something else but that is not shown has to be imagined. The mind needs to make connections that are not seen, perceived, or made explicit. We have to compare the acts and gestures of people from earlier periods to see the differences in ways of thinking, seeing, and, ultimately, acting. We who were born in this century think in terms of movement, and our perception has become adapted to an environment that is increasingly dedicated to mobility.

In the 1880 poster, on the contrary, the central object is shown in the foreground with a great deal of detail. The viewer of that period was engaged in examining a new tool. To see it properly one has to be standing still; the tricycle is shown in three-quarters view (so we can see the whole outline and the contours), as if it were on display in a museum. The man placed on top of it is like a mannequin. He looks as if he has been taken from a painting to be perched on the tricycle for this occasion. The man and the machine are there to be looked at, and aesthetics take precedence over the qualities of the object. When movement is to be expressed in this frame, it is achieved only by means of extremely classic, if not stylized, effects. The scarf, for example, sticks straight out behind his head. The speed of the train is barely suggested by a few barely defined lines (of force). It is obvious that we are being addressed in the language of another century. The sameness here depicted, here suggested, is of a different ideology.

At the end of the nineteenth century, people were torn socially and politically between stability (represented here by the countryside, by the hero in the image, by the monochromatic coloring of the image as a whole) and the desire for change (shown by the train leaving the countryside, by the tricycle—the new means of locomotion in the city—and by the color yellow, symbolizing the sun, wealth, and violence). Thus, the elements that are meant to signify movement are linked to the expression of a political ideology rather than to a true perception of the universe. Refinement, order, precision, and nobility characterize the icon on display here; the man on the tricycle, like the paintings of the period, is fixed in two dimensionality. Posters were made for viewers who were used to looking at paintings. This was the beginning of advertising posters as such. These are not placards to look at for two or three seconds as one walks or drives by, the way we do today. These are not placards that have to divert attention away from all distractions. Contemporary posters project in an instant the main quality or qualities of the item to be promoted. The present generation is more interested in the effectiveness, the advantages of the product in people's lives. People in the nineteenth century were not used to gadgets, constant change, or novelty. The industrial revolution, rapid urbanization, and the advent of department stores forced the nineteenth-century mind to focus its attention. This was why people at first spent time just looking at new products; they were astonished at the very fact of their existence. "Twentieth-century man"[7] is so used to speed, to scientific discoveries and new technology, that we are sometimes astonished by the slow progress in certain fields. Our lives feed on the unusual. This creates a curious creature constantly in pursuit of what is new in the realms of physical sensations, art, and morality but at the same time one very difficult to impress, surprise, or enthrall. The tricycle in the 1880 poster is drawn to be looked at for a long time, to be contemplated in and of itself. In the twentieth century we no longer have the time.

But what exactly is being offered to the twentieth century?

However different the Howe and *Easy Rider* posters may be, their logic is profoundly the same: *the disease is the cure*. The hustle and bustle of the twentieth century become cures for the pressure created by bustle and hustle. In precisely the same way a century earlier, industry became the cure for industry. In a deft sleight of hand, freedom will come only from what oppresses, even though, in its essence, the *Easy Rider* poster provides the key for transforming the elements of civilization into a force for liberation. But add to this item that you should free yourself here and now, and then at that point when the circuit of occultation is complete. The subversive is transformed into sameness and creation is recuperated.

The uniform green of the 1880 poster corresponds to a profound need for homogeneity. It must not be forgotten that the middle class, particularly at that time, strove to uphold its system of values at all levels of society. Only the strip of gold at the bottom of the poster evokes the frail revolutionary thought that was stifled by expansive capitalist organization. The *Easy Rider* poster, on the other hand, assaults the eye with the violence and plurality of its colors. We get the impression that ours is a century in which everything is exploding; politics, morality, and social codes are changing at an alarming rate. Through films, television, and a press that highlights scandal, this century assumes the right, if not the mission, to live marginality, to know the underside as well as the flip side of an entire organization, to take things to the logical extension of their own contradiction. This love of risk taking and danger is admirably captured by the coloration of the *Easy Rider* poster.

But to claim that everything is possible in the land of the free (as they say), that everything can be expressed, and that in the *United States* there is plenty of room for every kind of singularity — is this not, precisely, a subtle recourse to ideology? Isn't this just an underhanded way of stifling the cries of a standardized civilization, of a people mired in uniformity and predictability while they are made to believe in so much difference?

The 1880 poster is divided into foreground and background, upper and lower sections, which corresponds to how society is divided: between the middle class and the others, country and city, the past and the brand-new industrialized present. Both centrifugal and centripetal, the 1970 poster is based on the diagonal line onto which circles, curves, and valleys are grafted and stacked one on top of the other. The diagonal seems to underscore the mobility of all existence at any level of society. The overall effect of the poster would tend to show how the contemporary world is less stratified horizontally and vertically, and to what extent all individuals live in their own cycles. But isn't this just the same old line about America the free?

This question, of course, leads to a double consideration. As an art photograph, the poster conveys a subversive message. I have taken the liberty, the artist informs us, of using the technology of this civilization to construct an arbitrary space of imaginary liberty. And as a consequence you, the spectator, are invited to do the same.

When this same photograph is used as advertising, it takes on a completely different meaning. Instead of appealing to a potential desire for "self-symbolization," it encourages the spectacle (here cinematographic) of a "good society,"[8] capable of producing its autorecuperation (the film) but, finally, incapable of tolerating marginality (the violent content of the film).

Living in America, one eventually learns to distrust the ideological elasticity of a country that claims an ability to tolerate all forms of dissidence, but that, in general, produces only the identical. In this context, the abundance, if not in fact the superabundance, of forms in the *Easy Rider* poster becomes somewhat suspect.

Prolegomena to a Theory of the Advertising Act

At the end of the previous chapter we drew a parallel between the construction of the advertisement and psychic defenses. To be even more explicit we noted that advertising tends to reproduce and set in motion certain unconscious defense mechanisms (projection, displacement, intellectualization, compromise formation, etc.) with the apparent aim of separating or distancing interlocutors from their desire, under the pretext of protecting them from it. Having taken a more diachronic view of advertising, we are now in a position to go beyond this first approach, not to reject it, but to broaden its meaning and scope. And this initial theorizing, as we indicated at the beginning of this chapter, brings us back to the strategy of desire.

The first condition for the appearance of desire is none other than the presence of a tension, a sort of imbalance in the internal harmony of the subject that calls for the restoration of equilibrium. Lacan, corroborating Freud's theory, points out that this imbalance amounts to a discrepancy between demand and need. We have by and large adopted this interpretation of the phenomenon but must now consider what unfolds in its wake.

This tension, which is akin to the distress felt by the infant, first of all demands to be represented, in other words, to be stated or formulated in such a way as to bear witness, on a psychic level, if not to the meaning, then at the very least to the presence of this desire.

In the process of this representation, the chains of association are of major importance. By means of displacement along associative pathways, an image may come to represent for us another image close to it in association. Similarly, through condensation, an image may simultaneously represent two or even a great many intersecting associative pathways.

To put it briefly, this process may in turn bring about two extremely different derivative processes. In the first case, in attempting to reconstitute the sensory context of a primary state of satisfaction, we develop, from its mnesic traces a phantasmatic that fulfills desire. In the second case, refusing to consider the tension that is experienced as a valid representation of the primary distress state, the subjects bring this tension, to some extent, back to everyday experience. Searching through their memories, looking for circumstances of satisfaction, they work out a plan for a specific action that is likely to satisfy the impulse, in other words, to reduce the tension.

Here it is important to note that the mental processes of condensation and displacement are not, in fact, specific to construction, but instead preside over the elaboration of all representations. Only subsequently do the events become separate. Condensation, displacement, and even representation are perpetuated in dreams. The dream is entirely composed of representation, and therefore of condensation and transference, following the well-known laws of figurality. What happens in order for desire to become drive, or, to put it another way, what sets off the reduction to everyday experience is not necessarily obvious. And it is at this precise juncture of deviation that the advertising act is actualized.

In the many advertisements we examined in chapter 1, as well as in the Howe tricycle and *Easy Rider* posters we have just been analyzing and comparing, we can bring out the presence of condensation and displacement. On this point, demonstration could not be more simple.

One example is the train in the background of the Howe poster. This is without a doubt an image with remarkable powers of condensation and displacement. Using the paradigm of means of locomotion, we are easily led from the train to the stagecoach, if not brought back to the tricycle. At the intersection of several associative links, this same train brings us back to the machine, to the phenomenon of industrialization, but also to the crush of public transportation. Essentially, this image registers as a locus of unquestionable polysemism.

One will recall the analyses suggested by the golden swath at the bottom of the Howe poster as well as by its monochromatic effect. Similarly, we will remember the multiple symbols evoked by the colors of the *Easy Rider* poster. We considered, for example, the opposition between the diagonal/biker and more pure, elementary forms. The question therefore is not to know whether or not the advertising image is the place of condensation/displacement, but rather to locate what it is in this image that blocks desire.

As early as chapter 1, we partially resolved this question. Clarifying the parallel between the construction of the advertisement and psychic defenses, what we established, though without explicitly naming the process, was that *advertis-*

ing discourse has to mask desire in favor of drive. Psychoanalytic practice has taught us time and time again that patients are above all neither beings without drive nor, for that matter, without specific actions. Whether obsessional, hysterical, or borderline cases, to the contrary they still spend their lives in a world of what are termed specific actions, namely, those thought to help reduce tension. It is abundantly clear, however, that these defenses and specific activities do a wonderful job of keeping patients at arm's length from their deep desire.

Rationalization, for example, is not an antidrive force. To the contrary, it encourages the development of a very complex and sometimes shrewd discourse and leads its author to actions that apparently bring relief. Yet these actions — and this is their essence — disguise desire and render it capable of being mistaken. Perhaps they protect the subjects from an overload of desire, but they push them to the wayside of a phantasmic path that would be more satisfying.

In a sense, we could leave the argument here and finish by demonstrating the recourse to psychic defenses in all advertising. We believe, however, that such an approach would be both too hasty and in many cases inconclusive.

In the Howe tricycle poster, for example, it is fairly easy to establish the advertiser's use of the formation of compromise. Between country and city, industry and artisanship, we are told to adopt the compromise of the tricycle. But is that enough to make the Howe poster an advertising act?

In our view, something else happens. Something else along the lines of the memory screen: what we will call the image screen.

The theory of the memory screen suggests that a scene is connected to a significant traumatic experience, but very indirectly. This memory, which is usually remarkably clear and detailed, linked to the other memory by associative displacement, masks it more than represents it. It distracts the subject's attention by giving the impression that it is important and significant, when in fact it is only a mask or (above all) a pretext for an accepted belief.

It seems to us that this double notion of clarity and recognition is also to be found in the advertising act, and precisely on the level of the screen image.

Following this same line of thought, if we come back to the Howe poster it must be admitted that the contrast between the precision of the tricycle in the foreground and the ephemeral vagueness of the background very probably has more than a single function. In fact, by becoming very attentive to this hazy and indistinct background, we were able to discover several pieces of information about the real conflict. The train: overcrowded, industrial, suburbs and city. The village: nostalgia, clean air, community, and the rest. It is probably there, in this indistinct and blurred background, where subversive elements are drawn, that is to say, those that might, by way of analogy, evoke a state of distress and, consequently, lead the viewer to a phantasmatic elaboration, to make contact with desire, and, eventually, its fulfillment.

This possible projection is blocked by the image of the tricycle screen. Even more than a simple defense mechanism, it suggests that the viewer's eye stop at the tricycle and go no further, just as the memory screen of rape prevents the patient from probing more deeply into memory.

Moreover, since this image of the tricycle is in perfect accord with the ideological tenor of prevailing opinion, it seems a very obvious and acceptable place to direct one's thought and actions. From this point on, it seems to us, the die is cast.

In chapter 1 we concerned ourselves with the role of writing and typography, beyond any reference to text, as a sign of the sacred. Indeed, to the actual point where theorization develops form and volume, this sacred element itself appears as a screen image—an intentionally clear place but one that also keeps the gaze from going further to join with desire; an obviously acceptable point of focus because it is in agreement with tradition, history, and a context: a place of *sameness*. For here is where, ultimately, the question lies: how does the advertiser incite us to produce *sameness?*

On reflection, the question can be approached from another angle and leads us to discover that access to desire carries with it the risk of a difference. For an advertising act to occur, a construction that, on the one hand, is calculated according to known psychic defenses, but, on the other hand, offers the viewer a representation that is completely acceptable since it agrees with ideological sameness is brought into play.

Within a broader frame of reference, there is little reason to think that desire is set in motion each time that a tension is felt. One might even think that most of the time, tension is interpreted as an everyday occurrence, one requiring a specific action. It must also be added that the specific action will appear all the more plausible if it fits in with the subject's values.

Advertising transposes this logical argument point by point; since it cannot know what is acceptable to everyone, it weighs its acceptability on ideological statements that are frequently tested and verified through periodic surveys of public opinion. To put it another way, advertising exploits our need to resemble, to agree with the world around us, and in this sense, our need to produce sameness. Inevitably it reinforces the fear of desire, the only possible place of a *self-symbolization*.

Examination of static advertising alone limits our possibilities for theorization even more. Though it is clear that the characteristics we have pointed out here to be pertinent to the advertising act seem well-established enough to be set forth as constants, we consider it essential to extend our investigation to include kinetic advertising, in other words, commercials, which make up an important part of what we see on television.

Chapter 3
Associative Drift

To this point, we have limited our inquiry to static advertisements, and, because of the fixity of the medium, we have necessarily had to reduce the field of our analysis to a sort of transparency through which, beneath the manifest image, a latent image could still be seen. At the same time, it appeared to us that the psychic defenses that forced the spectator's predilection for the advertised image very readily recuperated mechanisms of waking life (projection, identification, development of symptoms or compromises, and so on). Dream defenses, those of nocturnal life, for their part presided over the advertiser's elaboration of films that until now we have been content to examine shot by shot, from the bias of a degree of fixity and stability.

As we begin to consider cinematic advertisements, from the outset we have to acknowledge that here we are dealing with an infinitely more complex situation. In each shot of the filmic sequence, on the one hand, this play of transparencies is ready to work. But on the other hand, in the very construction of the series of images, in the successive engagement of motifs of representation, much more subtle mechanisms will in fact be engaged by the spectator. Here we will touch on dream defenses themselves.

This is a major change of direction. It requires reflection on the associative life of the psyche. It demands that one examine certain fundaments of symbolic life and the reasons for attachment to certain representations. This shift in direction also sheds light in the field of psychoanalysis on certain elements of psychopathology and, in particular, on perversion.

˙Unconscious Association: The Law of Series

It would seem that one of the most constant laws of the human psyche is that no representation ever survives alone in the psyche.

On the contrary, representations regroup among themselves, form series, sequences, cohorts from analogous elements. *Signifiance*,[1] consequently, would never originate from an isolated representation, but instead from series of representations — as if it were only faced with a series of representants that a certain validity of analogical linkage could finally be established, as if it were only in culmination and reciprocal connections of elements that what is actually trying to express itself could finally be perceived.

Psychoanalysis makes extensive use of this phenomenon as it strives to extract meaning from the associative sequence, whether from the session or from treatment. But this phenomenon extends well beyond what happens on the couch: it is a mode of understanding specific to the human mind and its consequences for psychic life to this day remain barely measurable.

What concerns us more immediately, what we retain from these signifying sequences, is their strange power to qualify, to specify, but also to work their way around, if not pervert, a primary meaning. It is, in fact, on this very ground that television commercials polarize their messages.

But first let us imagine a banal example and suppose ourselves confronted with the image of a violent scene: let us say, for example, a particularly grisly crime. It is clear that this image in itself has no meaning. It has yet to be qualified. Are we the perpetrator or the victim of this crime? Is it a friend or parent? The recurring memory of a traumatic spectacle? None of this becomes explicit without subsequent associations. Exactly as numbers originate from the convergence of a series in mathematics, here meaning originates from the *convergence* of the *associative series*. Meaning, moreover, has nothing fixed or permanent about it; it is always in the process of being elaborated since, in a way, every series always remains open, always remains to be completed.

What is also obvious is that subsequent associations can easily come to corrupt the original representation, connote it in an acceptable or tolerable way, transform it in an effort to mask its immoral intent. Hence the gory murder of a family member you thought you loved can be transmuted into a desire for self-affirmation and for overcoming a certain dependency. Evidently, the switch works and the connotations provided by association become absolutions of guilt.

The connotative and corrective importance of subsequent associative linkages to original representations is thus crucial: they can transform a devastating spectacle into an entirely pleasant image. In most cases, the original will be repressed or diminished: it will be disarmed. Only the acceptable and satisfying image will remain—a useful lure, no doubt, without which the burden of anguish might be unbearable, but would all the same remain the lure of an essential illusion.

In this perspective of psychic associations, advertisements constitute what we will call—even if this abuses language—a simple situation.

Advertisements are made up of two images.

The first is latent. It speaks of death, despair, revolt, of desire, homosexuality, and subversive freedom. But because it is articulated according to a desire of some sort, it is equally shocking or troubling, unacceptable at least short of a continual reopening of the question for every advertisement in every magazine.

Upon this first vision, a second, manifest, socially acceptable representation is superimposed; it is articulated not on desire or on fundamental lack but on drive and need.

Uncontestably, this manifest image will appear as an utterly privileged substitute of the first, because it is less menacing, to begin with, but also because it offers an analogical transcription of the first image, one that makes it desirable.

In associative terms, we are dealing with an analogical series that has two representants. The too-disturbing original is repressed in favor of its substitute. The phenomenal problem of urbanization in England gives place to the image of the Howe tricycle, and the original disquiet remains willfully misconstruable [*méconnaissable*].

What happens in the television commercial is not entirely of another order. All the same, here advertisers have at their disposal a series of longer and more elaborated shots. To dupe or redirect the look, there are ten, twenty shots, which, by turns, can contradict or shade the first—to divert desire. The substitutions, in principle, can thus overdetermine one another. For the first substitutes, second ones will follow in rapid succession. The panoply of resistances can be refined over and over again. The staging of this scenario will in particular call forth the play of dream defense mechanisms. One can, in a way, play on all of these levels.

Print advertisements in effect resemble a psychic situation of the waking state. An unconscious image tries to surface. It is necessary, somehow, to get free of this image: it is rapidly followed by a projection or a rationalization; the urgency of everyday life calls for immediate substitution. It is, in fact, fitting to set up a kind of counterscenario, a process that appeals to dream processes.

Obviously, the advertisements we are considering here are the opposite of fixity. To begin with, they are made up of several shots and offer a *sequence* of images. Some television commercials are not cinematic per se. Their only advantage over printed advertisements is a larger audience. Single shots, on television, can be analyzed on the same psychic level as print advertisements.

Thus in the case of truly cinematic commercials, we will see the organization of a sequence that attempts to make possible meanings converge toward a desired

Figure 3-1

meaning. From the initial polysemics of original representations, one will at-tempt to conclude with a kind of final monosemy. The technique merits illustra-tion and dissection.

The first shot of the commercial we will consider here is an urban scene. Near a window, a young girl with a sweet face is alone in an apartment. A voice says, "On Sundays, light has a melancholy flavor" (fig. 3-1).

If one limits oneself to this introduction, everything is, in a way, plausible. The stage is already set by a sweet, pretty young girl, but she is alone. Sunday refers us just as much to possible pleasures during this day of rest as it does to the dreary solitude of days when there is nothing to do. Melancholy seems, in effect, to qualify this turbid atmosphere where flavor and vision get mixed together. Ev-erything invokes a warning: sight, odors you can taste, the sound, in the very wording of the phrase, of a voice that is at once gentle and solemn. Already, in each of us, certain associative chains are summoned forth. Sundays, melancholy, maybe the rape of a sweet young virgin. How is the advertiser going to get out of this polysemic mess? Such is, in fact, a question that could come to mind, even when we know full well that there is no profit to be gained by leaving us in a state of melancholy.

If we examine the situation attentively, we find the following plausible associative chains:

Associative series in the Bell commercial

boredom	young girl alone	wish for love
desolation	at the window	
week	Sunday	holiday
blackness	light	brightness
distaste	flavor	flavor
emptiness	melancholy	emptiness filled
seriousness	voice	soft

A melodramatic author could easily use, for subsequent developments, the left-hand series (boredom, desolation, blackness, distaste, emptiness, seriousness) to establish the scenario.

Contrary to all obvious expectations, the advertiser's scenario refers us to a curious balance: it praises reduced rates for phone calls made during the weekend—even while heavily stressing their financial dimension.

Yet, on second analysis, this sequence no longer seems so improbable.

The series on the left, that of boredom and desolation, has in the end been retained by the advertiser, but reduced to an expression: that of *affective poverty*.

The unspoken aspects of boredom are interior emptiness and the feeling of emotional poverty. The image of *material poverty* will pick up the cue. Thanks to reduced prices at the end of the week, we are (momentarily) no longer quite as poor. From this moment on, the series can be inverted. Material poverty having become banal, loneliness and poverty are disarmed. Melancholy has the flavor of Sunday's light: it fades away.

Associative circuits of the advertising message

Manifest message	Associative paths of overture	Latent messages	Analogical series
Young girl alone at her window	double	The human being is a being alone and you live from emptiness.	melancholy = sadness = solitude = affective poverty
Sundays, light has a melancholy flavor	nostalgia emptiness		

| the telephone =
savings | light and rejoicing
images of
memories and
pleasing calls | It costs little to
fill up all of your
emptinesses.
It is crazy to
remain nostalgic. | emotive
   poverty =
material
   poverty =
banalized
   material
   poverty |
| Isn't there
someone? | Separation is in
fact just distance | Finally the feeling
of aloneness is
ridiculous like any
idea of castration.
You are not
castrated, after
all! | banalized
   melancholy |

A print advertisement alone could have tried to convince us to use long-distance telephone service: it would have been enough to set forth, for example, a latent image of loneliness and superimpose upon it an image of reminiscences. Inevitably the argument would have been less elaborate, the passage through affective poverty to monetary considerations much less certain, the gestalt much less complete.

What seems to be happening here is that from the start we are offered a theme—boredom—that appears to be monosemic, but it is a theme that, according to the usual workings of the unconscious, will have to be inscribed in a connotative series. In order that the spectator not veer away toward complete nostalgia, this *series* amends what everyday language rightly calls a *first impression*.

It is interesting to notice here how much, from one country to another, from one culture to another, profound human themes are the same and how, as a result, the same advertising problem, continents apart, comes to be stated according to the same argumentation.

In 1981 France had to develop an advertising campaign for its national telephone ''traffic.'' The problem was to be dealt with from a perspective closely related to initial pain and rediscovered happiness. The campaign was made up of a series of four testimonies, thirty seconds each, that were, in principle, supposed to incite the spectator to make use of the phone network. They had a clear effect, according to the phone company. Let us consider their general content a bit more closely.

''I was furious with him, he called me, he explained, now everything's fine,'' declares a young housewife, smiling next to her telephone (fig. 3-2).

Anger is thus dissipated, transformed into an amorous call, muted into a re-

Figure 3-2. "Cheap happiness."

assuring discourse, into a totally secure sense of well-being. How, in effect, could one not come to rely upon this electronic bearer of happiness?

Elsewhere, the initial discontent is of a professional nature. "Even though the weather's perfect, a call to the weatherman could save a harvest." The initial concern here is just barely sketched, is just as quickly smoothed out, and is replaced by the affect of pride, linked to the expectation of success. The problem is no longer without solution. The cost of a telephone line in no way measures up to the cost of losing a harvest.

Standing in front of his inexpensive compact car, a young man who displays the unflappable composure of a stockbroker declares, "I ran a little ad with my phone number and in less than twenty-four hours, I sold it." How efficient!

Behind these testimonies, only fragments of which we reproduce here so as to not overburden our text, one perceives, transparently, an affective poverty not unlike the disarray in which human beings flounder from coast to coast.

The tangible smoothing out of material or concrete difficulties occupies the forefront. Behind it another order of resolution and conflict stands out, namely, the passage from solitude to communication, from ignorance to informed knowledge, from empty to full. Such a materialization-concretization of intimate experience can be shocking at first: why not, in effect, deal with affect directly?

Séguéla (1982) and many others try, after a fashion, to clear up this question. Being and having, he asks himself—don't they become confused? *To have* the telephone is *to be* more communicative, isn't it? To have this wife beaming with reassurance, to have this stockbroker's confidence following a favorable transaction or this farmer's smile while in full possession of his means, is it not, in a certain way, a *being more?*

The question is subtle to the extent that these charming exteriors camouflage the real drama they cover. What Séguéla tells us, in sum, is: the advertisement works to the extent to which we willfully confuse *having* and *being.*

Our reading of the national telephone campaign confirms, at first glance, Séguéla's claim. The advertiser has oriented the connotative chain toward material representations of affective content, banalizing, by the same stroke, actual anguish just as much as potential happiness, reducing them both to a factual tangibility. A quick call makes life much easier.

By acquiescing to the phone company's proposal, we in effect agree that it is *easier* to consider having than being, easier to endorse the false self than to endure the patient, steady forward progress of the work of mourning and of auto-castration.

Séguéla pushes language too far, however, when he presumes that the two levels become confused. If we choose the tangible way it is because the other, that of affect, would here confront us with the archaic, the violent, with solitude, with relative incompetence in the face of technological change. If we have chosen stereotype and ease, it is because the alternative, more tortuous in itself, in these thirty seconds finds no support nor any alibi. An excellent advertiser in his own right, Séguéla displaces the problem. It seems more fair to assert that, faced with a potential choice and being encouraged to take the side of the mythic or the idealized, our attitude, which leans in the direction of ease, does not necessarily implicate the totality of human response. The complicity of the advertiser and the spectator here aims to maintain a silence on the other, more reflexive choice made up more of mournings and assumed castrations. The affective steady forward progress we forget, in these advertising situations, in order to let ourselves be duped by the provisional euphoria of Séguéla and his colleagues' messages, does not justify believing that such will always be the case.

The Principle of Contiguity

In fact, the subject at hand, that of *associative logic,* is one of the most complex our modern knowledge has had to consider. Just to name these few, pure mathematics as well as anthropology, psychoanalysis, and linguistics in their own way come to grips with associative logic, and the debate is far from having run its course.

In mathematics, the question of associative logic takes form in the vast field of Boolean algebra and mathematical set theory. But since the advent of the computer, its perspective has been squarely inverted. When in the algebra of sets one produces arguments based on classes of objects that have in common a single given characteristic, a new branch of mathematics is slowly emerging. Symbology (Collectif, 1975) tries, in an irregular set, to perceive common traits among the elements of the set, to enunciate the characteristic that founds Boole's conventional algebra. One speaks of symbology because one is convinced that this common characteristic is a kind of symbol for the set, in other words, a representation capable of accounting for a group of elements. The computer calls for such research to augment its artificial intelligence. This theoretical sector is still only in the dawn of its development.

Psychoanalysis studies the question from an entirely different perspective. From a given associative chain, produced in certain clinical situations, it attempts to locate *signifiance* as if, in its very postulations, it presumed that a meaning is fundamentally never acquired but runs the length of a chain that defines it and draws it into a convergence. Understanding this logic is essential here: how, in fact, does the analyst understand what is said on the couch? Are the analyst's commentaries or interpretations not supplementary associations in the associative flow of the other's thought? How is the analyst led, for example, by a dream of a hit and run accident and a memory of lemon sherbet to speak of the need to kill a child inside oneself? An analytic space, says Serge Viderman (1970), constructs itself between the two analytic protagonists; it is a space that eventually produces meaning. René Major (1979) speaks of the associations of the analyst that come to complete that of the analysand.

The point of view we are here considering constitutes, in a certain manner, another aspect of this debate. We maintain that no word, no representation is in and of itself clear: that it always, if only to make it more specific, calls for other connected figurations, meaning being in no sense a static phenomenon, but on the contrary a *dynamic* one that is to be treated in a relativistic perspective, a little like Einsteinian physics.

So, in this perspective, the whole question remains to know what, faced with representation X, calls for the following representation Y.

The rationalists can happily claim that Y comes from a logical need to refine its perception. This position is utterly untenable; it would be necessary, in order to stick to this point, to put the whole of psychic supports into mothballs, to forget that many representations are to begin with unbearable to the mind, are thus repressed, and are transformed in order to make themselves over. Here we will set forth another hypothesis.

Until the contrary is proved, we will in effect postulate that *any representation is reducible to an interpsychic conflict.* Consequently, we will posit as a corollary that all the following associations aim at reducing this conflictual tension, at reabsorbing divergence. And, supporting this hypothesis, we will try to make explicit which of them have currency in the field of advertising.

The first association of the series having been given, the others, according to this hypothesis, will be chosen as successors to the extent that they bind themselves together in a certain manner but also to the degree that they are capable of *reducing* the tension the first association provokes.

This "in a certain manner" is extremely fluid; it should remain so. The subsequent links of the associative sequence can in effect attach themselves to sonority, to rhythm, to evocative potential, or to any other subtle dimension of the first link. Examples no doubt will illustrate a theory that would otherwise be too abstract. We will first of all borrow them from the brand names of certain products.

"Sveltesse-Taillefine" [slenderness-thin size] names a certain commercial brand, and its residual representation of course goes along with the thinness certain women, according to the advertising hypothesis, are looking for. But, if one looks closer, one ascertains that the expression leads not to one series but to two conflicting associative series. Obviously, *svelte* and *fine* [thin] suggest elegance. Surely, too, *sveltesse,* by the bias of its suffix, leads to phonetically similar terms: caress, princess, *jeunesse* [youth], goddess, and so on. But, on the other hand, isn't it also true to say that *tesse* refers to "test," namely to "trial" [*épreuve*], indeed to "detest" [*détester*], then to test your size [*teste-taille*], then to hate your size [*déteste-taille*]? *Svelte* and *fine* are acquired only through a size test. *Taille* [size] is also a somewhat cutting verb [*tailler* means "to cut"], but one that is not so far removed from the phantasm of flesh to be taken off in order to attain the desired slenderness.

The expression, for good reason, has a good chance of being remembered because it states both a conflict and its plausible solution. Some representations that, absurdly, are neutral do not hold our interest: *without a gap in signifiance,*

f. Advertising did not invent this rule;
iaximum.
iap brands such as Lux, or of certain
n-bec products? Or Lois brand jeans?
to light. It also recalls the secret guilt
to one's own body—to deck yourself
iomes down to certain prejudgments:
nd water are not luxuries. In "Lois"
"leisure" [loisirs] and warm affects
the austerity of "the law" [la loi], of
ein, Jontue perfume (fig. 3-3) links je
ll [tuer]? Or wild herbs of the nearby
:, à moins que Je . . . on . . . tue?
kill . . . someone?"]. Love and hate,
no mistake about it, is for a femme
i to the pertinent absence of an r in the
s what best establishes the double as-
products in general—a double chain
y the reassuring statement of a sensu-
words, precisely that of a "chanelle"
: lacking the r of "carnal"—Trans.].
more than in isolated images that one
laborates itself, in this context, much
more freely, stems out into an or its ..tual possibilities, and, consequently,
leaves much less room for problematic equivocations in interpretation. Around
isolated representations there is always a lasting aura of imprecision and doubt
that certainly lends them a kind of charm and mystery but that also causes the
representation to escape an analysis that is anything other than projective.

The television commercials that we are now going to examine illustrate, in our
opinion, this function of orientation and of the advertiser's control of the spectator's associative drift. We will analyze them in this specific sense, leaving the
more properly ideological aspects to the subsequent chapter on cathodic homily.

The Reign of the New Woman

If we have chosen to initiate our reflection with the help of a television commercial for perfume manufacturers, it is more than simple convenience; it is linked
to, among other things, the fact that perfume is in itself a more or less connotative entity. Before it, a person exists and is agreeable; thanks to it, a person appropriates a connotation. The smell, whether of mint or of periwinkle, of rose or
of lemon, is a representation just the same, in the olfactory order of things. The

Figure 3-3

perceptions of the sense of smell, we know, are not always consciously elaborated. It is nevertheless useful and from our earliest childhood arouses recognition of the other on a primary and archaic level. To choose for oneself musk or lily means to agree to be recognized on the most instinctual level of human contact, to give oneself over to pre-view or, better, to pre-s(c)entiment.

At this olfactory stage, easily repressed because it is archaic, everything operates according to drives and repulsions, taste and distaste. Wildness here has the taste of a dependence elsewhere disavowed; the body invokes the body without saying so to the overly rational mind. The scene is, by all appearances, ready for a potentially "violent" enactment. The advertiser here is walking a tightrope.

Yves Saint Laurent (1978) accepts this risk in an ingenious and representative way. His perfume, remember, is not for shy women.

In the first shot, a woman rushes down a staircase as fast as she can. Her hurried pace and the rapid movements of her body evoke a race that the spectator can associate with a disastrous or catastrophic event, if not with the actions and gestures of an athletic woman short of time or with an enthusiast who is a little "wild." Her gestures are the associative opposite of the elegance of her Cardin clothing. The image of this woman on the loose denies, in particular, the dependence on classic "feminine" models one finds in other advertisers.

A subsequent sequence shows us a car speeding along, abruptly screeching to a halt, and parking utterly illegally by a sidewalk café. Further on, this same D-S (goddess [déesse], MerceDeS) brushes up against the pant leg of a passer-by she almost runs over because she is going so fast, at such an uncontrollable speed.

The associative drift orients itself: we are faced with a car—and by extension a woman—capable of anything. She mows down anything in her path. Nothing stops her. She is a Fury, an outlaw. One thinks of the Mafia, or of Al Capone and Chicago. The woman on the screen deals in evil, murder, or, maybe, the affair of the century. Romance here no longer goes by the name of blue flowers and a whiff of periwinkle. We have before us a woman of action.

Next, a long corridor, which she follows, still running, then a long stairway, which she climbs four steps at a time. Where is she going? Where is she running to? What is she looking for? Our curiosity is on edge. Is it passion that drives her in this way toward some Romeo? And what kind of furious passion is it that knows only the laws of love, that sees only the empire of the senses? Wild, dying of passion, this woman is certainly not one who would let herself be held back by frivolous nonsense (perfume, for example).

The staircase leads us to the meeting place: the hall of justice. The spectator is astonished, recalling the equivocal relations this madwoman has had with the law.

The overview of the hall gives us a sense of the location without our being able, from the outset, to determine its meaning. This image structures the ambiguity of the commercial. Is this woman the defendant? Her driving style would persuade us of her guilt. Now—what a surprise—the only actor missing from this court is the lawyer.

Everything vacillates. The complicity of the judge and the assassin, a situation treated by the filmmaker Bertrand Tavernier, comes to mind, just like the ambiguity upon which lawyers thrive.

The outlaw suits the lawyer the same way a savage suits formal dress. The crazy submission of this woman to her legal appointment has no equal other than the needs and duties of a profession where she has to be the master (mistress?) of the destiny of her colleagues, to be on hand in case of exploitation or humiliation. Her passion, her mad rush, the delirium of her actions here constitute a counterbalance to the mind that litigates, rationalizes, argues, and demands respect.

Still, the conflict is contained, is set aside and repressed. In a quick gesture, during the only pause of the entire sequence, she sprays perfume behind her ears just before entering the courtroom.

Would she thus, by this gesture, resemble those women of current advertisements who are aggressive but sweet, catty but conformist? Feminine beyond an apparent virility? One has the feeling throughout that she hates delicacy, finesse; this gesture, though furtive, suggests that she is capable of caress. She caresses herself, granted, meaning she does not yet deal with the world of relationships, but soon she might (Joyce McDougall, 1985). On the other hand, does anyone here want a relationship?

Left bank, right bank: passage from hopeful fantasy to the realism of power. "This perfume," the voice-over says, "is not for shy women." We could even conclude that it suits aggressive, tough, delinquent, or phallic women. We are in the midst of denegation, disavowal of the need for relation and masturbatory or narcissistic claim to autosufficiency. Subterfuge relies on our fear of dependence and of relationships (Searles, 1979).

This product promises to liberate the consumer from the need to count on anyone and, by extension, from the (legal or other) hindrances of life itself. We go along to the extent that drift, without this regulation, would lead us back to reconsider the pain and sadness of separation, the necessary reality of mourning and of the law.

The position once again becomes aconflictual in the play of supreme narcissistic effacement by which the suggested phallic exhibitionism disappears. This perfume is meant for women engaged in the murder (of the mother? or of the father?) or in the assertion, on the fringe of the law, of a grandiose ego; it appeals to women obsessed by (dreamed of) control of their passions. It is meant for all those women who would find life so much easier were there no *other* (Lacan, 1977)—which is to say, for this grandiose ego that all of us spend our whole lives unmasking.

Is this the avenue of feminism?

Conflict Minus Guilt: An Ethic of Ease

The second advertisement we will consider could just as well have been called "the more problems there are, the fewer you have." In fact, this 1979 advertisement for Carlsberg beer hardly differs from the first as it identifies a problem in order to make it go away immediately, as if by magic.

The first scene shows us a man held within a recess that could be a doorway. This could just as well be a motorcyclist with a knapsack on his back wearing work overalls. In fact, he is a sky diver. In any case, he tells us, "Me, I like *action*," then throws himself into the void.

A second character is climbing a slope, knapsack on his back. We will later see him sitting at a campfire. He declares simply, "For me, it's nature."

In the following scene, a narrow stream, tall grass, a small boat, and a man who leans forward, about to grasp something, and says, "Adventure's my passion."

The woman who appears next is young. She toys casually with a silk scarf she is wearing around her neck. The scene is the seashore. "For me, it's the ocean," she announces.

Then we hear folk music.

Each one of these sketches could, of course, be the specific object of analysis. For the moment, we will retain this quadruple proposition as a thematic ensemble: here are, to be sure, four relatively young people who have in common the fact that they love something—earth, air, fire, and water, as if they had all read the Greek philosophers.

But the advertiser is eager to stress something else. The screen subdivides into four equal parts. A jingle starts: "We're different, still we're alike."

Here then a first key. We have been boldly solicited by the individualism of these enterprising, happy-go-lucky people: the reference is to some state beyond difference, to some deep resemblance.

The quartered screen is like them: on the level of the group shot, they come into contact and continue to evolve; their difference certainly does not get in the way of their lives. This is even a clever way of showing belonging.

Anyway, it is easy to see: each one continues to go about his or her own business, which, and what could be more natural, leads to the same gesture—open up a Carlsberg, proof of their common interest. What is more, each in his or her corner of the screen recites in unison, "Carlsberg's my beer." Everything is perfect.

Clearly, it is not necessary to have spent a lot of time in analysis clinics to know that for everyone the feeling of difference constitutes an extremely conflictual zone. And even more specifically, that this difference almost always opposes itself to the symbiotic phantasm of a total resemblance.

What the advertisement is juggling here is nothing less than a stick of dynamite. In any case, following these same premises, we can elaborate more than a social theory, more than a political project as well, extending from anarchy to the most totalitarian repression.

The images locked together by the associative opening could thus easily lead to the awareness either of a castration or of a desire or both at once, since, in any case, they are intimately linked.

Yet what has to be seen is that such a reflection — requestioning, which could run through all of these possible questions ("Am I different?" "Am I alike?") — would have something trying and exacting about it.

The "still we're alike" thus presents itself from now on as a precious token of relative calm. To believe it would mean not to worry about a deeper question. The moment has come to associate the product not (and this must be stressed) with the initial divergences, but entirely with the "still we're alike." The association between product and divergency would resolve absolutely nothing, but would send the spectator back to personal conflicts so that, in principle, the spectator would refuse this association: *ease obligates*. Psychic life, in any case, is made up of millions of conflictual representations that one thus disarms by means of banalizing associations, the conflict never surfacing until the moment when defenses stumble.

The scenario of these messages is then *not* read by the television viewer, but is from the start transformed. The narrative is condensed into a generative difference of resemblance — beer. The throw-oneself-into-the-void of the beginning magically turns into an allow-oneself-alcohol-of-forgetting; the taste of adventure or of the sea [*la mer*] becomes the bitter [*amer*] taste of beer. Displacement and condensation are fully at work, and when people claim that they do not hear advertising messages, you probably have to believe them: these messages are dreamed.

To Dress a Narcissistic Wound

It could seem improbable, at first glance, that an advertisement for adhesive bandages, just like one for a beer, might provoke dreaming. Nevertheless, if we examine it closely, the Urgo campaign in France (1980) seems to achieve this feat. We will see as much in certain representative fragments.

In our reflection on static advertising, we signaled how Urgo could dress urban blight. The emphasis then (1970) had to do with the elasticity of the strip of bandage.

The 1980 series first presents a little sketch, which in most of the individual commercials depicts handiwork being done. But it could be a playground scene: a close-up of a child's leg with a roller skate. A voice warns us: "There's Urgo in the air.'' We hear, "Ouch!" The hammer's head lands on a stray finger. A voice reassures us: "There's air in Urgo.'' A close-up shot on the product and its container: "Extra-flexible Urgo.'' Every sort of tool is shown, or nearly so. We see a saw whose teeth are pointing up instead of down and an X-Acto knife—in short, the everyday instruments of potential mutilation. The structure, from one message to another, is sufficiently univocal that we can treat the campaign as a single entity.

Moreover, the lettering and its dynamic mobility on the screen serves this unification in an admirable way. The first appearance of the phrase "There's Urgo in the air'' is on two lines whose characters are spaced conventionally. In the following shots, "in the air'' divides itself and draws to the right, leaving between "in'' and "the air'' a void that plausibly represents the wound or the gash [*la béance*].

"The air'' stays to the right, but rises up to the first line, separated, this time, from "there's'' by an identical solution of continuity. On the second line, now, "in'' and "Urgo'' are separated by an important void. The following shots bring together the letters (by some elastic bandage technique, one would think) in order that final representation be at once full and justified, on the right as on the left.

The words that spread apart shape lips and the wound, and their subsequent coming together is that of a potential scar and the return to a whole unity, similar to that of a printed text. Honor is secure. One does even better with Urgo than with nature, since the first text displayed two lines of unequal length: there's Urgo / in the air [*il y a de l'Urgo / dans l'air*].

One could then read these first sequences, through associative drift, as a warning of the permanent danger of bodily harm or of psychic hiatus, as an advertisement to the ego always threatened to a certain extent with becoming dispersed, to go so far as an act of self-mutilation. The image of a handyman who does not know how to use his tools in a professional manner or a child learning some new sport is explicit in this regard. The ego, tempted by grandeur, can forget its limitations just a bit. Happily, Urgo is extra flexible and will be able to corral the straying limits of the self. Or else!

Or else—what, exactly? Or else what could emerge or rise up is sadism or masochism, the "accident waiting to happen'' in the wings of each of these sequences.

What can take over the ego, if it is left to its own devices, is on the one hand the possibility that it will allow itself everything, even that which clearly is beyond the field of its competence, and on the other hand the chance that it will self-destruct, lacking supporting, stabilizing constraints. Narcissism, just as the egotism of the two sides of the image, is a double-edged sword (Green, 1983). To dress the narcissistic wound (to not be omniscient), the ego needs a relative solidity, or else the eventual choice will be the irruption in the field of consciousness of a primitive phantasmagoria, in particular one that is perverse, sadistic, or masochistic. The advertiser here acts in conformity with this hypothesis: the wound, figured forth in the words, is more tolerable than the sight of blood, but on the other hand it evokes a multitude of possible lesions, including more symbolic injuries (Bettelheim, 1954).

There is air in Urgo to the extent that Urgo restores or brings back to life an ego that, left to this associative drift, because of it will have come to disappear, giving way to a pretentious and sadistic false self. There's air in Urgo—what do you know, it almost doesn't hurt anymore!

As we can see, the structure of the message is here finally analogous just as much to the message of the Bell commercial we analyzed earlier as to that of the Carlsberg advertisement. The basis remains the same, a kind of tryptic: a conflict, a product, a conflict resolved—namely, one avoided or repressed. And we invest all the more in these messages in that they speak to us both about our confused human uncertainty and about plausible avenues of escape. Beyond a truth that matters to us, they provide us with a way out.

Incitement and Erosion

Without moralizing—this is not here our aim—one could nonetheless oppose to this strategy a line of inquiry. Why does the advertiser, consciously or not, in order to seduce us, resort to a fundamental, eye-opening gash [*béance*], a gash from which the advertiser then steers us by reassuring us that it is really only a scratch? The process is surely doubly perverse: the fundamental is evoked in a properly accessible real situation and then, right on the spot, a needlessly sparked flame is extinguished. Well beyond the consumption such maneuvers incite is the corrosive and constantly banalizing usury of an authentic desire that, from one message to another, repeats itself insidiously. If it is not certain that the (accidental) tactic leads to the consumption of product B, it is clear, on the other hand, that the (global) strategy leads to the everyday apprenticeship of the perversion of self. It is there, it seems to us, more than in the market economy, where analysis should remain extremely vigilant.

On the other hand, what a perverse mode of operation such as this very probably justifies is the unanimous disavowal of consent to advertising. Listening to the testimonies on public affairs programs or reading texts about advertising, one is surprised by the small number of people who say they watch, listen to, or even hear and see advertising messages—so much so that we would have to conclude that we are dealing either with an extremely selective population or with an effectiveness of advertising that would originate only on condition of not being perceived. These two hypotheses of course remain interesting, but it seems to us that the disavowal reflects another phenomenon. Advertising is dreamed and makes itself dreamed—we suggested this earlier—but as a perverse act it remains unavowable. Basically, the seemingly banal question "Do you listen to or read advertising?" would harbor another, along the lines of "Are you perverse?" or, at the very least, "Do you sometimes let yourself be perverse?" To which, almost without exception, one would respond, "Who, me? Of course not."

Still the proof is there: products sell and owe their success at least in part to advertising. Some government television stations concentrate all their advertising messages in a single televisual block exactly the way some reviews group together the whole of their advertisements, and no one accuses them, in either case, either of bankruptcy in the share of viewers or of reduction in the share of readership—even to the contrary, in certain cases. The phenomenon thus has another explanation, and our very complicity with an interlude of ease, even if it is perverse, seems to take root in a more infantile reflex. Are we not told, when we are reading a specialized review or a research article, that advertising distracts us or make us relax? As if, in the final analysis, we never get over having lost the illustrations of our childhood in order to plunge definitively into the dry abstraction of a typographic text!

Metonymic Value of Associative Drift

At the beginning of the present chapter, we considered the extremely complex question of the associative logics of the unconscious and expressed the hypothesis that any representation, conflictual to begin with, tended, by associations, to be disarmed into a residual, "deconflictualized" representation. It is clear that such a hypothesis would eventually require a demonstration that would greatly exceed the limited scope of the present work. This assertion will have to retain the character of a temporary theoretical construction.

What gradually becomes clear in the course of our discussion, however, is that a representation locks onto, forcibly summons, other representations, which are called associative in order to avoid the problem of defining them. It is this "association" that calls for our undivided attention here.

Far from drifting away from the first bylaw of linearity, an associant (an element of the associative chain) is rarely linked to its precursor by its semantic value. Rather, it attaches itself to one of its "accessory" values, all the more so when the precursor is polysemic.

Thus, for example, if we consider a whole one-minute advertisement in its entirety, that is to say, as a metaphoric syntagma, we can presume that what will be retained by the subject-receptor will be rather vague characteristics, such as the profusion of color and tone, the dynamic of forms, the rhythm of movement. If these qualities permeate more than others, if they call forth more associations, it is above all because they speak to primary movements, to the fundamental logics of the psychic apparatus.

Sveltesse calls forth associations far more by the law of phonetic contiguity (suffix-prefix) than by its semantic value. Equally, a minute of cinematic advertising appeals to our mind much more as a result of its cinematicity than of any other value. We retain from it the cadence and the vivacity to which will often be added the brand's theme song or jingle, itself also reminiscent of childhood rhymes, simple songs, traditional ballads. As if the laws of the unconscious were not enough, this same relation of fragments of representation will be taken up again on every phase of the one-minute television commercial by constantly forcing us to retain from the image or from its statement only a bearing fragment, so as to reconstruct for each a metonomy where the part manages to *invalidate* the whole.

What our psychic apparatus knows how to do at once best and least well is no doubt the resolution of conflicts, that is to say, how to protect itself from all of the probable or eventual tensions that could assault it in order to reestablish directly its attentional equilibrium. It is for this reason that the associations that will be chosen to complete the circulation of a meaning, indeed even that of a signification, will be chosen in terms of their apparent innocuousness and of their complaisance with the process of equilibrium.

Whenever a representation is presented to the mind, the psyche runs up against the problem of *giving* the representation a meaning.

The advertising message can in no way avoid this situation. On the other hand, it counts on the fact that we are going to retain from all of its rhetoric only the least troubling aspects — that we are ourselves going to collaborate in the repression of what is problematic — and in this sense we are ourselves authors of our own perversion.

The very abundance, in the text, of all the polysemic *I*s, *you*s, *they*s, the construction of an irreal temporality, be it past, present, future, or even conditional, are there only to attract the unconscious, which, banking on the fact that the message will elaborate itself by itself, will tend to condense or displace everything for its own comfort, to construct its own dream by way of this pretext or rather this predream.

The product, it should be made clear, is here merely of secondary importance. To begin with, we associate to take into account characteristics such as physical proximity, sounds that draw us somewhere else, rhythm that promises life, nostalgia that emerges when someone calls, an opening that leads to ease or even to the necessity to dominate.

The advertiser counts on the simple fact that we would rather have dreams than lucidity, perversion rather than integral respect for the wholeness of the other.

Drama is there to hold us captive, so that desire might be invested, but also in order to introduce *the process of drift*.

What finally dominates the associative flow of the message itself is probably these holes, these interstices, left there to be interpreted, that is to say, made up, grease-painted, filled in or transformed, reread after having been scotomized.[2]

Montage, in this sense, represents first of all a kind of conflict of continuity and discontinuity. It breaks up so that, shortly afterward, it can reconstruct; it chips away, it crumbles into pieces so that it can just as quickly be put back together. Here is the real substance of associations. Here is the element one clings to in order to *give* a meaning to the glimpse of the void. Overload becomes potential opulence. Haste becomes a way of life.

We associate to begin with because we refuse to listen, and all it would take to be convinced of this would be to just once hear your analyst accuse you of as much.

In the first meaning of the expression, it is then first and foremost *we* who produce all this advertising.

Does this then mean that the unconscious is so stuck on representations that it will accept any pretext, any protodream, and will from the outset start disarming associations?

We should above all not believe as much naively. In part I, we cited several advertising failures. The television medium is not in itself a guarantee of success. And the fact that associative sequences willingly call forth other associative sequences in no way assures the positivity of the result.

The relation that here unites the one who looks with what is looked at, even if it is bilateral, contains its own fragilities and stumbling blocks. All roads do not necessarily lead to consumption. On the contrary, just as in the case of the print advertisement (see chapters 1 and 2), a sort of equilibrium is to be maintained between the void of despair or desire and the overabundance of the passive solution—a sort of equilibrium, more precisely, between the art form and an ineffective insignificance. Recourse to the cinematic work will here allow us to illustrate our analysis to some degree.

It is important to note right away that the three advertising thematics we have in particular considered in the preceding pages—nostalgia (Bell Telephone), difference (Carlsberg beer), and pleasure and necessity (Urgo)—could each constitute the problematic of a major motion picture, one that is profound, moving, and pertinent.

It is thus not through the banality of its subject matter as such that the advertisement diverges from the work of a great filmmaker, but indeed through the treatment of the theme.

What one could not imagine from a film made on one of these themes is that it might *deconstruct itself* just as rapidly as it starts, that it might evoke its subject no sooner than to repress, to annihilate, it.

Fellini or Bergman would leave us with one or more real questions, would have us see that we both differ from and resemble one another or that distance evokes separation but also is what unites us.

When the film *Cria Cuervos,* for example, takes up the problem of the solitude of the child, or when *Scenes from a Marriage* sketches the love drama of both solitude and real sharing, one does not especially feel, as spectator, shielded by the screen. On the contrary, one is confronted by a real void, by a manifest gap so subversive that it sends us back to ourselves and suggests that we make sense, all of us for ourselves, of this void.

The gigantic fresco that is the film *1900* cannot be explained solely by the theme of "We're different, still we're alike!" but it deals with this theme in a broad manner. By finding a solution therein? Never. Even if it is clear, throughout the film, that the proletarian and the bourgeois set against him are somehow linked, their friendship never hides the look of dissemblance.

Carlsberg divides the screen but reunites all its protagonists around a single beer. Difference no longer exists. Or, more exactly, after having drawn in desire, difference is metamorphosed into a resemblance that denies desire. The hole, the void, the yawning gap by which the subject, eventually, would have been able to accede to the necessity for it to take on meaning, is sealed before being able to exert its subversion.

Just as in the Rothko painting, it is the interstice, the flux, from the lack of representing from which the *freedom* of the cinematic work of art is born; it is from the hole or the void between the sequences that subversity is born. The fullness of advertising presents itself, on the other hand, as a stopgap against authentic desire, as a blinder, but above all as an avenue of perversion.

In short, the work of art invites us to transgress meaning and the signifier in order to take up signification again on its own account: to kill Laius, empty oratory, and discourse in order to come to *its own* way of speaking.

Advertising films, thanks to the commercial principle to which they owe their existence, have to block this transgression, at least partially, in order to entrust to another object the trouble of *making sense*. It is around this axis that their construction pivots. If they are too empty, too little constructed, they will not take and will hold no more privilege than the illustrated page holds over cursive writing. If they are too full and stuff the television viewer full before fundamentally evoking the image of a certain void, then this will not work either, since the bait that the investment of our libido fixes on is in this case absent. The failure of some commercials is relatively well known. Nothing is gained by leaving no room for the television viewer, nor, inversely, by leaving the viewer alone. Films are figural places, that is to say, virtual spaces where looker and what is looked at attempt to enter into some relation. To forget either one element or the other makes any such relation impossible.

The polysemics of the image are such that it can lead to an infinite number of representations. Now, when what one is looking for is a precise direction of the look, polysemics can be a major obstacle. Some advertisements stumble because the multiplicity of meanings they evoke is never recentered on an object. In general these are advertisements that are the most respected in the advertising business, that win prizes or satisfy the artistic wishes of their authors, but also that least often appear on television.

In any case, to mitigate this risk of the polysemics of the image, advertising agencies count heavily on the corrective value of textual statements, to which we will devote the next chapter of our study. Faced with the vertigo of desire and transgression, the text, as we will see, offers itself as a supplementary guardrail.

Chapter 4
Cathodic Homily

We know that, generally speaking, advertising is a system that operates within a much broader system that, for short, we call a social system. But what we all too often forget to specify is how we understand the notion of *system* and how, following this notion, we feel ourselves authorized to speak on the subject in question of a *system* of any sort. To avoid this complacency, we will try to establish here the perspective from which we intend to support this discussion.

The notion of system to which we refer is extremely close to that of Berthalaanfy, Bateson, and Barthes, which means that it describes a *whole* made up of various parts just as much because of their aspect as because of their function and linked together by a synthetic task, which, eventually, can be grasped on the operational level as a common one.

We are therefore dealing not with a mechanism that has only one function, nor with an agglomerate, since there the parts would be linked to one another only by chance or by a history whose workings do not show (a mineral aggregate, for example), but rather with an ensemble of mechanisms.

In this perspective, right away it becomes essential to locate, in the *system*, certain elementary functions in order to read their organic or operational interrelations. On the subject of advertising, we have already glimpsed some of these elementary functions—*to inform, to attract, to start over*, but also, on a deeper level, *to excite* and *to forbid*, *to solicit desire* and *to provoke defense*. We thus already possess, in systematic terms, a brief lexicon of functions.

The question that consequently waits to be asked might be framed in simple terms: To which medium or to which fragment of such and such a medium does one usually commit, impart, confide which function? Can it be gauged, or characterized? Unfortunately, no simple answer seems to exist for such questions.

There exist, of course, all sorts of possible generalizations—for example that, in America, television advertising is committed to the function of informing and seducing, whereas static advertising is asked to occupy the role of recall: ''girl in window, as in ad,'' a Bell scenario specifies. But beyond this, everything seems to become complex. Each advertising medium fulfills several functions at once. Posters solicit and recall, excite and forbid. Usually, it is writing or the name of the product which, in a given mechanism, works as a hook; but we know that some writings univocally play out a solicitous role. Should one, therefore, from this fact alone, renounce any systematization of our intuitions? Surely this would be easier. But we will suggest another avenue.

We will postulate, in effect, that each advertisement, whatever its form, is itself a dynamic and multifunctional ensemble bound both by its intention to the overview of psychic representations and by its very origin to the more overt fabric of manifest and latent social representations. We will postulate, therefore, that there is no way to account for the advertising act without accounting for both these multiple functions and these complex bonds.

Concretely, it seems to us that it is not enough, in order to speak about advertising, to assert that it willfully exploits sex or that it reproduces so-called bourgeois values. If it is true to say, for example, that such and such an advertisement in part utilizes a woman's body, in our view one also ought to acknowledge the way this image is both offered and forbidden, advanced and withdrawn—the way, therefore, what is going on is not an infantile and simplistic game but is rather an extremely elaborate, complex art. By the same token, it is false to interpret the advertisement as an exclusively social phenomenon: it is not in the social, in the strict sense of this term, that the advertising phenomenon unfolds, but indeed rather at the fragile border that barely separates an unconscious in waiting from a magic proposition. This border zone also makes up a part of the system we are here attempting to locate.

In the logic of this dynamic-systemic perspective, we will adopt, for the analysis of televisual advertisements, a slightly unusual point of view. Most authors are fascinated by the televisual image. We are interested in the sound track. The temptation is great to assert that the sound track of television commercials is primordial with respect to the image track, but, in the interest of maintaining rigor, we will not succumb to this temptation, at least not entirely. Certainly, we believe that the importance of the sound track has been strongly underestimated in various studies and we intend to situate it as absolutely fundamental, but it is not a question of falling, in our turn, into the trap of aphorism. The sound track is, in effect, a major component of a dynamic system of representations: it responds to the image track by complementing or even by contradicting it in extremely subtle and shrewdly organized ways. It is therefore, in a sense, just one element among others in the system. But, thanks to its characteristics, for us it occupies a special place in the specification of the advertising media we are considering.

This position is obviously inspired by psychoanalysis. It issues in particular from the notion of the primal scene, that is to say, from the phantasmatic elaboration engaged by a scene that is only heard. But it refers to preverbal, and thus archaic, qualities of music and sound, to the incessant apprenticeship of the mother tongue, and to the fact that ears, unlike eyes, are never closed.

Starting from this point of view, necessarily an arbitrary one, we will consider one by one certain advertisements in terms of a classification aligned first according to their sound construction, but one that fundamentally takes into account the dynamic relation between the images and what is heard. We will see, in each of these circumstances, how each track directs and challenges its complement. Our review will include the primary contemporary televisual advertising formulas: the announcer advertisement, the narrator advertisement, and the conversation advertisement. We will devote particular attention to background sound because of its connection to the unconscious, and we will take a specific interest in advertisements that have characteristic refrains so as to be able, finally, to state in its first traits the central hypothesis of this work, which postulates the existence of a contract of a perverse nature in the broad sense of this term between the consumer and the purveyor of consumer goods.

Announcer Advertisement: Promises of Technology/Knowledge

Generally speaking, the announcer is taken to be a strictly informative advertising institution. Presumed to be experts in relation to an object, to a product (whereas in fact they are expert actors, businesspeople, and sometimes sports personalities), announcers deliver speeches whose most important meaning is to inform us about the existence, and the advantages, of something for sale.

In a first formula, that of *announcer-demonstrator,* the person remains immobile facing the camera throughout a sixty-second advertising message. Usually, the announcer is at the outset the object of a medium close-up shot, and then along the way the camera executes a traveling shot that provides a glimpse of the object for sale, the place where the object is made, the makers at work (twenty seconds of a worker taking a steel ingot out of a blast furnace). Throughout this process, however, the announcer-demonstrator remains the central motif of the image. Only the camera moves, in a traveling shot moving laterally or to the rear, following our strolling professor in a self-explanatory setting. The voice never leaves the camera's field of view. Many tire manufacturers, car repair shops (for mufflers, for example), automobile dealerships, and technical services (computers and others) have adopted this formula. It connotes a didactic dimension useful for "scientific and technical" products; it can also have the attraction of a revelation or a demonstration of the abundance of a product or the importance of an effort (a construction site, for example). Because of this, the formula has become one of the options most frequently chosen by advertisers.

The second type of announcer we have identified is the *actor-announcer,* shot in close-up (head and shoulders). The camera will remain static throughout sixty seconds, so our characters have nothing to do but be expressive, to make their faces count, to use the role to ensure that the words transmitted are well understood. The person chosen to assume this kind of role is most often a soap opera actor or a model whose photo might have been in a recent magazine. Sports celebrities are also used, though they are more often seen in advertisements of the announcer-demonstrator type.

Obviously, the actor-announcer formula introduces important nuances with respect to the "competence" of the announcer. Whereas the announcer-demonstrator is, in principle, a technician or a specialist, the actor draws "competency" only from phantasmagorical relations into which his or her public image is invested. One trusts what Mr. So-and-So has to say because, in such and such a film or television series, he seemed like a fair-minded father. Given this effect, one could even permit oneself the luxury of an anti-expert. This is what happens in the Gésal-Conseil advertisement in France in which the announcer is neither an expert in television nor an expert in horticulture. But, dreaming like many of the French of having a green thumb, he puts his trust in Gésal products. Following this same logic, we have, over the past few years, seen a series of commercials in which the designated expert is none other than Mr./Ms. Everyman. He has tried one product or another; she washed her clothes with such and such a soap; they participated in a soft drink taste test (Coke versus Pepsi, for example) and voice their opinions publicly.

One can see, in these three kinds of announcers, a gradation of identification desired by the advertiser. The more sophisticated the product, the more the expert has to appear to be out of the ordinary; the more one wants to present the product as popular, the more the expert ought to be close to "the people."

This hypothesis is verified in a recent IBM campaign for personal computers, a product of relatively wide distribution. A technical expert would have rendered the product forbidding; Mr./Ms. Everyman would not have been credible. Instead they used Charlie Chaplin's Little Tramp character from the film *Modern Times.* If the Little Tramp himself, he who has justly and tastefully criticized the pitfalls of modernity, gets behind the idea of a computer, how can we not go along with him?

Elements of Analysis

Once one attempts to analyze the inherent logic of the announcer advertisement, one expects to address functions of identification. But this notion need not, in its turn, cause us to lose sight of a subtle system of references nor of the establishment of a skillfully administered conflictual apparatus.

On the level of identification, the manufacturer of top-of-the-line stereo systems addresses the public from the angle of an image of competency. The consumer will spend a considerable sum for the product and does so in the name of a technical understanding either real or fantasized, of which a faithful, that is to say, complaisant image is returned.

High-tech products are not the only ones to take advantage of this staging. We have seen, for example, that certain banks and other service-oriented institutions are happy to resort to it.

Our first comment has to do with the leader of high-tech knowledge in current ideology.

The announcer-demonstrator is an *expert,* who from the outset makes reference to a carefully orchestrated idealization of the technical competency, and the film demonstrates the force, the breadth, the high-tech quality of the product or service. Thus, in many instances, we have a simple convergence of discourse and image: the reference is linear, nothing more.

What should not be neglected is that the function of an advertisement is not only to make a product or a service known, but also to *situate* it within the current *order of things*.

Thus, the reference to knowledge from the outset points to a product in harmony with current wants. But, equally, by *reference* to advertisements of the same type, it gives to product or service A the virtues of product or service B as reference. In other words, one witnesses a veritable system of interadvertising and, consequently, interideological references.

In *Publicitor,* Brochant and Lendrevie aptly evoke concepts such as "to position the product in an adequate referent" and "to occupy a specific communicative loophole." Our opinion does not diverge on this matter, if only because, unlike these two authors, we believe it is of primary importance not to forget the symbolic function of these loopholes. The idea of "positioning" the product reads, for us, in terms of assuring for the product a precise symbolic valency, in other words, of situating it in a certain "order of things," of its occupying a determined ideological space. Whereas Brochand and Lendrevie perceive their objectives only on the level of communication, which reflects the usual position of advertisements, we believe that the image they try to produce will eventually occupy a place in the universe of our personal symbolizations, that is to say, will become buried in our unconscious to the extent that it corresponds to other elements of collective symbolic propositions. From an advertising point of view, one could thus say that the interadvertisement reference "positions" the product; from an individual point of view, this same reference suggests a symbolic place for the product.

An example here will clarify our argument. The Canadian National Bank experiences certain financial difficulties. Technically, the solution to these difficulties seems to lie in a merger with another bank, namely, the Provincial Bank. After the appropriate administrative maneuvers, the merger takes place and the new bank, National Bank, launches an advertising campaign. The television commercial is relatively simple: one sees images evoking the fusion of metals in blast furnaces. Dofasco, around the same time, publicizes its metallurgy with similar images. Behind this very simple strategy one can perceive the allusion made by the National Bank to an industry that is, so to speak, enduring in the public's phantasm. Steel evokes perennity, blast furnaces, high technology. Here, then, front and center in the image, is the idea of solidity even though the merger was in fact the result of economic difficulties that put the Canadian National Bank in a precarious state.

On another stage, on the level of interadvertising reference, by authorizing its own use of metallurgical images, the new bank attempts to position itself, in the phantasm of the spectator, on the same level as metallurgy. To invest with us, the bank seems to promise, is like investing in the very prosperous metallurgy industry.

This type of interadvertisement reference is made possible only by taking for granted a certain advertising culture in the spectator. But this is the least concern of our advertisers. This culture exists; it is even extremely widespread. They can count on it as upon the strength of . . . steel.

Similar systems of reference are at times extremely subtle, at others somewhat crude. For example, in a reference to the well-known advertisement "September 2, I take off the top. September 4, I take off the bottom," the Santa Claus of a 1982 ad announced: "December 24, I take off the sack." The allusion here is obvious. It is a wink in the direction of the spectator. But its existence shows that a particular advertising structure does not just sell a product; it gives the product a place among objects, situates it in a certain "order of things" that is itself, more than is generally believed, one of the priorities of advertising.

Mi-Cho-Ko, publicizing its little chocolates, introduces in a television commercial with romantic overtones a sound track of "classical" music. Certain advertisements for Eram refer to the films of Tati or Fassbinder. Manufrance refers us to Defoe's *Robinson Crusoe*. Here one will recall allusions to Michelangelo in advertisements for Levi's jeans. In short, the advertisement in this regard is like Mr. Smith, who from time to time likes to let drop in conversation a remark like: "Oh, you know me, the latest Derrida!" And finally when, in order to present its dining products to us, Saupiquet imitates Marcel Pagnol's texts, we are invited to agree to a shared meridional culture and therefore to an original complicity. In order that a French consumer might agree to buy pre-prepared food, perhaps the advertiser first had to reproduce a cultural complicity. In this way a more established order of things can be transgressed so that a new one can be installed. What the advertiser says is that, in this case, there is no transgression.

Sound/Image Dynamic

Even if, as we have indicated, we mentally accord priority to the sound track for its effective relations with the unconscious, we must pause at the working conjunction of the visual and sound tracks in order to grasp the actual constitution of television advertising's space.

Here, in the case of the announcer-advertiser, the two are complementary. Not that they move in the same direction—absolutely to the contrary; still, they complete each other by associating to state a conflictual psychic representation and then resolve it by eluding it.

For example, in the simplest case, that of the expert demonstrator advertisement, one initially thinks of a simple explanation of one track by another, the image *illustrating* what the voice says or the voice *directing* the look, whereas ambient noise would represent the *reality* of a place. In shorthand, this kind of analysis is accurate enough, but at another stage it is not adequate. Most of us are familiar with neither industrial blast furnaces nor sophisticated research expeditions to polar regions (oil company advertisements). The calm textual mastery of the commentator contrasts in more than just name with the images of *size* that occupy the background of the image. The manifest presence of the announcer comes, like a guardrail, to avoid the always potential straying of our unconscious either under the weight of a collapse or in a flight toward the grandiose. The conflict of an interpsychic nature here opposes (ravished or submissive) vertigo to mastery. The image itself refers to the *tamed forces* of nature. For us the question is, finally, an everyday one: deciding, more or less every step of the way, how the *instinctual* forces that live in us become *civilized*. The reassuring mastery of the commentators, the very neutrality of their objective tones, thus play out the role of heading off drive and megalomaniacal or depressive postures.

Ecstasy (or would it be servitude?) is resolved while it is under control; castration becomes achievement and the advertisement is bearable.

Here it is certain that verbal excess is lying in wait for us and that the temptation to blame the advertiser is a simple trap into which we could easily fall. Rest assured. Our position on this subject is clear: advertising messages are never, in themselves, more ill intended than any other message. To tell the whole story, in an example such as the one we have just quoted (the demonstrator-deployment) the advertiser has, in fact, absolutely no choice. Within each of us lives a child frightened in the face of the immensity of the forces of nature that *embody* and *surround* that child. These forces trouble and fascinate us all. And advertisers are just about the only ones to invite us into a serious appropriation of this interior/

exterior world. Even more, advertisers are alone in drawing us out into this world on the archaic level where it most affects us. When in the preceding chapter we stated that the advertising message acts as a cathodic homily, we did not mean to condemn advertising but rather to signal that it might be one of the rare televisual institutions to speak to us intimately of the phantasms that matter to us.

After many years of research, Bion, who for a long time believed in an epistemological drive—a desire to know—changed his mind in order to claim that, in fact, the unconscious does not want to know, but that we try to be, and be more and better.

Advertisers know as much and, despite the utter failure of all sorts of television commercials, they take this fact into account.

This trait is also clear in the example of the advertisement based on the competence of Mr./Ms. Everyman.

Doing the laundry is a standard, everyday activity. We have heard enough protests from housewives to know that the thankless world of cleaning stains evokes more spite, envy, or aggressiveness than spontaneous sublimation. "While I keep to my wash, others live extraordinarily!" is close to a common feeling. Some might add: "While *he* takes part in a life of high technology, in debates concerning the world and life, *I* slave away."

Ms. Everyman, having become an expert in the choice of a detergent, suddenly sees this banality, this exclusion, reversed: "You too, dear lady, are an expert. You belong to this scientific world where truth is conquered by means of sociological inquiries."

Lies?

This is obviously too quick. We must instead ask ourselves who in the world seriously dreams of revalorizing the household universe, of giving it place and meaning at the heart of the evolution we are going through? Feminist groups? Their intervention it is not situated on this level. The great intellectual debates? They do not touch upon the affective dimension of the question. Soap operas! Maybe we had better take another, closer look.

When Ms. X, in one of these messages, discloses the drudgery of laundry to a cheery husband, this does not mean we are saying that we are witnessing revolutionary propaganda, but it also does no good to proclaim the univocal bad faith of the advertiser.

Banality is transmuted, in the melting pot of these messages, into competency. Solitude becomes solidarity (with current evolution). Precariousness becomes solidity. Saupiquet pardons Ms. Jones for transgressing tradition by no longer preparing stews herself. Thus, Saupiquet transmutes transgression into conformity with tradition.

Unfortunately, it is not obvious that other voices have tried with the same emotive justice to deal with the questions that preoccupy us intimately. Once the image is in danger of turning into a transgression, we know that the sound track will become reassuring, since desire has to be dulled when suddenly it threatens to emerge with too much force. The material the advertiser juggles is plainly *explosive*.

The Narrative Advertisement: From Anecdote to Legend

To be rigorous in our terminology it is important to define more specifically what we mean by advertising "narrative."

We are dealing with a narrative, in other words, with a story we are being told, either by someone who has experienced it or by someone who has witnessed it. The immediate technical consequence of this formula is that the narrator is almost always off screen. Sometimes the narrator is seen on screen, but rarely in the process of telling the story; rather, we see the narrator's involvement in the tale.

A second characteristic is that the argument does not depend on the competence of the narrator but rather on the conviction conveyed by the anecdote.

The voice is neutral, warm, animated, or troubled, depending on the circumstances.

The image illustrates the anecdote with common situations that are both banal and eccentric.

An architectural consequence of this advertising vehicle is that the weight of what is useful rests on two opposites: the quality of the image and the narrator's ability to communicate.

The Bell advertisement analyzed in the preceding chapter is a perfect example of this model. We propose in the following to examine several others, including several radio advertisements based on this model.

We will draw our first example from a radio commercial. Here is a partial scenario:

A woman's voice: Nothin' ta do 'bout fate.
Whadda y' know. This morning, I g'w out.
First, it's raining.
Usual, since I'm going out.
I get to the office, spot right 'n front. I try to squeeze in but I bet I won't. Well, I was right. It was too small. Smashed my headlight. Nothin' t'do 'bout it: I'm jinxed.

The narrative is in the first person. The voice is extremely expressive. The event related is at once banal in its everydayness and extraordinary to the extent that it marks a point of exasperation near the breaking point. One could easily see it as a prototype of narrative.

The second part of the scenario does not correspond to the structure of the narrative, but instead comes from its counterpoint:

A man's voice: Mini Mini   (music)
                 If the city gets you down
                 Take a mini, morning and night
                 You'll make it through.

                 Mini Mini   (same music)
                 It sneaks in everywhere
                 It's not at all long
                 Three meters zero five in all.

                 Mini:
                 starting at only 20,950 Francs
                 at your Austin Morris dealer.

                 Mini: it's good for the nerves.

For the moment let us reserve our commentaries and analyses and instead present other advertisements, this time televisual ones, constructed according to the same model.

On the screen: a black face in successive close-ups. An off-screen male voice: "No, you're mistaken. I'm a journalist for *Actuel*. I wanted to spend fifteen days in the skin of a black. I got myself hired as a steelworker. I told the rest in *Actuel*." A second off-screen male voice: "Read *Actuel*. You might be surprised" (1980).

Another 1980 advertisement for this same monthly magazine (fig. 4-1) takes the following form:

Off-screen female voice: This weirdo is NINA HAGEN,
                           The biggest German star
                           Since Marlene Dietrich.
                           Before *Actuel,* who had heard of Nina Hagen?

Off-screen male voice: Read *Actuel*. You might be surprised.
The image: Shots of Nina Hagen, disheveled, extravagant, some
                           might even say hysterical.

                 Actuel: the monthly of the eighties.

Finally we turn to a last subgenre of the narrative advertisement, a narrative made up entirely of images. We will deal with two French examples.

In "Silk," a young, stylish, elegant redhead advances toward the camera dressed entirely in silk: a pleated beige suit and a lacy blouse. The decor: an apartment with Regency period furniture. Striking a pose, she takes off her jacket. Then her blouse. Then her pleated skirt. Gently, she lets a strap of her bra,

Figure 4-1

also silk, slip off her shoulder to reveal a breast pointed at the viewer. Then she takes off her panties. The camera moves up toward her hips. Close-up of the small of her back. Finally, we find her in bed, under silk sheets. Written titles and off-screen voice: ''Silk. Nothing replaces the natural.''

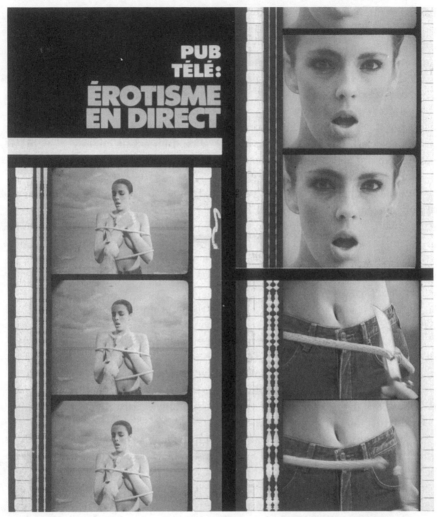

Figure 4-2

In "Buffalo Bill" (fig. 4-2), we see blue sky, blue sea, and well-known model Nina Klepp, alone, breasts bare, bound by thick ropes. A hairy, virile arm moves toward her with a knife—and frees her. Text: "Buffalo Jeans. I've got you under my skin, Bill."

Elements of Analysis

Here our microscopic overview comes to an end.
The first element to emerge from this brief enumeration is a certain diversity,

indeed a certain wealth of this body of advertising. In the case of the Austin Morris Mini advertisement, the narrative is only discourse; it is the kind of anecdote told at a café, with the sounds of movement and voices in the background. It is the catharsis narrative, the expression narrative. At the opposite extreme, the images in the silk advertisement speak for themselves. The voice is no longer present as an explanatory support, yet there is a narrative in the sense of a fiction that unfolds sequentially. This is the extreme case of the advertising narrative—by far the most effective, but also by far the most technically demanding. In any case, here the films are signed by the filmmakers up front, which was not necessarily the case for the demonstration advertisements.

But let us return to our analysis.

Beyond this apparent diversity, we quickly note an astonishing uniformity of argumentation. Whether it is suggested that we read *Actuel,* buy silk, or drive an Austin Mini, there is obviously no plan to induce us to do so through rational arguments or elaborate technology. Instead the method is affective consent.

Regency decor easily places "Silk" in a wealthy part of the city and at first seems to be everything that is most civilized. What follows is more ambiguous, as we have seen.

Actuel also appeals—oddly enough—to our primitive side, our dark side: Nina Hagen the "weirdo."

The Austin anecdote refers to anger and even to rage. But like a good doctor (a technological allusion?), Austin recommends: "Take Mini, morning and night, it'll pass. Mini: it's good for the nerves."

Despite their tendency to simplify, one could easily be led by these examples to believe that the narrative advertisement essentially consists of secretly inviting people into a kind of primitive state.

There is a grain of truth to this, and we will come back to it later. But to begin with we want to state that the question seems to us more complex, that what appears to us to be illustrated here presents itself in the form of conflict not just between civilization and the primitive, as is often the case, but equally between banality and eccentricity, between phantasmatic poverty and phantasmatic opulence, between modesty and audaciousness. In short, the advertiser confronts us with the difficulty we *all* have in inserting originality into the habitual, drive within a life of control, the eccentric within the banal or the normal.

In a sense, the advertiser insults us. You do not know how to live with your phantasms: read *Actuel,* wear jeans, rediscover silk.

But this insult is not just a single one. The message contains its own reference as much to prudence as to the norm. Mini calms the nerves. Read *Actuel.* Even the excess of the Buffalo Bill images is, in a certain way, a gauge of normality. We know perfectly well that the spectator will not go that far.

The Advertiser and the Law

Faced with certain "excesses" of advertising, faced, in particular, with the use of female anatomy, governments as well as feminist organizations have deemed it prudent to take a stand. In France, in the United States, and in Quebec, this movement is notable. The intention of the protests could not be less in doubt. The virtue upon which they are based could not be more worthy of respect. From a certain point of view, however, the attitude of the legislator in such matters runs the risk of proving to be more ideological than useful. The real underpinnings of the debate are more subtle than they are typically thought to be.

In the case of Buffalo Bill jeans, for example, and in certain similar circumstances (Aubade, silk, Atal), it is true that women appear on the screen almost naked and, most of the time, in submissive positions. It is absolutely justifiable to assert that such images degrade the female body and perpetuate an ineluctable phantasm of female submission. But is this really what is essential here? Or, to formulate the question in another way, what finally is it that messages of the Buffalo Bill kind announce?

To respond to such a question, first we have to reiterate that the advertisement that gets results is the one that aims true, one that in a certain way connects to a problematic felt to be fundamental by the interlocutor who reads or receives it. Advertisers earn their living by knowing better than anyone what will not work for each one of us.

From such a perspective, it seems pertinent not to disguise the fact that Myriam's naked breasts (Avenir), the promise kept by the advertiser (as opposed to the unkept promise of the government), and the blue of the Caribbean speak to the profound malaise of a collective body.

The appeal to freedom that shows here, the reassertion of a desire to recover a certain primitiveness, bears witness to a lived experience of constraint and restriction that can be harmful to disavow. Advertisers could here be seen as privileged observers—observers whose salary depends to a large extent on the precision of their perceptions. When such observers remark that the dream of a population harks back to what is primitive, to what is natural, or to freedom, it is perhaps proper, before condemning them, to examine attentively the general well-being of this population and to ask oneself what could bully this population to such a degree. Otherwise, censorship has no meaning. It is merely repression or a return to silence. Death of a question, death of a subversion.

It is clear to us that the animal who lives in each of us and the taste for nature that survives in each of us very plausibly have something to do other than consume silk or denim. The buildup of drive is both highly individual and a question of civilization. The fate the advertiser offers to our yawning psychic gaps [*béances*] is never the most noble or the most sublimated. On the other hand, it seems to us that silence never resolved anything either.

The real problem our governments face is perhaps that in the final analysis advertisers might henceforth be the only, or nearly the only, ones to bring us basic questions concerning our existence. What do we do with the primitive? How do we manage the sadism that haunts us? What is to be done about melancholy? How to find a way to get along together in huge urban developments? For all of these questions advertisers have only one answer: consume. One might disagree with this answer, but then it is fitting to ask ourselves what we have to offer in the way of symbolizing metaphor.

Sound/Image Dynamic

Some will perceive the preceding commentary on the relations between law and advertising to be unjust or misguided. In our opinion, on the contrary, this commentary opens up a development that could eventually be explored much more directly. In fact, advertising and the law have much more in common than one might normally suspect. Both are concerned with the world of drives. Both pretend to manage the "how" by which to act upon these drives, not the "why." And both, finally, hope to seize the truth on this subject. Law punishes and constrains. Advertising directs and orients by promising to gratify those who obey. It is not astonishing that these two moralistic neighboring schools of thought so often thrive, between themselves, on quarrels of unanticipated power. But for the moment let us leave the world of politics and return to sound and image.

We were saying that advertising, like the lawmaker, is concerned with how drives work. The case of the narrative advertisement is an apt illustration.

Want to be primitive? There is a little "animal" in each of us? Sensuality? Frustration? City life? Read *Actuel*. Rediscover silk. Try on a pair of jeans. Get behind the wheel of a Mini.

As we said in chapter 1, it is not as much to desire that advertising is addressed as to the *defense* against desire. Accordingly, the conjunction of the sound and visual tracks acquires, in our opinion, major importance. The rule can be formulated very simply: when the image becomes excited, the sound reassures or envelops; when the sound provokes, the image inhibits. But what happens when there is no image, for example on the radio?

Here we can agree on the importance of the two stages of the Austin Mini advertisement: a state of rage, hate, and despair and a state of calm, (musical) joy, and solution. And when there is no sound, as in the case of "Silk"?

To begin with, let us make clear that there *is* sound, since there is music, and we will return to this sound later. But let us add too that the image here is double. It is sensual, granted, but also restricted. Striptease and the elegantly dressed woman respond to one another in this film in a remarkable, precise, and calculated way. Vulgarity and class, meaning and measure, it is thus to a portion of the image that one has accorded the responsibility of representing the law.

As for the Buffalo jeans advertisement, it is here to the almost grotesque *excess* of the situation that the surreptitious reminder of the established order of things is accorded. It is not much, and it is probably because lawmakers feel, in circumstances such as this, that their patrimony is threatened to the point where they want to enact laws. It is not much but, in our opinion, it works.

Conversation Advertisement: Familiarity

Television advertisements' use of conversations conducted among several individuals does not in itself raise a logistical problem. Several protagonists exchange comments addressed not to the camera but rather to one another. In most cases, the shot is from a medium angle; sometimes it is taken with a wide-angle lens. To this point, then, nothing very astonishing: the technique resembles that of any movie dialogue or conversation among multiple interlocutors.

From this point of view, the first established fact that commands our attention is the important feeling of *familiarity* that emanates from the conversation. The banal tone — at least it appears to be banal — coincides with this familiarity, but so does the decor and the relaxed bearing of the participants. Despite the vigilance of the authorities on the place of spoken language, despite, in effect, the more or less avowed imposition of the code of an "international French," the tone remains playful and many typically local expressions easily make their way into the scenario. The location does not just resemble places familiar to the spectator, but is often one of those places where a television is on (living room, kitchen, little corner restaurant, neighborhood grocery). The design of these locations is shrewdly calculated according to the social situation. The target public quickly feels right at home — no models or superstars, no one inaccessible. Everything should be — dare we say — within arm's reach.

Initially and thus generally we could assert that conversation allows the advertiser to comfort the spectator: *the product offered is not foreign to the surroundings of the spectator's everyday life*.

Upon examination, however, this proposition reveals itself to be much less vague, much less imprecise than one might at first imagine. The strategy of conformity, of nonrupture, of continuity with the prevalent ideological context extends to the slightest detail. The conversation device in television advertisement thus becomes the vehicle not for cultural differences in themselves, but for the differences ideologue advertisers would like to see culturally assimilated. Thus it is clearly to the psychosociological or, better, to the anthropopsychoanalytical perspective that the study of advertisements leads us. But let us look rather more attentively at one of these advertisements.

Figure 4-3

Wishing to highlight the quality of its service to its customers as well as the importance it attaches to the notion of *performance,* Imperial Oil proposes to its public a little advertising sketch articulated around a slice of family life (fig. 4-3). It is night (when, obviously, it is even harder to find a mechanic than during normal working hours). A woman is alone at home. She has made dinner. A man enters. He is around nineteen years old and would seem to be the woman's son. A conversation starts between them:

	French version	*English version*
Mother:	Late *again*.	You're late.
Son:	What a day, Ma. I fixed sixty-four headlights, ten tires. I'm beat. But service comes first.	Mom, don't.
Mother:	(smiles) That's, it's . . .	Don't tell me you had to replace a fan belt, a tire, or whatever you may call it.
Son:	. . . performance, tonight, is not to move a muscle. I *want* to watch TV.	Right, when you have an Esso station, customers come first.

Mother:	(seriously) We're having a special guest. Your Uncle Antoine is on his way over.	What about your poor mother?
Son:	(reacting) Oh, yeah!	Mom, please.
Mother:	Actually, he has a little problem with his car.	Eat and run, I suppose.
Son:	Oh, no!	I'm staying home to watch.
Mother:	You know it . . . (pause): performance!	Good. Your uncle Max is coming over and wants you to fix his car. (pause) You're such a good boy.

An anthropologist so inclined could use this material for fascinating transcultural analyses. Oedipus *figured,* represented, or proposed—Oedipus reflected—is clearly not the same from one text to another. So susceptibilities differ, but probably so do psychological interplays.

Justification of Delay

In the French version, it is the son himself who wants to justify his delay. He does not mince words in his explanation: sixty-four headlights, ten tires—and even more than that, so it would seem—which accounts for his late arrival. Maybe here it is a question of his day's work or who knows what else, but not of his reason for being late. The mother of the English version is not as possessive, at least in appearance. To begin with, she gives her son a way out: "Don't tell me . . . " This time it is a question of just one tire or a single fan belt, which seems if not more realistic then at least more limited just to the circumstances of being late.

The Adolescent Is a Man in the Making

The anglophone mother obviously considers the sexual awakening of her son to be an important dimension. "What about your poor mother?" casts guilt and clearly indicates that her son has already started to direct his drives elsewhere than within the family circle. "Eat and run, I suppose" puts us on the trail of the son's autonomous activities in the realm of seduction. In the French version, the allusion to the son's sexuality is much more discreet. Evocation of this reality is entrusted to the single word *performance*. It appears in the text twice, both times in an unclear and ambiguous way, as if one ought not speak of such things, as if it were a question of taboo.

What is more, in the staging of the French version, when the son comes in he kisses his mother in a way that is not very sonlike (maybe the kiss is even a romantic one). Staging of the English version shows relations that are clearly much more easygoing.

Uncle Max/Antoine

Very explicitly, Uncle Max/Antoine is a representation of a real or possible lover of the mother. This lover, though virtual, obviously is going to take the place of the son and supplant the son's oedipal role. Thus we have to witness the recastration of the son in favor of the mother's sexuality. Is it just by chance that the English text puts in the son's own mouth the ambiguous phrase "I'm staying home to watch," without specifying if by this he means watching television or something else? In order to watch over a primal scene, might one think? As for the francophone son, he is not going to move a muscle; he finally has an evening alone with his mother. He is, from the beginning, more submissive: if he bristles, it is all for show. The anglophone son does not bristle: his mother is in fact more submissive toward him. First she asks him if he is going out, then she suggests that he repair Uncle Max's car. It is his acceptance that earns him the "You're such a good boy" at the end. In the French, the mother's last words remain ambivalent. They could easily be read as "Your Uncle Antoine is coming. He might be my lover, but the one who knows performance is, after all, you."

In the final scene we see the son lying under the uncle's car, in the process of fixing it. The Esso logo comes across the screen.

From the point of view of the advertisers, it is obvious that Franco-Canadian culture is perceived as a matriarchy or that, at the very least, one has understood that the average Quebecer wants to be seen in this context. Here the mother plays a dominating role that the anglophones would accept only with difficulty. The Quebecers prefer, it seems, to perceive the woman as all-powerful, and the advertiser sends this image back to them.

We find this same basic schema again in an advertisement for an anti-inflammatory analgesic. After the son uses this product, the mother has no problem with saying, "You seem so much better now, honey. Could you take out the garbage?"

In the anglophone context, nothing of the ambiguity of these scenes would ever be dared. The suggested relations between members of a single family would from the outset be based more on competition than eroticism; they would be more easygoing, less troubled—and on the other hand, more aggressive.

In the American context, the notion of competition and aggressivity extends to the phantasm of a breakup of the family, to members of the clan having nothing to do with one another. Visual and textual montages will not, for example, avoid devoting separate shots to each individual, bits of text or speech that are absolutely discontinuous with one another.

One of these advertisements was rejected in Canada because it was too different from the Canadian lifestyle.

The father, the mother, the son, and the daughter in this advertisement appear separately, each profoundly exasperated (abrupt movements, wincing faces, mouths wide open). The shots follow one another without link precisely because no actual conversation takes place. No one listens, no one gets an answer.

Obstinately, the mother repeats, "Put the salt on the table . . . " Exasperated, she will finally add a spiteful "please." To whom are these words addressed? No one knows. You might say she is speaking to the air.

The shots that show us the daughter follow one another at more or less regular intervals. She says:

"Daddy, Michel took my record."
"It was my very best record."
"It was my very best one."

Their words are punctuated by dreary remarks from the father:

"Where is Michel?"
"He should come to dinner, it's time."
"So what is he up to?"

Does the mother really answer this question when she says, indifferently, "Doesn't he seem out of sorts?"

Father: "Oh, he's okay. He studies too much, but he's okay."

Cut to Michel's room, where he is giving himself an injection in the arm. Without a shadow of a doubt, it is drugs, yet another reference to an absence of communication.

The son comes downstairs, and the image is transformed into a blurry, shaky, drug-filtered vision. In a calm, neutral voice the announcer intercedes to talk about Metropolitan Insurance and the ravages of drugs among the young.

The overall impression is the solitude at the family core. To counter that solitude, the announcer proposes a solution that is at once exterior and derisory: insurance.

Advertisers did not believe that in 1972 Canada in general and Quebec in particular were ready—even on the ideological level—to be confronted with a familial division of this sort. Scenes around the dinner table, conversations in the living room where the family gets together were the preferred tools of advertising discourse, which has nothing to do with reality, it goes without saying. All sorts of Quebec families are divided. The American family has a hard time dealing with its solitude on different levels, and, in more ways than one, the phantasm of symbiotic and romantic love still survives. But it is clear that, ideologically or mythologically, the representation of division is easier to take below the forty-ninth parallel than in Canada. This reinforces the idea of liberal and capitalist individualism and returns to Protestant morality and the wholeness of moral consciousness. Christian experience would reject a message of this sort.

In a certain sense, familial unity seems even more sacred in France than in Quebec, but it is different in that it is aligned to the father and a patriarchal model. Medium-distance shot of a whole family (four people) inside a car, the father at the wheel; a couple in their late twenties and the driver's in-laws; a scene of family life where the man cooks for his little household; a man who rents a big car so that he can take women and children along with him; a successful young man who buys himself an expensive car and *allows* it to be driven by his sweetheart: here are the instruments that in France will privilege advertising discourse. None of this provides us with a real clue to the affective life of the French or the Americans, but all of it gauges the lives these cultures *dream* about.

Finally, let us note that on the level of desire, the technique of conversation offers numerous advantages. The product in this familiar context is no threat to the consumer since it comes, in a double movement, to *consolidate* already held values and the system of received beliefs even while proposing a *novelty,* a satisfaction essential to the need for change and rejuvenation in the face of life's routines.

Thanks to the atmosphere of *intimacy* created by this context, the advertiser can address more fundamental questions (*love, the future, happiness*), proposing for these great existential enigmas gimmicky solutions that unconsciously are welcomed by the viewer since at the moment they are stated, they comfort an anguish with no real solution or, at least, with a *uniformly vague* response. In simple terms, they say:

—We know you well.
—We know how you speak.
—(We're butting into your life.)
—We know the issues important to you.
—Of course they can't be resolved.
—But instead of worrying about all of that, which is pretty complicated, here's an easy solution.
—Shop and forget all about it.

Stressing the desired absence of major upheavals, the camera stays fixed throughout, stable like a reigning ideology, immobile except to make room for a product or logo.

If the psychic representation remains the same—we are like you and you are like us—the scenic formulations to understand this idea diverge from its ideologies. In the table that follows and the examples elaborated above, it clearly appears that advertisers adapt to their public, and especially to their public's ideology.

Nationality — Ideology and Familial Representation

Family	Advertising representation
American	Family in pieces but unified Independent and complicitous relations combined Example: Metropolitan Insurance
French	Organized around the figure of the father and his authority Example: Dunlop Tires
Quebecer	Pronounced mother/son oedipal situation Allusion to matriarchy Importance of "being together" Example: Imperial Oil
Canadian Anglophone	Mitigated warmth Relative autonomy of family members "Fair play" Example: Imperial Oil

To demonstrate the generalization in use for a product/solution or the exposition of a new practice, we will refer to aforementioned techniques of reverse traveling shots (exposition) where little sketches are multiplied (generalization).

The drive engaged, in the final analysis, is most often that of a person who, within a given culture, has resolved most basic problems — a successful citizen who, in this sense, makes all the right moves.

This advertising law of engaging specific action is well known enough that Brochand and Lendrevie, for example, can routinely refer to it by the term *conation*. There it is a question of impulses that lead to action. Such action constitutes the basis of most of the marketing manuals we have consulted. Yet what these texts in general do not analyze is how this action derives from impulse rather than from desire; how, even while seeming to satisfy "desire," this action only appeases impulse. The distinction between desire and need does not exist in these theoretical devices specific to their implementation since no one here believes in the unconscious.

If we then attempt, retrospectively, to reanimate the four stages of analysis to which we have become accustomed, we need to see that the trick of this subsystem on the level of *image discourse* is to manage to have familiar protagonists speak the content of an advertising message. Familiarity favors identification if not ideological identity. In the *system of advertisements,* such a solution avoids, even more than the narrator system, any thought of the grandiose or the threatening. It situates the product in a familiar order of things. Companies that want to provide an image from an everyday and very intimate service here will therefore have recourse. From beer to gas, from the grocery store to the phone company, those buying into a formula such as this one are very numerous.

In the broad scope of these structures, we might say that, in the final analysis, what we are given to consume consists more of a mythology and an order of values than products. The accompanying homily is always the same: here is *the* vision of the world to be entertained. Here is heaven, here is hell. Here too are the gods to whom you owe it to consume.

The Sonoreal Background: On the Plausible and the Irreal

At the beginning of this chapter we attributed a fundamental role to the sound track of the advertising message and, following this hypothesis, we classified different advertisements according to categories that to begin with took into account the textual aspect of the messages. Yet in order to grasp the role of the sound track in depth, we now have to go beyond this first glimpse and analyze certain specific traits.

For example, one of the ideas we have supported so far is this: faced with the unfurling of the polysemics of visual images, the sound track operates like the text of a print advertisement, that is to say, as a recourse to law or to the order of things. This is often true, but sometimes, as one might suspect, the situation is more complex.

As one moves along the continuum from the announcer-demonstrator to conversation, the authoritative tenor of the sound track decreases progressively. In conversation, for example, sound participates in the polysemics of the message.

In many instances, one will even attempt to avoid the legitimating aspect of voice. And, although certain images favor desiring mechanisms and others favor psychic defenses, symmetrically one part of the sound track sides with the law and the other supports dream and desire.

Sounds, just like images, have the power to awaken the archaic, to stimulate associations on the register of desire, to suggest themselves as potential exchanges throughout associative links.

Obviously, on the other hand, the more these sounds remain out of the field of legitimating articulation, that is to say, the more they are music or noise, the more they have a polysemic power.

It is to these sounds without definitive semantic value to which we refer when we speak of the sound background.

Theoretical Background

If we have chosen to place the sound track of advertising media at the forefront of our analysis, it is above all in relation to psychoanalytic theory concerning the concept of the primal scene. This concept, it is well known, is first of all an abstraction that attempts to designate the relation of the child, alone in his world, faced with the nocturnal life of the parents. This life, with its strong sexual connotations, intrigues the child, who is, de facto, excluded from it. A primal scene? The child is ready to imagine as much. But his phantasm is for him the only guarantee of reality. He does not see what he hears and what he hears forces him to invent what he does not perceive. Castrated by the fact of this exclusion from the matrimonial place, the child fumes in silence, imagines revenge, makes up reprisals that will console him for being neglected. His ear here is his first point of reference. It provides him with his sole reference material. In his mind, sounds thus take on monstrous or eminently tangible proportions. These are more than signs in the limited sense of this term: they become the necessary relays of an essential fiction.

As an abstraction, this concept could obviously be applied to a number of analogous situations in infantile and adult life—situations of exclusion where one is led to wonder what is going on, noises in the next room, things that go on in secret. Each of these situations recalls what remains of the old oedipal defeat. Each is also articulated as if by magic on a sonoreal level, which has the value of support for the phantasmatic elaboration that aims to explain it. The waiting room of a professional's office is an example. A part of our unconscious would really like to know what goes on behind the lawyer's or doctor's closed door. Sometimes imagination, in moments such as these, can be particularly productive.

Still other situations are perceived in the unconscious as primal scenes. In a 1981 advertisement for the monthly *Actuel,* a woman makes gestures intended to be associated with sexual relations. One hears her "take pleasure" for several seconds. Then a voice informs us that the Americans have invented a chair that massages the buttocks. Read *Actuel;* you might be surprised. The allusion to a primal scene here is obvious. Nobody is going to talk about it. It is a matter of a primal scene in the most genital sense possible. The listener, very clearly, has no choice other than to imagine the scene that is evoked.

Most advertising uses of this unconscious schema of reference are, we should recognize, far more subtle. But to speak more casually, let us put ourselves in the setting of a typical evening in front of the television. During the course of such an evening, the broadcaster's use of all sorts of sound techniques in effect corresponds to certain precise limits. News broadcasts are rather monotone (on the sound level); soap operas use very few specific sound effects, little background music, in general no sound highlights, either. In short, there is little diversity on the level of sound. Often, on the other hand, families know perfectly well who says what while the show is on; the sound does not get in the way or gets in the way very little.

A commercial intervenes. What one then hears marks an obvious diversion from the rest of the programming (if it is not a film): sounds and fanfares, multiple melodies and rhythms, shouts and outbursts, sound highlights and special effects. The ear, beyond dispute, is seized. For the unconscious, *this* is where "it" is going to happen.

Is this supposed to mean, you will object, that we watch television to witness primal scenes? The only answer to such a question might seem an unhappy one to some, but it is an absolutely affirmative one. On the rational level, of course, we watch television to stay informed about politics or to be distracted, to watch a sports match between Colombia and Argentina that we cannot attend in person. This does not mean that the unconscious does not look to the television screen for the trace of an entirely different memory. The encounter it tries to perceive, the vengeance it wants, the blood it sees flowing—all of this concerns, at an initial stage, the event of the broadcast, but on another stage definitively concerns only the primal scene of our childhood. In the monotony of a typical evening of television viewing, the unconscious relaxes. When there is a confrontation, whether it be literary, as in the case of "Apostrophes" [a long-running French television program on which writers were interviewed, as popular in France as, for example, "60 Minutes" is in the United States—Trans.], or less intellectual, the unconscious is already even more interested. When television sound is modified by advertising, the ear is absolutely riveted. Children show this clearly: they pay no attention to monotonous broadcasts, but their ears perk up as soon as a commercial comes on.

One could thus, at least by extension, compare a typical evening in front of the television to the long waiting moments a child spends "spying" on the nocturnal life of the parents. And the advertisement itself can be compared to a kind of sound peak where the initial scene risks being reproduced. But this analysis deserves to be developed in its own right since, within the message itself, certain segments of the register will work as evocations of the primal scene. Noises here will serve as relays. We will now listen to them more closely.

Noises and Track Functions

In its relations to the primary sound level, noise or what takes its place occupies a privileged place to the extent that it enjoys a power of evocation that is both discreet and absolute, attracting us even while surreptitiously going unobserved.

Whether it is the crunching of a snack (Croc-en-dip) or the squeaking of snow under the shoes of a solitary walker, a noise, as soon as it is heard, seems to be everything that is most natural. One suspects noises of nothing at all, other than that they add to the realism of a description or present themselves as counterpoints to conversation. The unconscious does not hear it this way. The manifest sound track in effect superimposes another track, which we call a latent sound track. Skis gliding over snow, the squealing of tires in a car race, the opening of a bottle of beer, children crying, ringing bells announcing a marriage, the characteristic screech of a car's brakes, laughter, the metallic clanging of machines — each of these noises refers to its associative series of psychic representations; each one evokes a particular universe.

In many cases, these noises have no importance, are there only to increase the realism of the representation. Yet in other circumstances they can become sound actants, that is to say, can provoke a phantasmization without apparent relation to the manifest text of the broadcast message.

In such instances, we will be dealing with a sound construction calculated on the abstraction of the primal scene, which is to say that we will be intrigued by an unusual or inexplicable noise upon which we can only project our personal images. To illustrate such an instance, we will put ourselves, oddly enough, in the shoes of an advertiser who has to create a message for a high-tech product for which a demonstration advertisement by a real expert is required. Following the usual laws for this model, the manifest image will show us a serious man and an impressive factory. We already know this prototype and can easily predict that the latent image track here will try to associate technological force and strength with the product to be advertised. The text, the manifest sound track, is likely to inform us of the latest productions or the most recent research in a specialized sector.

Now here, from an advertising point of view, we face a problem. Among the elements at our disposal, none refers the spectator anywhere but to the real. No space is left to the imaginary or to dreams. Now if we do not succeed in engaging a minimum degree of dreaming, even if only to block it off quickly, we will not construct a workable advertisement.

To get us out of this bind, there remains the latent sound track. On this level we can introduce dream or metaphor, allusion or allegory. Melodies and cadences are available to us on this level. We could thus forge an atmosphere of more archaic evocations than the real within which we are confined. A military march, for example, could add a tinge of humor to the cadence of machinery. Or circus music could redramatize the sight of impressive integrated circuits. The primal scene effect will here hinge on unexpectedness. The attentive ear could fabricate all by itself a representation of this discovery. These representations, because they are produced by the spectator, are infinitely more pregnant than those offered directly.

Contrary to this scenario, one could easily imagine weak advertisements that address only the imagination of their spectators. O.B.A.O. in 1976 presented suggestive images of mousse and women's bodies on the screen while the sound track gave us suggestive music. Brador (Quebec, 1978) filled the screen with shiny gilded blobs and shapeless bubbles while on the sound track a rather seductive instrument played music. Mutzig made use of lovely drawings to express the art and nobility of its beer. On the level of the construction of a space that is specifically one of advertising, such documents can initially pose a problem. Where, in effect, will the spectator be given access to the real? Since if it calls for the evocation of the real, the primal scene also demands its repression. Such advertisements, if they just evoke, can end up as failures by not barring desire, by not preferring repression.

Here again, the latent sound track can play a primordial role in the restitution of the necessary equilibrium between desire and inhibition at the heart of advertising. As in the cases cited here, it is the indefectible complimentarity of these various tracks to which the message will finally owe its effectiveness.

Discrete noises, banal, everyday ones, ones that are quasi-surreal might here be enough. Mutzig sets a limit to our sentimental drift with a rhythmic appeal to the name of its product. The S.N.C.F. [the French railroad] in 1980 balanced the surrealism of its presentation of a blue train against an entirely artificial background by the discrete evocation of the train's movement. Thus the equilibrium of matter and irreality can be reestablished, which by definition grounds the advertising medium. Outside of this equilibrium, one might present all sorts of qualities, but it would not be advertising.

From this point of view, the latent sound track holds a singular trump card: loud and clear, it can plug in the nearly unconditional consent of most of our unconscious; it touches directly on the preverbal zones of understanding. And, by way of this single archaic point of anchorage, it is capable of short-circuiting most of our defense mechanisms.

On the other hand, the bottom line of manifest tracks, whether they be sound or visual ones, is that they never work except on the level of reason. Reason is where psychic defenses live. To counter an argument, one can always defend oneself; to counter a thesis, one can always find an antithesis. Preverbal sound elements bring to the encounter rationalizing structures and avoid fields of potential debate—making for an incontestable advantage over other tracks.

If we add to this argument the fact that ambient noise analogically recalls the reconstitution of a psychic state pertinent to the primal scene, the latent sound track will easily prove to be the most powerful of registers at the disposition of the advertiser in the elaboration of a message.

To our knowledge, there are few televisual advertisements without a word being spoken or sung. What we find more and more, however, are advertisements in which the preverbal sound track accompanies fifty of the sixty seconds. This is achieved by one of the brief characterized refrains we will consider later or by the image/product conjunction on the one hand, and on the other the voice that names the product.

This type of advertising derives its great effectiveness from the fact that the unconscious or the whole psychic apparatus becomes extremely permeable to a discourse that is evoked rather than stated. It is as if, faced with a verbal silence, suddenly we are ready to listen.

Now, there is nothing so surprising about this phenomenon. The human imagination of course needs some freedom, some "craziness," or, even more simply, just some breathing room; but at the same time it has to obey certain specific orders of the psyche. Among these laws, one seems to stipulate that the absence of representation is, for all intents and purposes, intolerable; that in the presence of a diffused or imprecise stimulus (for example, sound), one of the first responsibilities of the apparatus of phantasmization is the production of images to fill the perceived void. If the image is furnished by an exterior source (in the advertisement, for example), the unconscious, which is by nature lazy, will gladly prefer this image to any it would have to elaborate on its own, especially if this elaboration risks drawing it into the conflictual zones of its psychic existence, as is almost always the case in, for example, the primal scene. One thus understands just which trump cards advertisers hold. But by the same token, we also see the point to which we as spectators choose the path of ease rather than that of confrontation with a conflict we are given to resolve.

Such techniques can be seen at work in propaganda and in political discourses as well as advertising. What characterizes, from this point of view, what is called the advertising apparatus is that it never modifies the content of an ideology or a culture, but constantly consolidates it. But come to think of it, is this really so characteristic of advertising alone?

The Musical Television Commercial: On Rhythm and the Casual

The musical television commercial is, of all televisual advertising genres, surely the most complex and the most demanding, as much in terms of production as of analysis. A truly filmic work, often directed by a famous filmmaker, it takes form both in a sophisticated image track and a sound track articulated as much rhythmically as phantasmatically. Its cost alone limits its use to products of wide distribution: films are often shot abroad and as a result entail great expense. The audience they reach is huge and their appeal is popular. An ethnologist who wanted to grasp the soul of a population would usually discover in them a fairly accurate commentary of a privileged observer—the advertising agency, a witness whose job it is to know what fundamentally motivates a given population.

In commercial terms, the musical commercial has several specific requirements. Since the product is popular, it should appear on screen as easily accessible. Moderate cost and broad access will be stressed. But, at the same time, the allusion to popularity should not offend the targeted public. Judgment and tact are necessary. The elevation of perceivable social character would here be the norm. The British would stress their sense of humor, the French their love of culture and history, and Quebecers their desire for simple and more than hospitable friendliness.

Another element of the musical commercial, its characteristic refrain or jingle, will be the object of very careful selection. Its aspect, its rhythm, even its complicity have to evoke either the sweet familiarity of national folk songs or more contemporary music. It has to have the quality of seeming to have been known forever while being sufficiently original to be perceived as specific. Casual or playful, in most cases it provides support to a text that is sung and whose function is praising the merits of the product. This is not an insignificant detail. It is no longer to a speaker that the textual function is entrusted, but to a singer, like a little opera. The register of reference to the law mechanism will find itself thus very clearly modified.

Since our study has not allowed us access to complete scenarios of musical commercials other than in Quebec and in France, we will have to limit ourselves to these two countries. Yet we are certain that a transcultural study on this subject would be very illuminating.

Friendly, Hospitable Quebec

The first advertisement we will consider dates from 1971–72. It might seem out of date to some readers. In fact, it is not, at least from a structural point of view. Besides, it has the advantage of providing a complete scenario, as well as a certain analytic distance that is not negligible. Like many Quebec beer advertisements, it exalts the theme of friendship and camaraderie. Its structure relies largely on a "hero," Tex, a popular Quebecer singer who has since become a comedian. Extremely casual in dress and in manner, nevertheless of a rather imposing stature, he represents at once the jovial, down-home side of the Quebecer and the somewhat more sophisticated artistic or poetic side. He is a sensitive bon vivant from the country but is not the least bit effeminate. This detail is more important than one might think, since above all one must not evoke the homosexual phantasm in connection with beer commercials. The world of bars is a homosexual world, but a blatant awareness of this fact must not be provoked.

Around this charming character, the following scenario has been constructed:

Shot	Image track	Camera	Sound track
1	Tex at the table with friends pouring a beer (4 sec.)	Forward traveling shot	"Oh Tex, I'd like that, see people on the move."

2	Tex, in close-up, glass in his hand (2 sec.)	Traveling shot	"You want to see them? Hold on tight, here we go!"
3	Horse race (2 sec.)	Long shot	Music
4	City (1 sec.)	Aerial shot	Music
5	Tex (1 sec.)	Close-up in plane with ground in background	When you're a Quebecer . . .
6	Bird's-eye view of turnpike interchange (1 sec.)	Long shot	. . . you're proud of your choice.
7	Tex (1 sec.)	Close-up with city from above in background	And because we have taste,
8	Street and Molson truck (10 sec.)	Long shot	Molson is what we drink here (repeated by the chorus).
9	Three beers and glasses being set on a table (6 sec.)	Close-up	You enjoy yourself. You love life. You pay your dues. You don't count the rounds.
10	Uncapping (2 sec.)	Close-up	You like a beer
11	Pouring (2 sec.)	Close-up	full of pleasure.
12	Beer in a glass (2 sec.)	Close-up	When you pick it, it's for a long time.
13	Racetrack (2 sec.)	Medium shot	Molson is what we drink here.
14	A girl watches with binoculars; she turns away from her friends (2 sec.)	Medium tight shot with camera traveling forward on the girl	
15	Boy watches (2 sec.)	Close-up	
16	A toast raised by Tex and his friends (4 sec.)	Medium shot	Music
17	Beer logo (letters MOLSON) (3 sec.)	Close-up	For us, beer no longer has any secrets.
18	The profile of a girl walking by (2 sec.)	Close-up	A real pleasure, you know what that is.
19	Tree and motorcycle (2 sec.)	Medium shot	You get an idea, then it's serious.

20	Racetrack (1 sec.)	Long shot	Molson is what we drink here.
21	Tex (1 sec.)	Close-up	Molson is what we drink here (repeated by the chorus).
22	Boy and girl (1 sec.)	Close-up	You see how it goes where we live.
23	Tex and his friends (4 sec.)	Close-up	Cheers!

Twenty-three shots thus follow one another in the span of a minute. In appearance, they come together like a mosaic of disparate ideas. In reality, they are elaborated like a musical construction following the first three shots, which serve as a theme or central motif. In a nutshell: friends, beer, sports.

But to begin with, Tex is with his friends. And, cleverly, this notion will be repeated in shots 14, 15, and 16, then again in 21, 22, and 23 — in other words, in the middle of the montage and at the very end, as if in order to close the loop, to come back to the point of departure.

Meanwhile, the theme develops, branches out. Within a parallel montage, these motifs come back to us barely transformed. In shot 14, it is the girl; in 15, the boy; in 22, the boy and the girl; in 16 and 23, Tex and friends. The guiding principle is very explicit. Everyone likes each other, nothing is wrong — after all, we are among friends. In other words, everything is fine.

The montage that serves to sustain these connotations is a syntagm in brackets. It is a montage that expresses fun not only in time (multiplicity of events), but also in the diversity (gatherings of all kinds).

This variety of events, this diversity of moments introduces the second panel of the thematic: sports or, better, fun, special occasions on which to get together. Announced as early as the third shot (the horse race), this second theme henceforth develops all by itself. In shots 13 and 20, we see the horse race again. Then shots 6, 18, and 19 return us to this same notion: a motorcycle race; the quick stride of a young girl; a plane flown by Tex. The allusion is of course to Tex's seductive charms, to his phallic power (plane, motorcycle), but above all to fun, to incredible ease. Everything unfolds without the slightest difficulty; the scenario, one might say, shoots forward.

Why? Why all this nonstop fun? This is what shots 4 to 12 try to explain: *because of beer.* This answer was suggested as early as shot 2, but it is elaborated on its own authority in the following. Shots 9 through 12 describe in a quasi-ceremonial fashion the ritual gesture of pouring beer. Shots 4 and 8 compose an alternating montage of Tex and a truck transporting the beverage around the country. No risk of running out: this beer is sold everywhere, so you can have fun any time you want. What is more, a simple wave of the hand is all it takes to order it and enjoy it.

The equation beer = fun = get-togethers is established by parallel syntagms, which, from shot 13 to shot 23 in an *identical formal manner* treat sports (motorcycle and horse races), friends getting together, love (boy and girl), friendship (Tex and the group), and beer drinking to the point where these are no longer solitary images bracketed together in this way but are underlying connotations. The two seconds each devoted to beer, love, friendship, horses, and motorcycles give the impression that all of these elements bear the same weight since they all merit or require the same treatment.

Similarly, it is not only to the abundance of shots or images that such a profusion of means and illustrations wants to invite us in such a restricted time frame. We have stressed parallel and alternating montages as well as time spans across the whole of the commercial, which means that we have yet to worry about technical matters. An equal abundance has surely produced its effects. Spectators, faced with such a wealth of information, are from the outset bewildered, as much on the sound level as on the visual. They watch from scene to scene and are carried along by the rhythm. To begin with they do not understand anything whatsoever, unless it is *shoved in their faces*.

It is the figuration, Marxist analysts will say, of capitalist opulence that is here at work. That is obvious. But there is more: this abundance, this opulence are above all those of our unconscious, within which there exists no limit. Totally saturated by images, you dream, you release yourself to the wave of illusions of an overwhelming aestheticism. For an instant, you live in the irreal, in the phantasmatic.

The abundance of shots, finally, copies the abundance of what is dreamed to be found at the base of the psychic apparatus. Advertising, we once again find ourselves led to assert, is constructed like a phenomenon of the unconscious, of defense and censure but also, we will note, of manifest primary processes. What such an unfolding of images resembles most is phantasmatic unfurling. This maximum condensation of scenes in a minimal period of time, this incessant and continual deployment of views both new and incongruous together, this implausible figuration of life: all of this, in fact, is found only in dreams. In the final analysis, this is what this abundance and the motif that constructs it mean to signify. In our opinion, if there is such a thing as subliminal advertising, it is on this level that it takes place. Such a similarity to unconscious structures can only elicit the consent of our psyche.

To stay in agreement with dominant ideology, however, this message cannot allow itself to run the length of its own phantasmagoria. It too is constructed like a censured dream, like a dream that has been interrupted. Morality is secure; or, rather, nothing will be disturbed. All the same we are reminded of what is everyday by various, more realistic insertions, by, among other things, corporate logos, by cityscapes, by a limited evocation of political reality. When you are a Quebecer, you are proud of your choice. In reality, however, the choice of being or not being a Quebecer is not made; even in 1971, this choice was far from being enacted. Simple recuperation? The national question is resolved? Of course in this sense one could interpret this text as though it were a negation of the national question. But there is something else, in our opinion: a call to the order that impedes a too-subversive hallucination, a return to the real, which intervenes as a kind of protective guardrail. It is useful to engage desire, of course, but at the same time it has to be kept at bay—it has to be tamed, redirected back toward products. Friendship here serves as a relay in this important mediation. Short of expectations of national autonomy, what is suggested is nothing other than the actualization of certain dreamed-of characteristics of the "typical Quebecer."

An ethnologist might be curious why it is so important, in an advertising medium, to stress the value of friendship. Is it an authentic cultural trait? Or a self-congratulatory definition of the average Quebecer? Are they alluding to the tradition of "pitching in"—to the old custom of helping out that is particularly prevalent in rural areas? The cooperative is surely part of what is unique to the economic infrastructure in Quebec. Nevertheless, there is in this friendly populism an ease that on inspection appears to be a little suspect, if not troubling. Societies without fathers are often fratricidal. And it is not in itself clear that Quebec should be the exception to this rule. But there, for the moment, is where our commentary will end.

France: A Civilization, a Paganism

The corpus of advertising messages is immense, and the mere fact of having to choose from it already poses a problem. In effect, we are trying to remain both representative and demanding in terms of the quality of production. We regret that many significant advertisements are not reproduced in these pages. Our selection aims not at exhaustiveness but at illustrations of certain mechanisms at work. Thus, what motivates our preference refers more to the process than to the breadth and diversity of its application. Consequently, we will cite only the examples that seem to us to be the most telling from a didactic perspective.

This is the case in the following advertisements chosen to attempt to gauge what, in France, seemed to be conceived as an ordinary typecasting of the average French consumer.

Our interest is not so much in knowing whether this portrait is complete or definitive. What is important is to perceive, through a number of advertisements, the portrait that is elaborated or which shows itself, for this portrait, even if not fair, has the advantage of prompting consumption—the French, we might offer, at the moment of recognizing themselves. Let us note again that this portrait sharply differs from the image the Quebecer advertiser projects to the television viewer.

For the friendly hospitality of a moment ago, here a new human type is substituted. The French see themselves in their *advertising mirror* as very clearly differentiated. They like to hold to their opinions and have one on every subject. They claim, in their uniqueness, not to be like anyone. In their heart and soul they are adventurers, and, we might say, underneath their exterior of extreme civility, they are deeply pagan. Other traits might emerge from a more thorough study of the question. These have in every case appeared to us to be central and relatively constant. We will now try to speak about them with more precision.

Renault; or, Cheap Freedom

From 1972 to 1981, Renault advertising relied on a singular assertion: this economical little car can drive you to adventure, literally take you from the Sahara to the North Pole. Despite its diminutive appearance, it can swallow anything. A forgiving object of the sadism of its owner, it will dutifully submit to every fantasy, culminating, in 1981, in a Renault in the middle of a Roman arena freeing itself from chains. The image, created by Publicis, is effective and, in principle, flattering to the consumer.

Among the directors of these commercials, one finds names such as Tavernier, Leone, Trintignant, and Gainsbourg. In other words, nothing has been left to chance to make sure the message is conveyed.

The campaign opens in 1972 with a film that looks like a well-made documentary. We are taken to the Sahara, to the north, to the shores of a huge cape, to Mont Saint-Michel, then up a stairway and into a painting (as in the expression "to fit right into the picture"). The music marks the jovial if not frenzied pace of this trip around the world within the range of every market punctuated by this refrain: "*She*'ll never turn you down."

The campaign moves on almost unchanged over the years, such that we find it in 1981 nearly identical to itself. This time the film bears a title, "Around the World in a Renault 4," and the landscape is limited to America and Africa. The Renault races down a swath of stairway to find itself in the middle of the display of an unbelievable treasure. America is identified by the FBI logo while the characteristic refrain specifies:

Sound	*Image*
Open a big picture book.	Encounter with Bedouins
The Renault 4 invites you to travel.	
Get ready for adventure.	
You can trust your car.	
Go, go farther away still.	

It runs really, really well.

The Nile or the Pyramids,	
only your fantasy guides you.	Camels walking
Leave the sands of Arabia	
for the forests of Africa.	Images of virgin forest
Don't take any shortcuts.	
It has a small appetite.	

Go to the land of the Raddajas,	Stairway and mysterious
in the grotto of Ali Baba.	treasure
Don't be afraid to load it up.	FBI logo
Its trunk can swallow anything.	
It's a hardy machine.	
It'll go all the way to America.	Manhattan

Go, go even further.	Surreal image
It runs really, really well.	a car between
Go, go even further.	sea and sky
It runs really, really well.	first shot of clouds

The last of the Renault advertisements we consider here is for the Renault 18 diesel. Despite the difference in products, the spirit is the same except that, we might say, this time the advertiser explores the unconscious dynamics more overtly.

The sound scenario is simple: Music. Choirs and ambient sound. Voice off: "Renault 18 . . . the diesel breaks loose!"

The images we see, successively, are:

—an aerial view of a Roman arena
—a Renault 18 held to the ground by four huge chains
—dust kicked up by the Renault in the process of freeing itself
—close-up of a chain link that breaks
—overall side view
—the Renault 18 inside the arena, its chains hanging loose
—the Renault 18 leaving the arena (5.21 by 100 km)
—close-up of the Renault 18, with a view of the arena from a distance.

Here one thing is absolutely certain: it is the idea of freedom into which the television viewer is being invited.

Yet an obvious paradox is that it is the Renault 4 that travels around the world—cheaply, granted, but around the world all the same—whereas the Renault 18 is burdened with the mission of resembling a Roman slave or a circus animal trying to get free. Is this in some way telling?

We think so. We believe that the advertiser is happy to think, much in the manner of many scholars, that an executive's life shows more in the way of bondage and slavery than the life of the average worker. Our point is not that the lot of the average worker is enviable, but that, typically, wages and domestic circumstances permit access only to consumer goods; there is very little potential for accumulating assets, except perhaps a house, but even that is not so easy. The worker's phantasm of freedom thus differs from that of the executive who feels tied down to work, to a house, to a mortgage, and so on.

The advertisement that targets businesspeople (Renault 18) speaks more directly to this bondage, whereas the first (Renault 4) opens ''the world'' to those who could only with great difficulty take advantage of such an offer.

Beyond the specifics of this example, still it is remarkable that the two messages speak with such force of this freedom, of this same liberation from hindrance. Without being able to prove it, we believe that the advertiser has tapped into a powerful feeling of constraint in the target public — a feeling of constraint that seems accurate enough for one to base a decade of advertising on it. Would typical consumers in their everyday lives feel hindered by what amounts to business as usual or even by the weight of history? Other advertisements, focusing on themes close to these, seem to justify such a hypothesis. In any case, the frequency of the motif of freedom in so many French advertisements at the very least seems suspect or, shall we say, worthy of mention.

Eram; or, The Art of Common Extravagance

The advertisers for Eram adopted a thematic motif that is very interesting from the point of view that concerns us here. The product is shoes sold inexpensively by franchised merchants. Thus it is a question of translating into advertising the accessibility of an affordable product. On the other hand, it is crucial not to suggest to consumers that by buying Eram's products they are sacrificing quality or originality. One has thus simply imagined the following general visual schema: in each of these advertisements, *groups* of people, dressed identically, present themselves to the screen successively. Chinese people, bikers, homosexuals, actors, ballerinas, sailors — visually they are identical yet eccentric.

From the outset one witnesses a profound confusion of the concepts of extravagance and uniformity. It is easy to extrapolate the concepts of originality and conformity, and this is exactly what the advertiser seeks.

As shrewd as can be, while in the shot these characters evolve at the limits of the bizarre, the text, sometimes spoken, sometimes sung, never stops making reference to madness. Eram: you'd have to be crazy to spend more.

We say as shrewd as can be precisely becausethe point is to convince consumers that they in no way abandon the crazy side of their way of dressing by buying from Eram. They are led to understand that by not being ''crazy'' enough to buy elsewhere, they can commit crazy acts of their own choosing. The proof lies in the fact that "crazy" people do not do these kinds of "crazy" things, but by the same token this does not mean that they are not "crazy" from the point of view of a certain uniformity/conformity.

In this sense, each of the following commercials will have to bring along its own sample of eccentricity. Thus we will see, one after another, rock 'n' roll dancers in white tuxedos, gangsters right out of Chicago mythology, women wearing coronets or veils, dancers in zebra tights (the voice-over will call them "weird zebras"), sailors who look like Fassbinder's Querelle. In short, everything will be set in place in order to convince one of the compatibility between the lived experience of uniformity and a clear-cut marginality. The argumentation here is very powerful.

One will perhaps recall the Carlsberg advertisement analyzed in chapter 3, which took as its theme the same conflict of difference opposed to resemblance. At the time we asserted that we were dealing with a universal question. We find a basically identical question expressed here in a different manner.

The problem confronting consumers in a situation like the one we are evoking is to assert their originality while respecting a budget that does not permit them to shop at expensive stores. In a context where everyone has an opinion, in a country where everyone is persuaded to maintain a share of inalienable truth, in a culture centered until very recently on little "specialty" shops, the shift to "mass" consumption can be suggested only with infinite adroitness and tact. Narcissism can easily be offended by a message that works against the impression that each of us is unique. Any advertisement that does not uphold this impression would fail monumentally.

Does this mean that average French people cannot accept being alike? That they do not accept the idea of identity with their peers?

The Eram advertisement shows that the question is an important one. What it seems to indicate, on the contrary, is that the French could accept being like someone who is like no one. To the conscious mind, this kind of argument seems fallacious; as for the unconscious, it is quite pleased to let itself be persuaded by the same sort of paradox. The sales of Eram tend to prove that, in an instance like this, the unconscious prevails.

Saupiquet; or, Carefully Tempered Transgression

It is to the same advertising agency that we owe the advertisements for Saupiquet, a maker of fancy prepared foods. This time the problem is of a slightly different order. It is a matter of transmitting to the spectator the idea of using a commercially prepared food when tradition says that one prepares good meals oneself, at home. The French typically are still extremely conservative when it comes to gastronomy. Everything depends on leading them to transgress without making them feel guilty.

One of the advertisements of this series is conceived in the spirit of Pagnol theater, in a meridional milieu (in the south of France)—in other words, one that is folkloric and traditional—an animated discussion in the public square in which exchanges are sung. Isn't the language of Provence by its nature singsongy? Everyone expresses an opinion; freedom of expression should not be scoffed at, either. Difference, tradition, even the spirit of friendly disputes are respected. So everything is secure: one can clear the technological hurdle. Instead let us look at the text more closely.

Sound track	*Image track*
"When it comes to Saupiquet	Meridional café scene
appetizers	people argue and laugh
I say that the one I like	
Is sardines with lemon,	
Sir.	
And I say you're a fool	they are playing bocce in a corner
And that the best is tuna	
In which Saupiquet puts onions,	
Imbecile.	
And the spring mackerel	
With lots of spices	confrontation men/women
Does that tell you something?	one of the men wears a chef's apron
Good mother, you know nothing of	
Saupiquet	
And the smell of tomatoes	
In the *escabèche*	
What will you make from it, acrobat?	
When it comes to fish hors-d'oeuvres	
Everyone can make it in their own way	
When it comes to Saupiquet hors-d'oeuvres,	they dance
Everyone can do what they like."	
Saupiquet	many Saupiquet products

The café discussion here takes on the value of argument: it establishes both the traditional and the contemporary context of the event in progress. Saupiquet hors d'oeuvres are discussed as if they were traditional cooking, in other words, as if they were important events.

The evocation of Pagnol [a member of the Académie Française], both in context and in spirit, gives this advertisement cultural reference value: you do not become uncultivated just because you eat prepared foods. This meridional discussion can furthermore acquire the value of a testimony for the rest of France. If the people of the region, who on the phantasmatic level are seafood experts, discuss among themselves Saupiquet canned food, then who, even in Paris, will be able to remain unaware of this new trend?

In the mirror of advertising, even the conservative French come out of this characterization without so much as a scratch. Their taste for discussion, their taste for divergence, and their respect for tradition are all represented. What more, in a sense, could they want?

Lee Cooper; or, The Pagan Festival

The last of the French advertisements we will examine here is a commercial articulated around lively and compelling African music (fig. 4-4). The initial scene shows us multicolored balloons against a black background. Dancers straddle the balloons, acting as if they were going to mount them. They are blacks who dance in a remarkable way. A tom-tom keeps the beat while, on a round stage, a black woman drums on the naked buttocks of a white woman who seems to enjoy it. The show continues with a scene of mutual body painting in which everyone is covered with paint. It is a festival. A stairway appears on the screen. Three characters (two women—the original black woman and a new black woman—and a man) slide down a pole like firefighters on their way to a fire and pass through a hollow cylinder to fall into jeans that mold onto them. Then we see the women from the back and the man from the front. A curtain of jeans. The brand of the product: Lee Cooper.

Analysis of this advertisement leads us to the limits of a civilization in the midst of trying to find itself. It is without a doubt one of the most expressive advertisements we have examined; but let us not anticipate, let us look instead.

The first sequence presents African dancers, that is to say, in the logic of this advertisement, people already used to primitive life. They know what to do with their bodies, they are in contact with rhythm and music and evolve elegantly in the world of drive. No need to point out that these are professional dancers.

The white woman of the second sequence is a newcomer, which is why she has to be initiated—has to be painted, has to have the secrets of her body, her sexual climax [*jouissance*], and her rhythm shown to her. But the body painting of the black woman renders the tableau symmetrical. She too here finds herself "initiated" into civilization, introduced into the festival. She can wear "subdued primitive" jeans.

The stairway that appears then represents the traditional way to go down (to one's deepest depths?). The protagonists, by now initiated, refuse this "civilization" in order to adopt a more primitive, more infantile mode of vertical descent.

Figure 4:4

The passage through the cylinder embodies in a barely veiled manner the initiation in process: it produces a second birth.

Beyond this theatrical uterus, the uniform that confirms the new baptism can finally stand on its own. The initiated deserve their jeans.

Some will say that we should not take the advertisement's initiatives seriously, that it is just a matter of creative visions on display. We believe, on the contrary, that these messages are extremely revealing of the state of our civilization, that they set forth important warning signals and not to listen to them is to close access to an accurate comprehension of how we live.

The pagan initiation staged here reveals, like it or not, a malaise and a feeling of suffocation in the overcivilized context in which spectators evolve.

The advertiser's lie is to have us believe that the fit of our jeans will resolve this huge question. Our lie to ourselves is to agree to believe as much and to consume "paganism" without having the sincerity to rebel. What we have to admit is that, beyond these circumstances, this shared lie suits us both equally well.

Few films or books go as far in decrying our loss of contact with the primitive. The advertiser here merely raises the question—names the problematic, sets up a barricade, and proposes the product in order to silence the drive that has just been awakened. All the same, it is not the advertiser's role to define a civilization's new avenues. But if we do not take seriously the views advertisers surreptitiously transmit, we risk remaining blind to the indices they have made a career of discovering and exploring.

Whether it is a matter of Leone's commercial for the Renault 18 or this initiation to the pagan festival, whether it is a question of Saupiquet hors d'oeuvres or Eram shoes, different advertisers seem to show a thirst for freedom and a desire for creativity that are anything but ordinary. Is this a limited phenomenon or a permanent cultural trait? Difficult to say. But this denunciation sells, not just its products, but also its music and images. Not to take into account reflection in the specular sense of this term, contrary to what some intellectuals think, could prove to be more harmful than one might imagine.

The Perverse and the Subversive; or, The Discreet Charm of a Life without Castration

There is of course more than a single point of view from which one can or might envision the dynamic specific to the discourse we call advertising. And we have already attempted (see chapter 2) to qualify the characteristics of the advertisement in comparison to the fictive tableau of the work of art. But here, for obvious reasons of convenience, and to remain faithful to the ensemble of our relativistic developments on the associative series, we will borrow the path that seems to us the most pertinent and the most auspicious: that of a fictive perversion/ subversion dialectic.

Our terms, as might be guessed, still need to be put into context.

It would seem that, to begin with, human beings are narcissistic machines, in other words, machines that, first and foremost, are never interested in anything other than themselves.

The other, in this context, is a kind of abstraction — is even, in the final analysis, someone who does not exist. If the other is imagined, it is, at best, as an exact self-replica, as a projection of the self's conflicts, as a support to produce a phantasm of the Other with a lowercase *o* or even with a capital *O*.

During the course of their history, human beings break away somewhat from this position of autosufficiency. Bit by bit they learn about the difference of the other, adapt to it, establish with the other and with what is different contracts that respect a ''narcissistic equilibrium'' satisfactory for the two partners.

Subsequent evolution, at least theoretically, would presume that we ought more and more to come to endorse, to respect, and in fact to like (and take pleasure in) this difference of the other. But in many cases, this will gets deflected, gets frozen in its tracks. The other, in all of its alterity, is rarely an object of satisfaction.

In this perspective, however, perversion presents itself as a situation ideally perspicuous for this study.

Perverts, for whatever reason, are incapable of recognizing the alterity of their other. In the place of this alterity, they presume and propose a phantasm of their own invention — seeing, for example, just the hairdo or the masochism of their eventual interlocutor. They neither understand nor perceive anything of the other.

Consequently, the pervert will negotiate with the other a relation that, on the one hand, will emphasize certain preferred fragments of the person and, on the other, will scotomize the rest of difference: in alterity.

In this sense, then, the perverse relation is extremely close to the psychotic relation. It proposes that an image take the place of the real.

On the other hand, some relations necessarily confront the one with the universe of difference of the other. These are relations about which people say, in everyday language, ''I got a lot out of it'' or even ''Our contact was stimulating,'' and so on. We will name such relations subversive ones.

The name seems justified to us to the extent that what from that point on confronts difference is manifestly more susceptible to provoking a reconsideration of a certain state of things, even if this state of things should be, among others, a closed narcissistic equilibrium.

Generally speaking, human beings have little tolerance for subversion, which means that they are not ready, to begin with, to requestion a whole series of adaptations, adjustments, or personal equilibria that often have taken years to define or elaborate for the sole pleasure (if it is one!) of encountering the other and, by this very fact, of confronting their own desire. In a general fashion, then, any encounter with an other will be interpreted, a priori, as an encounter with the known, with the same, or with that which conforms to certain personal archetypes. It will only be via exception, in certain relations that stand against the flow of everyday experience, that from time to time a breach in this alterity will open. For example, the practice of analysis abundantly illustrates this given: one hopes that the attention of the other as other will completely fill in the gap, but still the other escapes with the exception of single, very brief moments of insight. The same goes for many ongoing relations where, in their alterity, one almost always gets only a fleeting glimpse of the other.

All this to say then that, most of the time, we are the authors of a certain perversion of the other, of a reduction of this other to a "sameifying" vision of it.

This attitude, we repeat, has as its aim and purpose to preserve a certain number of narcissistic equilibria judged to be both precarious and precious to the human organism.

What is important to note, from another perspective, is the extent to which certain methods and institutions swallow such an attitude or, on the contrary, oppose it.

We stressed in chapter 2 what we consider to be one of the possible definitions of a work of art, namely, the opening out upon the possible breach of desire. We might now add that the eventual work of art is constituted as a kind of possible virtual place of encounter with what is other, with all of what this signifies for libidinal mobilization.

At the same time, we should add that the work of art does not exist in fact, *but sometimes takes place* in an encounter between spectator and screen at the moment when the spectator is ready to open out upon what is other and, as a result, upon desire.

Consequently recognized as works of art are works that are able to engage a large number of spectators in a pursuit of desire. In this sense, then, no painting exists without an active spectator nor any theater without participation.

Art would be a moment, a punctual event. Or, more precisely, art would be the art of making moments like these happen.

The other—theoretical, at least—side to this art is the challenge to show how what in everyday life we call the "social" in general attempts to evacuate all difference.

The reason for such a collective scenario is obvious. The group, the collective, has to think of laws, of group operations. It is thus, from the beginning, a priori the search for the lowest common denominator, for the *same,* that brings us together and reunites us. Individuality, singularity, difference—*even in a capitalistic regime*—thus appear, from the outset, suspect.

The collective cannot create difference; it lives by the very death of difference. At best, to mitigate a monochromatics that could become sterilizing, large groups or societies (to be understood here as collective authors of laws) accept or even propose the establishment of subgroups or social categories whose harmony or hierarchy then falls under their responsibility. In this context, the collective delegates to different subcollectives (the clan of the Tortoise Lévi-Strauss analyzes; the American Medical Association and the Hippocratic oath) the responsibility for a primary ''sameification.'' The collective reserves for itself a second ''sameification'' of these regroupings.

In so-called primitive societies, the partition of the ensemble is made with the help of the totemic institution of the clan. In a more developed context—the megacollectives of the West, for example—the partition is more complex and more subtle. Professions, sexes, and religions of course determine different partitions, but various factors such as age, social status, general behavior, and so on are also taken into account.

For each of these subcategories, the collective or the subgroup (or both) concerns itself with stating or regularly recalling opinions or behavioral suggestions. Thus, one will hear, ''Christians observe abstinence during Lent''; ''young people are relaxed''; ''we should be charitable to the elderly.'' Everyone will, of course, interpret these suggestions as a call to order and, notably, to the order called social.

It is clear that in the capitalistic megacollectivities of the Western world, advertising constitutes the privileged public announcement of such orders.

The Howe tricycle poster illustrates this process abundantly. The company starts by treating its customers with kid gloves. Bicycle makers prove to begin with that they are in harmony with the collective, in touch with current problems—urban or suburban life, overcrowded trains, massive immigration, the industrial era, and so on—and so they fall into the order of the Same. The spectator, by the same token, also falls into this Same.

But the poster makes its statement more specific. ''You live in the city (a social category) or you live in the suburbs. You do not exercise much (another social category) and you think that the industrial age kills all creativity or possibility of being an individual?'' (This last category alone brings together nearly 80 percent of the population.) ''Triumph over this situation (all you have to do is choose). Appropriate for yourself the marvels of the industrial age (a bike with all the extras). Individualize yourself (while remaining the same). Better yet, leave behind (in the distant monochronism of the poster) all of your worries. Live in harmony with a collective that, in its sameness, has foreseen all differences.''

The *Easy Rider* poster addresses itself to subcollectives that it identifies as the young, free spirits, people who are alive and active. They see the big picture.

Other advertisements will establish, on the contrary, that in order to belong to a particular subcollective (the rich, for example), one has to subscribe to a given condition (drink Chivas Regal or drive a Mercedes). The effect of partition is here explicit.

Brochand and Lendrevie refer to this collective placement when they speak of the need to come to an accurate social diagnosis of the "target public." This diagnosis consists in gauging the *needs* of this public, particularly in terms of status, then structuring the "communicational" message in accord with both these laws and these aspirations of belonging. Curiously, as a result one finds oneself again in the kind of interesting or troubling paradox — take your pick — in which it is advertisers who, maybe for lack of a better choice, end up defining the rites of passage of a class or of a clan. As if, elsewhere in our collective endeavors, hardly anyone were concerned with this task — or that, at the time, the regime of consumption could find only in agencies of consumption the necessary relays for the explication of its code.

Whatever the case, the net result of this operation is always a return to the same, or to an ideologically preestablished sameness. In other words, *a perversion to avoid a subversion.*

No collectivity, it goes without saying, can survive without the complicity of a certain number of subjects. And, in the case that concerns us, this complicity is of an overbearing importance.

The collective might well have proposed nothing but the same. At the very least, it will never manage to stress anything less than the fact that any ''I'' should find therein some interest.

The question thus requires a relatively complex analytical model of analysis that combines both microscopic and macroscopic arguments, a model in which the ''social'' and the ''psychic'' can (independently or in a parallel fashion) propel one another. We should now devote our attention to such a model.

In this complex and dynamic model, we will speak even more of a relation between advertiser and the subject of advertising or, more precisely, of an advertising contract rather than of advertising in itself.

What we have to note from the outset is that the *advertising effect* obviously requires both offerers and receivers. Most published analyses to date study the offerers and often accuse them of, if not obscenity, then at least immorality.

Such a conclusion is necessarily simplistic.

Faced with advertising, if the ''I'' becomes a receiver, it is because there is some satisfaction in it. The ''I'' consents to the *contract.*

This interest in the contract and this plausible satisfaction are particularly apparent in the televisual advertising contract. This contract, as we have said many times, continually comes back to the *same.* Sometimes, as we have shown, the offerers go so far as to show the receivers a disturbed image of a family where noncommunication is pathological, or offers them a sound track utterly discontinuous with a simple and static image track, conditions adverse to any advertising contract. But there is a contract to which the mercantile efficacity of the process attests: the receivers are interested.

What seems to happen, in fact, is of a curious nature. It is important to stress that receivers have to find absolutely no interest in the advertisement in order to find in it information about products. What captivates the receivers at the moment of considering an advertising proposition—or a television movie or a book of science—are broad, astonishingly fundamental questions about solitude, love, death, work, difference, everyday life, and intimacy. What the receivers look for in advertising, and elsewhere too, are satisfying answers to these questions.

Consequently, two broad families of answers become apparent: subversive answers, of the "artistic" type, on the one hand, and reductive, defensive, or perverse answers, of the advertising or ideological type, on the other. Now, everything happens as if defensive, perverse, or reductive answers had infinitely better chances of being understood than subversive answers. This is, it seems to us, a first major conclusion. The second conclusion—and it follows directly from the first—concerns the inherent limits of subversion. One seldom subverts, or so it would seem, one's own life: people do not change their psychic composition on a regular basis.

If proof of this human limit to subversion were necessary, we would suggest that the reader consult certain extremely refined advertisements by the photographer Hiro. These photos are works of art. The product—jewelry, a sandal—becomes the object of aesthetic transformation. These photos appear in art books; they have never been published as advertisements.

The aesthetic transformation they propose refers to subversion. Faced with these works one is not comforted but returned to one's *desire,* amazed because questioned. You do not buy: you think.

For—it is important to return to this—at the heart of the advertising contract, the receivers do not learn anything about the product. What they are looking for, confronted by the advertising proposition, is just the most run-of-the-mill psychic operation: solving a problem. It would seem that, in fact, we take immense pleasure in creating psychic conflicts for ourselves just so that we can then find our way out of them.

Faced with the work of art, the "I" enters into conflict—in other words, rediscovers its own desire and castration. But the work of art has no easy way out. To get out, the "I" has to rethink the very premises of its everyday nature.

Faced with the advertising proposition, the "I" enters into conflict—in other words, rediscovers its own desire and castration. But, just as quickly, it is offered an elegant way out. It is taught again how to repress, how to become defensive, how to console itself over its castration by being sent back to the idea of the *same.* This is the pleasure the "I" is looking for. And it will associate the offerer capable of procuring this pleasure for it with fun. The "I" will not buy the product right away, but will attempt, in buying the product, to reproduce this fun. Paradoxically, then, the more an advertising proposition refers to what is the *same,* the more likely it is to work. The more it refers to *desire* and the less it incites defensiveness, the less likely it is to be effective. We act, faced with an advertisement, as though we were in a game: we make up a problem for ourselves, for the pleasure of . . . solving it. Insoluble enigmas cannot function as advertising propositions.

In this dynamic context where receiver and offerer understand one another in order to play at resolving an enigma even though the solution is virtually at hand, the advertising phenomenon shows itself, strangely, to resemble a homily. According to one sacred text, homilies set forth problems of life and death. Preacher and preachee agree to resolve them, following certain principles. The more preacher and preachee introduce in the way of subtlety, the more the game gets complicated. But, beyond this subtlety, the operation remains the same: both know perfectly well that a coherent response will emerge. The subversive preacher, who would not play the game according to the rules, will simply be excommunicated for not fulfilling the contract. The artist who provides the advertiser with a keyline or a storyboard that is too subversive does not, in this sense, fulfill the contract. If the event is repeated the artist will be excommunicated from the world of advertising, because homilies, at the end of this century, have become cathodic and services, electronic.

Each of us, in the familiar confines of our living rooms, participates in a new collective mass that brings together more of the faithful than have ever before been gathered. The "Us" speaks to each of its subjects. Its voice is broadcast via a medium that, at the same time, signals by its color or by its sound quality the technological perfections of the whole. The "I" listens, understands. It seems to take great interest in this message.

But what sort of interest is really at stake? This is what we will attempt to elucidate in the following pages.

Chapter 5
Religion, Perversion, Consumption

For the interest the "I" brings to the "Us," to its discourse, to its language, to its argument, so far as we know there currently exist several schools or directions of thought. Whether one is interested in certain specific languages of the "Us" — such as, for example, science or mythology—following the point of view by way of which one observes this discourse and its effect on the "I"—the psychology of motivation or structural anthropology, again for example—one will construct strongly diverse theoretical fictions. The point of view we develop here is in its nature psychoanalytic and refers to *signs as bearers of representations of desire*. Here we are placing emphasis on a notion that is quite new, at least in its manifest expression, namely, the notion of problematic. This point of view, however, before being developed, needs to be situated with respect to certain contemporary works.

Contemporary Points of View on the Discourse of the "Us"

The advent of psychoanalysis has led certain sociologists and anthropologists, following a better understanding of the dynamics specific to the subject, to reconsider the mode of operation of collective mechanisms and, more precisely, of different social systems of representation. On the other hand, a certain overture of psychoanalysis upon the field of humanistic studies and, especially, that of semiotics, has permitted certain psychoanalysts—with sometimes questionable success—to set forth hypotheses with respect to the social field of representations. It is in this direction that the present work is oriented.

From the anthropological perspective, such a marriage of psychoanalysis and the human sciences, among other effects, will have given birth to the school of structural anthropology under the patronage of Claude Lévi-Strauss. For this author and his disciples, collective discourse, and more specifically myth, has as its function to ensure, in the heart of a community, *the permanence of a knowledge* fundamental to the workings of life. By avenues of successive dichotomies in the real, the *network* of myths and of stated traditions succeed in reconstituting the entire universe of nuance necessary for knowledge. Hence one will find, in mythic material, various radical oppositions—the raw and the cooked, the masculine and the feminine—to arrive at terms of an infinite complexity where a specific word, for example, will for a particular people designate an extremely precise ecological order.

The Lévi-Straussian discovery is shrewd, without a doubt, and one very naturally grasps that the network of myths and traditions, legends and customs, constitutes in certain circumstances a veritable oral encyclopedia of life.

One could nevertheless address the same reproach to Lévi-Strauss as to Jean Piaget: both, in effect, because they preoccupy themselves with knowledge or understanding, come to fabricate a model of human beings where the life of drive—other than intellectual—is remarkably absent.

The advertisement of the object could, for example, be analyzed by way of Lévi-Straussian criteria. And we, along with others, have indicated that any advertisement is necessarily situated both in the ideological whole and within a more particular panorama of advertising families. One could go further and assert that from these oppositions certain statements of knowledge emerge (the permanence of steel and the ephemeral nature of certain products of immediate consumption, for example). Still it would appear to us that in this light we would singularly neglect the dimension of the subject's drive, to which advertisements of things finally address themselves quasi specifically.

Sociologically speaking, certain analyses have truly fascinated us—those, for example, of Moscovici and of Castoriadis. We owe much to each of them—to Castoriadis because he sheds light on the fact that any collective apparatus is a fiction in the process of permanent edification; to Moscovici because he is interested in a subject close to our own in more than one way: antipsychoanalytic propaganda. But we were personally interested by a specific area of exchange—that of the rapport between ''I'' and ''Us''—and, from this point of view, what these authors elaborated seemed to us to be lacking in pertinence to the present discussion.

Both in his *Mythologies* and in *The Fashion System,* as well as in *A Lover's Discourse,* Roland Barthes more broadly traces the kind of elaboration we were seeking. Without systematically defining the readable play of the dynamic of the subject, he always makes allusion to it in an ample and stimulating way and with an enviable elegance. We want our discussion, however, to be more specific and more systematic from the point of view of the subject. It is on this analysis we would like to help shed light.

Thus, it would rather be from the direction of psychoanalysis that it would be useful to seek our peers. Psychoanalytic considerations on the discourse of the "Us," however, are often disappointing. Among the best known contributors in this field, one must of course cite Bruno Bettelheim's *Symbolic Wounds,* as well as his *The Uses of Enchantment.* These works are pertinent and show at the very least that it is not for nothing that fable and ritual appear in everyday discourse, that they show a subject in a state of conflict and an "Us" offering solutions. Bettelheim, however, insists almost exclusively on solutions (id, superego, ego) and sometimes leaves us unsatisfied, for example on the level of economic concerns. In no way do we presume here to fill the lacunae of analytical models in order to make them ready to describe the relation of the "I" to the discourse surrounding it; we believe, however, that, in this perspective, less static models might be set into place, by way of which we hope here to point to several potential mileposts.

Other psychoanalysts—Freud, for example—have kept to this decoding of the relation of the "I" to ritual, to totemism, to art, or to any form of public discourse. In most of these works, however, the thesis is to begin with a clinical one and relates to the realm of the social only by extension, which, in our opinion, presents several gaps. One will rarely find in such texts, for example, a study fleshed out either by literary material or even by anthropological material, which, obviously, will sufficiently weaken the pertinence and even the plausibility of these demonstrations. For us it makes no more sense to speak about any old banality of psychoanalysis without ever having undergone analysis than to propose the most astonishing semiotic hypotheses without ever having analyzed an image or a sign in a systematic manner. Few intellectuals have had the audacity or, simply, the patience to be doubly sure of the exactness of what they do. Yet the reality of this kind of study would demand as much. On the other hand, we note that when this double need is present and sustained, it produces works of remarkable insight.

Such is, for example, René Girard's essay on the repressive value of ritual with respect to fratricidal drives of the horde. But, because we know full well that we will fall short in any event, we will cite only a commentary by Greenstadt taken from an essay on the myth of Heracles where he tells us that myth exists *to warn and lead* anyone who enjoys hearing the myth repeated. This concise remark encapsulates rather well, were such a thing possible, the feeling that emerges from these various readings. Collective discourse, whatever its expression, assumes a *moral* task of counseling and of prevention. We are told just a little less often, on the other hand, that this mission, in most cases, is accompanied by a deviation of the individuality of the "I": by a *perversion*.

In the case of advertising, at the very least, this perversion has seemed to us patent and even, at times, disturbing.

The Exchange "I"-"Us" : A Theoretical Exploration

The "I" and Mythic Representation

When he attempts to elucidate the collective scope of various Greek and Judeo-Christian mythologies, Paul Diel constructs the (ever fertile) metaphor of a psychological combat—between a hero and the forces of destiny, between good and evil, between the feminine and the masculine. And, to reckon with this metaphor, Diel concludes that myth is there to *represent* a conflict of the existence proper of the receiver of such a narrative, that it is there also to denounce what the "receiver"—the "I," we would say—would tend to repress. In the same way, he suggests, myth would have a recall function of unconscious motifs that govern the human quest and, at the same time, beyond this avowal, a function of exaltation-sublimation of energies thus made available to the subject.

Pursuing an entirely different avenue and interested in the nonscientific content of contemporary cosmologies, Jacob Arlow postulates that the "I" reader of these cosmologies will be encouraged by the images of a beginning and an end of the world that they evoke. The initial "big bang" that gives birth to the expanding universe symbolizes, in a certain manner, initial coitus and thus gives access to the repressed primal scene at the same time that it projects this insight onto faraway, and thereby reassuring, cosmic bodies.

According to Bettelheim, the stories we tell to our children—complex yet at the same time simplistic narratives, full of dragons and beautiful princesses, charming princes and unbelievably sadistic ogres—allow, and precisely via the slant of their caricature, the rudimentary but no less fruitful staging of a heartrending experience for the fairy tale's audience. Through these narratives, children get a glimpse, Bettelheim states, of how their own difficulties are eventually going to be solved so that one day they can grow up.

According to Greenstadt, finally, the Heracles cycle is constructed as a vast mythic enterprise wherein readers will be able to test out, then see again and, better, learn not only about their own oedipal journeys but above all about the whole of the work of separation-individuation (from the mother) that determines all human existence.

The list could go on forever. For the moment, however, such a task would not add to our discussion. At best we would learn that other thinkers, Margaret

Mead, for example, are interested in myths and rituals, in the feminine-masculine relation, or in various other questions that are just as essential.

What interests us, instead, is to note that all of these authors, though they do not always make it explicit, recognize that in order to be able to read or understand myths, rites, fables, and legends, the "I" to begin with has to be in a state of *need*.

The question of the primal scene, of birth and death, of eternity and finitude, one might say to expand on Arlow, is always in mind. If we acquiesce to contemporary cosmogonies, it is not—at least not just—for scientific reasons but indeed because, to a certain degree, this question of finitude/eternity preoccupies us to the highest degree.

Fairy tales, like the tragedy of Electra, have a hold on us to the extent that, for each of us, questions as essential as the murder of the father or of the mother, fratricide, monstrous drives, or sublime virginity remain profoundly pregnant.

If the "I" reads the mythological cycle of the life (or is it not rather the lives) of Heracles, it is that the "I" is trying by itself to understand and figure out this complex dynamic, either of the emergence of identity or of the destiny of brute force in the circuit of models of power. In short, if the "I" is interested in a myth, in a fable, in a legend, or if the "I" lends its support to a ritual of cure or initiation, it is because to begin with the "I" carries anguish along with it.

Otherwise—and it is relatively easy to verify as much—narratives and rites will hold no interest.

This remark, however, draws us into a brief but necessary digression, after which, we believe, we will finally be able to take up, and with the necessary tools, the more specific case of advertising mythography.

The Concept of Problematic as Opposed to the Idea of Stage

In initial psychoanalytic formulations of the psychosexual development of human beings, the concept of stage occupies a central position. For Freud (1905–1923), it is a question of at once delimited and relatively discontinuous stages of life punctuated by the focusing of the development of sexuality on a particular erogenous zone—which means that one passes successively, according to the schema, from an orocutaneous polarity to an anal polarity, then to a strictly genital focus as the means for seeking pleasure.

The advantage of this theory is important. It allows for the location, in the life of the adult, of blockages, fixations, or regressions of stages particular to this original development. It is also used to set up a chronology, indeed a hierarchy, of diverse pathologies. In short, psychoanalysis is reconciling itself, in this genetic model of thinking, with the medical schema or linear or traumatic causalities, and it accedes, in this way, to the ranks of the "hard sciences."

In practice, however, this model presents many disadvantages.

The first of these flaws results from the relative imprecision of the stages that were delineated by Freud. Abraham, Fenichel, Klein, and various other authors have subsequently amply demonstrated that there was room, in several circumstances, to subdivide these stages (Abraham, Fenichel) or to present them in an entirely different perspective (Klein). Certain thinkers have believed it pertinent to add to this schema either the mirror stage (Lacan) or the breathing stage (Tristani). Where in this scenario should Winnicott's transitional phases be situated? Or recent research on narcissism that suggests both a prenatal stage (Grunberger) and the permanent *staggering,* on the grouping of these stages, of an important narcissistic component of human beings? In brief, short of persisting in infinitely dividing up the phenomenon of psychosexual development, or at least reconsidering in depth this play of hypotheses on its development, we find ourselves here at an impasse.

A second objection many authors have brought to the notion of stages has to do with discontinuity itself. It is far from clear, in fact, that once the oral stage is over, the whole of libidinal investment should become focused on the anal erogenous zone and equally, once this phase is over, that the libido should pass entirely from anal to genital zones. As a result, many authors stress the permeability of these different stages. Mahler remarks that certain processes of separation-individuation are staggered not just over a year but over a lifetime. Erikson, for his part, proposes the idea of *generative stages* whose cumulative integration would be staggered, once again, over the entirety of an existence.

It is only too obvious: such a variety of formulations bears witness to a profound theoretical malaise — a malaise upon which, in particular, certain women have not hesitated to insist, analysts fundamentally dissatisfied by the network of genetic explanations thus furnished at the origin of the development of female sexuality (Chasseguet-Smirgel, Irigaray, Olivier, and Montrelay, to cite only these few).

For our part, we propose a radically different perspective, and this perspective is articulated around the notion of problematic.

Like Mahler, Grunberger, and various other authors, we believe that the question of narcissism or of separation-individuation takes a whole lifetime to resolve. But we would add that the same goes for anal questions of power or more genital questions of pleasure in difference.

To postulate that these questions take a lifetime to resolve themselves, which then is to say that they will never entirely be resolved but will instead be engaged in a constant process of elaboration, we name these questions *problematics.*

We recognize the originary stages of psychosexual development, but, instead of stressing their discontinuity, we offer the hypothesis that these different stages (oral, anal, genital) are subsequently prolonged in life along the lines of the previously mentioned problematics of separation-individuation, of power and of sexualizing.

It does no good to suggest new theoretical concepts unless they are going to be both useful and enlightening. The idea of problematic for us works in both cases.

When we try to explain an adult's dealings with power or with control by singling out the notion of stage, by definition we have to appeal to the idea of regression-fixation. From the vantage we are elaborating here we will postulate instead that the problematic of power, always vivid for each individual, in such a circumstance will, with respect to this problematic, have a confrontational effect, or one of major restructuring.

In the context of the reaction of the ''I'' to public discourse, which interests us here, this formulation of the phenomenon by way of interposed problematics seems infinitely more justifiable. Faced with a myth, a tale, a fable, or an advertisement, it would be necessary, in fact, if one were to settle for the notion of stage, to presume that at every step of the way the subject regresses to points of oral, anal, or genital fixation. We prefer to think that the subject is the bearer of evolving problematics and that ambient discourse can always address itself more or less directly to these problematics to have them emerge, to make them be addressed again, or, if not, to see that they are silenced.

What is more, this formulation corresponds even more closely to everyday experience. It would be astonishing, as a matter of fact, if following an extremely brief duration at the orocutaneous stage an infant should, once again, have resolved all the ambiguities that have to do with narcissistic well-being. On the other hand, we know perfectly well that adults spend an important portion of their psychic energies resolving certain questions: Who am I? Where am I going? Why am I castrated? Why are women different from men? and so on. Without the permanent nature of these questions or, better, without differing problematics, the recourse of the ''I'' to ambient, mythic, religious, fantastic or, more specifically here, to advertising discourse seems, for us, impossible to explain.

Problematics and Advertising

As a result, we can postulate that it is not by chance that we are attracted to myths or fables, that we like the naive narration of epics or theatrical spectacles. It is, on the contrary, absolutely *actively* that in the exterior world we look for a plausible answer to the problematics that inhabit us, to the energetic seething that accompanies them to the dynamic quest they carry along with them.

To return, from this point of view, to the reading Greenstadt proposes of the cycle of Heracles myths, we would add that should the subject be interested in this mythic cycle, should be excited or be worried about what Heracles has to do with Hera, should identify with his labors of taming monsters or with his death throes, this is because, for the subject, this ''problematic'' of maturation-separation is still very much alive—exactly as one could think that the child about whom Bruno Bettelheim speaks needs the fairy tale to see itself *represented* living inside it (a kind of mirror transfer) and re-cognize itself in it (which is to say, recover a grasp on something of itself that escapes it). Adults, in a parallel fashion, when they read or consult a discourse of mythic order, re-turn to themselves a question that concerns them profoundly, even if this just means staying alive.

Occupied by questions of an oedipal, anal, or narcissistic nature, this exterior discourse seems to them of primary concern. These propositions, in fact, offer them a chance to share. They constitute an attempt to generalize certain human inquiries. Sometimes they even elaborate, if only on a basic level, explanations of mortal issues. This is all most people need. A kind of peace, at times even an amazement, settles in. They could not be happier.

In the case of advertisements of things, this play of the human problematic and its delight is particularly notorious. A public discourse on objects guaranteed to satisfy, advertisements of things, in fact, work no differently than any collective enterprise of answers. The thematics are organized and circulate around a fundamental disquiet and take root in these questions. It is rather in the range of answers they bring to these different queries that advertisements of things distinguish themselves from other expressive media.

If we reconsider, in this light, all the beer advertisements analyzed in the present work, suddenly we see their common theme appear: friendship, as we said; familiarity, thanks to the "jingle"; reminiscences, being together, but also parachuting, rodeo. What a lot of talk, we remarked at the time without being able to explain exactly why. And we even stressed this apparently paradoxical claim (Carlsberg, chapter 3): "We're different, still we're alike." There is, in this claim, in fact no paradox; what we are shown, clearly, is nothing other than this *problematic of separation-individuation,* which grounds any maturation. The advertiser brings us together by evoking a theme of life that causes us anguish and, by this very fact, gains our consent. Unlike the narrator of myth, however, the advertiser here refuses any conflictual exploration, any elaboration that would show the ambivalence of beings. The advertiser cuts short jealousy, expressions of sorrow, and any real dissatisfaction. Once a problematic is evoked, it is magically reabsorbed. The festival itself or human complicity, if it takes place, could only be of short duration. From the difficulty to differentiate itself, a difficulty governed at once by the anxiety of castration and the depressive fear of the loss of the object, everything here dissolves magically in the almost too sweet syrup of a friendship without rough spots, of an unconditional and undifferentiated love.

In mythic narrative, the real in question is clearly more complex. Gods and demigods love one another and hate one another at the same time, are rivals, spy on each other, and betray each other. In the narrative of the Trojan War, we see them as heated partisans of one or the other camp. Hephaestus is ugly, but Aphrodite is magnificent. Zeus gets incredibly angry; Hera displays her legendary jealousy. One thing is for sure: in the presence of such a narrative, the listener or the reader is confronted by much greater human diversity or multiplicity. Nothing, whether divine quarrels or magic spells, is easily resolved. Olympus, contrary to the paradise of the Judeo-Christian traditions, is not a place of complacent, contemplative inertia. Such narratives, we could postulate, had, in their time, a value of rudimentary psychological understanding. One cannot, in any case, say as much for advertising statements. Short and oriented toward consumption, they must not let the conflict spread nor let the look linger on it. At any cost, they have to conclude with purchase as a solution. In other words, above all they must not reopen the question.[1]

Earlier we discussed the advertising campaign for Marlboro, a campaign that, for some twenty years, essentially gravitates around a single image: a cowboy, his horse, and the Old West. It is interesting to note that, examined from the perspective of problematics, it refers very closely to questions relative to the masculine Oedipus. To become a man, the little boy, we might say, has to confront the threat of castration by the father, which, on the other hand, will assure him of a relative freedom and a capacity for a real intimacy with his peers but, in particular, with women. From the bias of the concept of stage, theoretically this question ought to be resolved at the oedipal moment. Clinical experience instead teaches us, however, that there it is also a question of a problematic (therefore never resolved) where masculine identity and the captivity of intimacy with the woman are, at best, always in a *progradiant* movement.[2] Here the advertiser counts on the fact that it is indeed a matter of a problematic that is very much alive. The advertiser addresses, in each consumer, this fragment of identity not yet consolidated, still in motion. From this point on, the discourse becomes limpid. In order to continue to become a man, in order to pursue the murder of the father and access to freedom, "Come to Marlboro Country," to the land of grown men free of the law (of the father). Is this just paradoxical? There you will find a sour breast, the link with the mother who kills, which is to say, at the same time, "Whatever you do, don't become a man. It is too dangerous." Everything works manifestly as though the advertiser knew both that we live off of our problematics and that we are at the same time not about to resolve them definitively. The exploitation of the death drive here makes one shudder.

The final example of advertisements of things that we will now cite is advertising campaigns for "European cars constructed with intelligence."

In fact, the problematic at stake here is power. An outcome of (sadistic or submissive) anal stages, the problematic of power is articulated at once on the important desires for control and supremacy and on a perpetual temptation of disavowal of these same drives. Ideally, over the course of the years, the desire for power progressively gives way to a situating, for the subject, of its power in relation to that of the other. But this situating remains always in movement and, potentially, progradiant.

The advertiser we evoke here is not trying to stimulate a similar process of maturation, which could, for example, be the case of certain mythic representations (one thinks of, among others, Aeschylus's *Prometheus Bound*). Thus the advertiser takes up strategically, as we described in chapters 1 and 4, at once the desire for power (you want to assert your might) and also defense and the forbidden, which risk bridling this same desire. So the advertisement evokes, at the same time as drive, all the defenses, rationalizations, intellectualizations, indeed reactional formations that risk guaranteeing the brutal nonemergence of this drive.

Whereas myth proposes a kind of catharsis and assumes, in a certain manner, the not unfounded risk of an at least diffused consciousness of the forces that regulate human behavior, here, in the psychoanalytical area, everything is blocked, controlled, clogged up. And, above all, the problematic in the sense we understand it cannot breathe. Such an elaboration is forbidden. The institution of advertising sees to its death.

Advertising and Stylish Thought

Here the temptation is great — and we will succumb to it provisionally — not to limit our commentary uniquely to advertisements of things. Other phenomena, in fact, unfold in an obvious way according to the same laws and principles as those that regulate advertising discourse. We would not be thorough if we did not say a word or two about them, especially since their manifestations are easy to see: they are current, they are concerned with popular singers, with best-selling books, with intellectual fads. They surely deserve our attention, however briefly.

Why, we might wonder, is Barthes popular? Why does Edgar Morin [Lewis Mumford is an American equivalent] captivate throngs? Why does John Irving sell *The World According to Garp* by the millions? Why do the tabloids enjoy the vogue we accord them? Or Asimov his great popularity? Why, in short, do these different efforts accede, at a given moment, to the rank of *public discourse?*

Of course, there are several possible avenues of analysis here, and the phenomenon of a statement's popularity cannot be reduced, very plausibly, to a single analytical gridwork. Nonetheless, from the point of view of the problematics we are elaborating here, a number of the components of this phenomenon acquire, in our opinion, a significant transparency.

The case of the tabloids will serve as a first example. Ms. Jones is worried about what will become of her family. Where are morals going? What sort of effect does a divorce have? How do homosexuals live? What kind of people take drugs and what benefit and harm do they derive from them? These questions and plenty more preoccupy her every day.

When she reads the gossip columns, she can for a moment magically enter into a marginal universe, that of the stars, where, she is told, these things go on.

This star uses cocaine; another tries to stay slender. Is it worth it or not? The tabloid answers. Yes or no, in the final analysis it matters little. But it answers. Someone gets divorced and becomes depressed, even on the verge of suicide. There: now Ms. Jones knows and can understand how Beverly, her niece, could be just as depressed. The gossip tabloid does not just justify her question but provides her with a network of answers that are more or less comforting and that satisfy her.

The phenomenon that unfolds at the moment when the intellectual community waits with great impatience for the imminent publication of the very latest book by Bernard-Henri Lévy [Susan Sontag might be an American equivalent] is of precisely the same nature.

Nobody — we leave the benefit of the doubt to the reader — is duped. The latest Lévy will not provide the definitive answer to all these questions, but there we will find, on the problems of the hour, what is essential for ready-to-consume thought.

Morin gives an inkling of a new synthesis in the social sciences. Barthes allows association and provides glimpses at how any sign ought to be productive of meaning. Foucault thrashes the institution brilliantly. Asimov explains science to us. Irving makes us dream, then reminds us that any dream can become a nightmare.

These authors bring to questions one asks oneself bits of peace, of calm, of apparent solution. And their text, on this level, operates no differently than that of an excellent advertisement.

And you, for that matter, you reading these pages right now, aren't you wondering: "Where are they coming from? What are they telling us we don't already know? What's their deal? Who are they against? What about this notion of 'problematic' they're trying to sell? I can't wait to read what So-and-So will have to say about them. Where are they on current intellectual debates? Who wins? Who loses?"

In the final analysis, we all spend our lives figuring out conflicts, solving imposing questions. In each of us, at each moment, questions come forth looking for answers. Answers crop up, creating a temporary illusion, only to emerge again elsewhere and in a different form. Without this unflagging process, life could not go on.

The discourses we have elevated to the rank of public speech are only those that, at a given moment, seem to be the best to calm or resolve these tumultuous movements.

The fact of their advertisement is not, in itself, directly linked to their more or less direct relation to the truth. Of course, it can happen that these statements can be very revealing, very honest, even profoundly penetrating. But this quality in no way prejudges their more or less wide broadcast. It is Asimov who broadcasts Einstein, and not the other way around. The more a work, a text, or a thought appears to respond to a question or the more it formulates it according to the givens of the moment, the more it has a chance of being retained as a public expression of a given problematic. Inversely, the less a thought chokes off anguish, the more it is in danger of being thrown out with the trash.

Advertisements of things have learned their lesson: they skillfully evoke but never make trouble.

Institutions, Problematics, and Death

Freud maintained that the heir to the oedipal complex was the superego, and, from a certain perspective, he was absolutely right.

We are presenting, however, the events of the psychic life from another perspective. At the moment of getting beyond the oedipal complex, we assert, for the first time the child has encountered the basic components of his sexualization. It has noticed the difference between the sexes, has had to deal for the first time with the anxieties of castration. It has come to grips with the forbidden, has competed for a place already occupied, has experimented a first time with its charms and its powers of seduction. It has managed, we might say, a first stroll through the garden of sexuality.

Ideally — that is, if things go smoothly — for the rest of its life it will feel itself free to explore with respect and pleasure the relation with an other both different and sexual. How far will the child go in this exploration? To what point will it be ready to mourn its all-powerfulness, to forsake a parental transfer to make room for the originality and different existence of an other in pleasure and eventual fulfillment? Here is a question that concerns us to the highest degree and that evokes, finally, just as many answers as there are individuals.

We know, on the other hand, that certain people will close in upon themselves, for all intents and purposes, into a fairly limited number of accepted forms of behavior and will limit their quest to a reduced number of human experiences where they will gladly repeat the same rigid attitudes. Others, for reasons that also belong to their personal history, do not feel wounded but, on the contrary, are delighted by the difference of the other, enriched by the discovery of rather than impoverished by contact with what they lack. Some, we would say, will bring to this operation a progradiant tone, whereas the more rigid ones will endlessly remain on the threshold of an eventual relation with this difference. For the progradiant ones, it will be obvious that sex is acquired and developed for as long as one lives. For the others, often, the sexual question will already have been solved once and for all. They of course will live on, but will sexualize little.

This, in our opinion, is the capital difference between an existence directed by life drives and one overcome by the narcissistic law of the megamaniacal inertia of death. There, again, is one of the fundamental questions human behavior addresses to us.

How is it that some progress, explore, or dare to take pleasure from life whereas others frown and sulk away their lives? It would be presumptuous to pretend to know why when in fact we have at our disposal a model at best valid only for research hypotheses. Yet the fact is there. And, without a doubt, there is truth in this half-truth according to which collective discourse extinguishes desire or progradiance. But there is also truth in the statement that one finds in collective discourse only what one puts into it.

The Destiny of Drives

Before examining more closely each of the most important problematics that occupy human beings, it is important to state, on a more general level, that in and of itself the fact of being a place of drive has something disturbing about it. One fine day, in effect, you realize that once someone goes into heat, that person is bent on destruction. A drive motion that was not expected, that you did not know was so strong, has just emerged. It is a need for power, a nostalgia for tenderness, an insatiable hunger, an incoercible revolt.

The first questions to be formulated before such an unusual situation strangely sound something like this: What am I going to do about it? How am I going to manage this at once fascinating and terrifying world of drives that are emerging in me? Libidinal overload, analysts will call it, especially analysts of children and of psychotics; weakness of the flesh, Saint Paul would say. How to manage this world of drives, mere individuals will ask themselves, so as not to lose the objects of love that I hold dear, not to confront myself with an eventual castration, not to experience a narcissistic wound?

Religious morality here plays on a sublime and radical shrewdness: drive has no possible fate other than to be purged. All desire is morbid, shameful, sinful. The ideal being gets free of this carnal hodgepodge to attain the spirituality of evolution. Dead before the fact because already disembodied, this being is, also, already closer to God and to eternity.

Such a conception of sin is astonishing to the extent that the claim is made that beings are made up of just that, of drives that course through them. And yet, if this notion has kept a little fragment of eternity alive, it is indeed because, somewhere, it consoles or reassures — not to the extent that it consents to a given behavior, but especially and to begin with in that it provides a mode of thought, a plausible model for metabolization of a case of drive overload.

Zorba's village in Crete does not operate any differently no matter who spies cynically on the death of the illegitimate Bouboulina. The nasty gossip that circulates in the cottages, the medieval Inquisition, the standard offerings of television do not operate any differently: all of them have only one intention, namely, to ensure the permanency of a single line of reasoning around drive-oriented becoming. In *Discipline and Punish* (1975), Foucault masterfully described the shrewdness of systems of incarceration: it is only in established prisons that such a surveillance of human actions, in view of their rehabilitation and normalization, is manifested; we all know this. The socius thrives in large part from this maintenance of the stability of the group that constitutes it. Now, in terms of overture and of closure, of progradiance and of regradiance, *the institutional is always on the side of inertia and death,* and one has to wonder a little what the advantages of such a position might be.

In fact, this advantage is at least double.

The "Us," it is clear, draws from this advantage a profound stability, a kind of unshakable guarantee of permanence and, in this way, in part insures the "Us" its perreniality. Thus the "Us" has a stake in encouraging the collective repression of the world of drives to the extent that this world threatens to turn anticipated and predictable modes of energetic circulation upside down. Consequently, the "Us" will incite its members to a disavowal of their own desire in favor of a normalizing pseudosublimation. And, from this, the "Us" will draw on the benefits of a certain "ruling order."

The first advantage the "I" draws from such a market of dupes resides in a certain harmonization of its interior world. In effect, thanks to this process of repression, drive tension is at least partially reabsorbed and the conflictual tug-of-war is alleviated, if only provisionally.

The second advantage the "I" draws from such a contract is even more considerable. From this perspective, in effect, that of the partial disavowal of the world of drives, the conflict of an interpsychic origin finds itself projected on the exterior of the self in a manifest way. Sin is the work of a demonic agency that lives in "hell," that is to say, outside the here and now. Capital and work, good and bad, chaos and the law are equally exterior to the subject, are abstract, and, by this very fact, are ungraspable inasmuch as they are *private* phenomena. The "I" draws from this exteriorization an important compensation. It no longer has to assume for itself a phenomenon that is repeated to it that it exceeds. It is in exchange for this relative peace that it is seemingly ready to disavow the space of its own desire — in exchange for this force of the "Us" to which it is ready to surrender its will to power.

We are struck here by the parallel between moral discourse and advertising rhetoric.

If we consider that the "I," in the grips of certain problematics that imply the emergence of a drive, in this regard consults either religious morality or advertising, we realize that, in both cases, it will get the same kind of results.

Faced, for example, with an "I want to be different," the moral response will oppose the narcissistic interdiction of the sin of pride and will lead the subject to a banalization of its problematic. The idea of fault will disarm the deep-seated project, whereas generalization (everyone feels this bad desire) will make the stakes communal. To the same type of question, advertising rhetoric will respond in the same spirit that "we're different, still we're alike," that the project or desire for individuation does not have room to exist since everything on this issue is foreseen: take beer, for example, which brings us all together in a perfect magma. The conflict glimpsed has no existence of its own: it is abstract, exterior; it is someone else's problem.

Human development, we stress, is not the cumulative result of a sequence of stages that are closed and unconnected to one another; on the contrary, it is the manifest product of an *evolving continuum* where stages and processes are perpetually synergized. To try to account for this complex phenomenon, we have introduced, to this point intuitively, the notion of *problematic*. To bring the object of our debate more to the fore, to attain greater rigor in the conceptual development we propose, we will now examine one of these problematics—that of separation-individuation—more closely in order to link it to the effect of certain expressions typical to advertising.

When a child is born—everyone seems to agree at least on this initial point—it feels entirely dependent upon its surroundings for the expression and satisfaction of its basic needs. Its relational universe thus gravitates, on the outside, around a bipolar axis of well-being and malaise whose zone of consciousness and of expression (pleasure-displeasure) is, in essence, orocutaneous. This description corresponds historically to the very first Freudian formulations of the oral stage.

For Abraham, the lived events in the very first months of life already show themselves to be more complex. Happy orality is layered with sadism. At the same time, the child wants both bonding paradise and a distancing autonomy. It takes delight but wants to bite.

Melanie Klein describes the articulations of the development of the infant as bipolar phases: passive-depressive on the one hand, schizophrenic on the other. With an Oedipus who, already, situates himself within the nuances of the parent-child struggle.

Lacan insists upon the role of the third-party father and of his law in the destabilization of the bonding project of the mother-child couple.

Mahler, finally, discerns in the very first months of life a process of individuation that would go through autism, symbiosis, blossoming, and a stage of attempts.

In short, if in place of opposing these diverse schools as we have too often wanted to do, we accumulate these different reflections in order to draw from them a kind of integrative image, we have to state that the life of the infant, far from a beatific state of vegetation, is constituted above all as pluripolar pins and needles of tensions and desires, as a pluriconflictual experience from which the infant, despite its extremely minimal means, will have to come up with a version of a synthetic solution.

At this stage of development, the issues are crude but nevertheless primary: finding love and warmth, attaching without dependence, getting angry, living in terror of being divided up into pieces, becoming detached, fearing cold isolation.

It is obvious that the infant can definitively resolve none of these questions. They will remain implanted in its psychic mechanism in the form of a fundamental problematic of its subsequent evolution.

This problematic results from several components: the other, the body of the other, the horror of the other (Kristeva), the wound caused by lack of power, the necessary narcissistic investment of the contours of the subject.

As a *problematic,* this network of questions will last for life. The transitional object will help the child tolerate the absence of the other. Thanks to symbolization, capacity for affective autonomy will grow even more. Other levels of questions are added as well: What is the meaning of the law of the other? What is the meaning of the sex of the other?

The question is insoluble or, rather, offers itself to just as many solutions as there are subjects. One sees it later on in the choice of a career, the choice of a partner, the decision to belong to a particular political or other group. The question persists as anxiety, and collective discourse knows it well. The problematic having as its principle never to be resolved calls for the study of a representation that might furnish it with relief or a boost—relief more than a boost, for that matter. Collective discourse busies itself with finding for it representations such as these.

In chapter 2 we tried to bring out the traits that distinguish art from advertising, and we stated the hypothesis that beyond their aesthetic merits, what especially characterizes works of art is a certain yawning gap of desire.

In the terms we are now using, we would even more strongly stress—or is it the same thing?—the nondisavowal of human problematics.

For Bergman and Joyce, the problematic of separation-individuation exists. The same is true of Rothko. As a result, the engendered representation can no longer take into account this avowal, mark its difficulty or hope, assume its majesty or miseries, suggest a commentary, offer a testimony.

Some works, on the other hand, remain blind to this dynamic deployment, deny it, or resolve it—they amount to the same thing. In this more or less lucid continuum of testimonies on the condition of desire, advertising represents the extreme pole of absolute blindness.

''When you're a Quebecer, you're proud of your choice,'' the advertisement insists. But what choice is in fact in question? Could one say ''When you're French, you're proud of your choice''? Or Romanian, or Argentinian?

''We're different, still we're alike,'' Carlsberg beer tells us. Nobody wonders any more if they are Marxist or fascist, atheist or Jansenist. Difference grounds resemblance. Everything is reabsorbed magically. Symbiosis and individuation are, after all, synonyms. Why didn't we think of that before? Everything becomes banal. Everything is spread thin. No wonder we find ourselves right in the middle of maniacal omnipotence.

Some will say—and rightfully—that it is impossible to sustain permanently the tension specific to the yawning gap, that places and moments of respite are necessary as well. Perhaps, in the final analysis, this is what guarantees advertising its appeal.

But this is where we have to agree that its appeal has nothing to do with raising a problematic or the implementation of desire. Advertising appeals almost exclusively to defense or to inhibition. Its function, we repeat, is that of flattening out destinies, which in the past used to be reserved for homilies or the witch doctor's ceremony.

Greek mythology, for example, offered to various human problematics a much more polymorphic and dynamic representation. Heracles defends himself from his mother, Hera, associates with various women, frees himself, falls madly in love, expires. Hephaestus is ugly. Aphrodite is superb. Zeus's role is that of an impulsive character; Dionysus is preoccupied with pleasure. Even more important, this register remains in a constant state of flux, is up to a certain point unpredictable. During the course of the Trojan War, the gods intervene according to a certain logic, but they can also change sides. Nothing is absolutely definitive. The subject confronted with its problematic of separation-individuation has plenty to feast on here; a panoply of possible choices is there for consideration.

In advertising, the more one is different, the more one is alike. Individuation is not a problematic. By the magic and religious ritual of consuming, everything is reabsorbed, is disarmed. Clearly, the two media of representation are not situated on the same opening-closing pole of human conflict. One is manifestly ''more open'' than the other.

Over the whole of his work, Lévi-Strauss demonstrates, with respect to American Indian mythologies, a similar diversity. Here, the mother is loving; there, she is ferociously hostile. Against the good father, certain ethnic groups establish an ill-tempered uncle. The ensemble of this system of representations offers a support to a diversified image of human behavior. The exploration of the problematic can, in this way, progress. There is nothing of the sort in the case of advertising.

Comic strips seem to offer another type of support for the representation of human behavior. Governed, like fairy tales, by the law of the happy ending, they show us a hero ceaselessly triumphant over multiple obstacles of existence. Tintin is a child who links up with inept adults in order to triumph all by himself over the threats of castration life represents. The problematic thus seems respected to a certain extent, but the ''happy'' ending guarantees its closure. We are halfway between advertisement and myth, halfway along the continuum that leads from the sometimes harrowing avowal of the yawning gap in the work of art to the most complete closure in the case of certain media such as advertising.

The Problematic of Power

The anal stage is marked by a libidinal investment of the corporeal zones of the same name and is punctuated by a search for pleasure articulated on the gestures of purging and retention. It is, by the same token, the occasion for the placement—and this, for existence as a whole—of a problematic that here we call power.

Abraham has situated the two phases of this first exploration of systems of power, the first masochist, the second sadist. Bouvet, for his part, has attempted to depict the type of relation to the object that emerged from such an encounter with the establishment of a possible control in the relation. His central concept, that of a relation from a distance, suggests many reflections in the subsequent development of the relation of intimacy. The fecal object is an object one takes pleasure in retaining or in purging following one's fancy, to be retained in a possessive or anxious manner, to be purged in a sadistic or counterdepressive manner. This dynamic, as we know, develops and spreads out over the entirety of existence—a possession of the maternal object, granted, but a possession also of the spouse or the partner, a control over the scientific object, a domination over subordinates, a critique of power or infatuation, a sense of propriety, transactions using interposing disembodied objects.

Once again, children can in no way resolve for themselves this ensemble of questions and propositions, which are much too complex. Comprehending them and elaborating a coherent personal position with respect to them will, in fact, require a whole lifetime.

All of us, by ourselves, have to devote ourselves to the renunciation of our own abuses of power, to rediscover or invent the security necessary to live and let live. We all have the responsibility of unmasking our own institutions, which from within attempt to analyze every object.

We all, following this rationale, also have to discover our own fields of real power and denounce our refusal of power. The question is subtle and polymorphous. Collective discourse tries, in many places, to bring to it answers and relief.

At the heart of Greek mythology, one rediscovers, precisely on this subject, an impressive variety of representations of problematics of power. Pygmalion wants to mold the object of his dreams with his own hands; the gods give life to his Galatea, but one learns that, by this breath of life itself, Galatea escapes her creator. Hephaestus dominates matter, creates objects each more ingenious than the last, but he gets angry when he finds out that he has been deceived. In the tragedies of the Oedipus cycle, one will find commentaries on power ursurped—in that Oedipus kills his father, of course, but also in the intrinsic drama of the rivalries that govern, for example, *Oedipus at Colonus*. The question of power is taken up again in the description of the capture of the Golden Fleece. Jason, Orpheus, Heracles, and Theseus, the heroes of this narrative, are so many "solutions" to this problematic. Jason wants to take back a legitimate power. Orpheus, the "weak," governs by his gentleness and his tenderness, calms the waves and quells the storm. Heracles, the man of steel incarnate, here again tries to exorcise the hold of his jealous mother, Hera. Theseus, finally, represents a kind of wise equal justice; we know he will defeat the Minotaur by accepting Ariadne's thread (allying himself with the woman) and will turn down royalty by founding democracy.

The universe of advertisers is, by far, much more impoverished in shades of meaning.

The documents that concern us here are those in which advertisers promote technical and semiprofessional devices: advertisements for computers and microscopes, very sophisticated devices, but equally advertisements for stereo receivers, cars, motorcycles, and all sorts of high-tech household appliances. These advertisements are, at least from one point of view, astonishingly unanimous. All of them propose, as *solution* to the problematic of power, *the ability of the object to control*. As if the allusion to the anality of these remarks risked being missed by its readers, Yamaha, in a 1979 advertising supplement, proposed a "machine" (motorcycle) constructed "in the down-to-earth spirit of muddy tires." "From the dirt up," these machines, their manufacturer assured us, allow a perfect mastery of any situation. A Mercedes-Benz, the advertisement for the German manufacturer tells us, is so well built that it will protect you from dangers of which you are not even aware. Canon cameras allow a perfect control of the image. Radiola stereo receivers are just what is necessary to seduce (a feminine position maintained by a lip to which lipstick is applied), whatever it takes to convince (control). Moulinex, manufacturer of household products, offers you "tomorrow" from "now on," thus promising you a hold over the future. We will stop this list here. In our eyes it exemplifies the dominant model of advertising strategy, which the interested reader will find on virtually every page of any magazine.

What appears to us to be significant here is that these discourses deny, for the most part, the very center of what we are calling the problematic of power. As a matter of fact, in order for the subject to evolve in its relation to power, it is indispensable that it be conscious of the limits of its mastery of the object, that is to say, that anal castration produce its effect and that the abandonment of sadistic control give way to a relation of real mutuality. This task is of course difficult, and some discursive productions withstand an initiation of this dynamic better than others. The various advertisements we evoke here are univocal in proposing their product as an ideal object of the buyer's unconscious phantasm of absolute control.

"You can infinitely mistreat your Timex watch." Or drive Yamaha motorcycles through all the mud holes in the world. "You can never be hard enough on your Volvo." Nikon resists everything. And so on. A relatively recent advertise-

ment illustrates everything to which you can make a Michelin tire submit—
without guilt and without anguish, and thus without having to perceive that the
drive appealed to in these claims is nothing other than sadistic and that it would
call for a requestioning of the subject.

In a situation of this type, the "Us" occupies a position—and plays a role—
that is absolutely comforting: to the desire for sadistic and tyrannical control of
the object (by the "I"), it proposes objects that are wholly acceptable and entirely submissive. The car, René Girard would say, is thus sacrificed to the sadism
of the buyer to safeguard something of the social order. For our part we will add
that, in this way and by swallowing the status quo of social exchange, the collective institution once more goes in the direction of inertia and of death. This is
a constant: *the collective cannot, by and large, stand life*.

Sexualizing Relation; Process of Sexualization

Considered from the angle of *problematics,* a sex is never truly acquired. As
early as the phallic and oedipal phases that mark the beginning of this long
evolution—and this as far as the synthetic reflections, which, in the final analysis
are existential—the sex of every subject is acquired and is elaborated bit by bit,
runs up against the other's sex, redefines itself, rediscovers itself, deepens or re-
invents itself more or less infinitely.

In this slow process, homosexuality and heterosexuality, for example, take
"their" place. Penetration and opening progressively acquire meaning, *are enriched* with new meaning. Virility and femininity are explored and are deployed,
are emancipated and are liberated in terms of a process that is nothing other than
life itself. This is, at the least, an ideal register useful for an understanding of
human sexual conduct.

Evidently, in this itinerary, certain forces are at work that, on the one hand,
will call for a halt to such a progradiance and, on the other, will encourage its
blossoming. It will be apparent to us that certain relations, in that they contribute
to an evolution of the definition of the sexual self, will be properly *sexualizing*
whereas others, more closing, aiming, so to speak, at the status quo if not overt
repression, will be clearly antisexualizing. From this will result, depending on
one's age, one's taste for risk, and one's particular pathologies, beings who are
more or less diversely sexualized. From this will result the human mosaic.

Sexualization presents itself to begin with and above all as a research spread
out over the whole of existence. Confrontations and complicities nourish and propel this research. Fears first stated then overcome punctuate it in their turn. Sex
is acquired through improvisation.

Evidently, according to the more or less satisfactory or more or less definitive
responses brought to the two other areas of problematics signaled earlier—power
and individuation—one will observe that the subject, even while pursuing its re-

search for a sexual identity, will at the same time try to respond to other questions concerning power-domination and individuation-pleasure-depression. An extremely complex area of human dynamism will result, rich in multiple levels whose breadth and depth can be discerned only in the field of analytic practice.

The "Us" is not unaware of the real complexity of this questioning.

The "Who am I as a man or a woman?" calls for consultation. "What do I do with my desire, this complex drive that emerges in me?"

The field here being subtle, complex, and, in a sense, almost explosive, so much does the energy contained in this debate matter, one finds oneself again, on the "Us" side, in a discursive bidding war. Religious or moral, political or mythic, these discourses will draw their power from the very ambiguity of the question of the "I." To close the question, they will obtain the at least momentary support of those who anguish too much over research such as this and its particular uncertainties. To open it more, they will gain, in general, little popularity.

The feminism of the early 1980s constitutes an excellent example of a collective discourse "conscious" of the problematic of sexualization. Feminist advances show in fact the point to which this question of sexual identity is never definitively acquired, to which it has to be ceaselessly restated not so that finally one day one might see clearly, but rather so that one might gradually see more and more clearly. And one can assert that by way of such a position, feminism has in its turn given a boost to sociology as well as psychoanalysis, that it is not done verbalizing what needs to be said.

The discourse of advertisers seems, from this point of view, a bit more ambiguous.

The first fact that has to be stated in this regard is that contrary to other discourses, advertising is not blind to the complexity of the sexualizing process. In the advertisement of the object, *allusion* is made to everything—homosexuality, fetishism, sadomasochism, the search for phallic affirmation, the workings of seduction, barriers specific to the laws of what is forbidden, the problem of the apparent and the authentic in the relation to the other.

Aubade and Kim overtly suggest homosexuality. Max Factor, Helena Rubenstein, and Clairol readily speak of lures. Real, Marlboro, and Winston overtly deal with questions of phallic realization. And the list could go on.

From a certain point of view—and, notably, from the point of view of the statement—one could then assert that advertising is more complete than many media: more complete than comic strips, for example, which, without exception, stay away from any allusion to sexual differentiation; more diversified than moral discourse, which, by reducing human expression to the idea of fault ends up disavowing the progressivity of every approach.

On the other hand, and contrary to the very spirit of what we are here naming

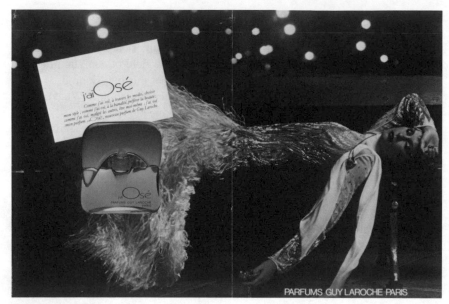

Figure 5-1

Figure 5-2

a process of sexualization, advertising denies these questions their dynamic or, better, their dynamizing value.

> How I have dared, through fashion, to choose my style; how I have
> dared, instead of banality, to have preferred beauty; how I have dared,
> despite others, to be myself; I have dared with my perfume. I Have
> Dared [*J'ai Osé*], a new perfume by Guy Laroche.

Such is the text of a well-known advertisement (figs. 5-1, 5-2).

If one examines more attentively, to begin with one notices an allusion to at least two of the problematics already cited, namely, individuation (to choose *my* style, to be *myself*) and sexualization (liberation with respect to the forbidden "despite others"): I chose my perfume (my sex). But one notices in this, almost as quickly, a will for closure. The choice is made, past, done, and definitive; there is nothing more to do and this is in no way an object of a permanent transaction.

But is this woman's choice of "I have dared" so clear? We see her, ascetic and almost asexual, on the one hand dressed in showy feathers that look fake, on the other in clothing with a masculine allure (a very elegant suit), but in both consenting to the stereotypical attributes of the woman as object. What has she really dared to do, if not conform?

The process of sexualization such as we are presenting it here is by far more complex than a simple access to attributes stipulated by fashion. It is the traversal from infantile sexual theories to personal and creative theories of maturity of a being who bit by bit goes beyond the prejudice to come to a kind of autodefinition of her rapport with her sexualized body.

Here, once again, the product offers a solution. It lets us consider the ensemble of the problematic as closed.

Jontuc is "sensual but not too far from innocence," whereas by falsifying hair color, Nice 'n Easy lets the subject be even more herself: "It lets me be me."

The paradox dissipates. Every contradiction that might be a possible place of evolution is disarmed. The wager is closed, dead, banalized. One consumes answers to the extent that every open question remains a vector of anguish; one consumes repression to the extent that nonrepression presumes the installation of an unbearable lucidity.

Perversion As Relation to the World

We have been postulating, since the beginning of the present chapter, that the questions the many stages of psychosexual development address to the child are — a priori — much too vast and too complex for the child to be able to find, at the very moment of their first formulation, a satisfactory response. From these various stages of development thus results a kind of dynamic residue, an ensemble of open questions about individuation, power, and sexualization that we have called, because of their very insolubility, problematics.

It is now suitable to consider the fact that these problematics determine, in their turn, and for everyone, what can rightfully be called "relations to the world."

Owing to our subject, namely, the advertising effect, one of these relations to the world, notably the perverse relation, will attract our attention in a very specific way. But first, however briefly, we will have to put into context what we understand by these relations to the world.

Return to Psychopathology

From the psychoanalytic point of view, one is accustomed to bringing together the ensemble or a part of an observed clinical tableau to unexpected developmental "errors" in specific moments of the individual's evolution and to speak, consequently, of diverse pathologies as regressions or fixations upon these stumbling blocks of development. This theoretical schema explains a certain number of observable phenomena, but it also carries with it serious limits to exploration at the present time or for future projects or, again, in ways that allow situating a useful or workable model of mental health.

We prefer a schema that takes account of both problematics engaged in the life of relations and the type of answers privileged by a given individual. This schema is like the first on more than one point, yet it differs from the first in postulating that once the oedipal stage is over, the subject continues to live dynamically and thus remains mobile up to a certain point.

If we consider the three principal problematics dealt with to this point—individuation, power, sexualization—we can see that they concern different persons to differing degrees. Some formulate their relation to the world around them almost uniquely in terms of sexualization, others especially in terms of power, and already we can distinguish particular typologies. Similarly, the responses or attitudes a person adopts when faced with these problematics can vary in terms of progradiance or recursiveness, creativity or stereotype. And it becomes clear to us that those who read all of the events of their lives by way of a single problematic and who always bring to them the same recursive answers will be less "healthy" than those who are able to situate diverse events in terms of diverse problematics by daring to bring to them more original—less predetermined or stereotypical—answers.

The neurotic is characterized by the predominance of problematics of power (obsessional neurosis) and sexualization (hysteria/phobia). The kind of solution that neurotics propose to these problematics is particularly recursive and bears witness to a field of reading drawn from the world around them.

An obsessive person, for example, who reads every event in terms of domination-submission and who has a hard time staying in the bathroom for fear of a cost to be paid for this surrender to a drive amply illustrates this phenomenon. Yet what is important to note is that despite the recursiveness of the neurotic's adopted solutions, the problematics remain—and in more ways than one—open.

The problematic of separation-individuation, like the underlying questions it engages, dominates many people's existence. At what distance from the other is it acceptable to live? Why the necessary suffering of separation? How to fill in its contours? What is the place of love?

Psychotics "choose" to carry with them answers of their own invention: a reality they hallucinate. A "borderline," without quite hallucinating, will always be looking for a gentler, more forgiving world, whereas the depressive, confronting this same question of separation-individuation, will live in anguish and paralyzing despair over the object gone astray.

Of course there is much to reflect upon concerning these problematics, and we will come back to them in a subsequent work. For the moment it is important for us to state that, in the singular field of psychopathologies, *perversion* has a specific calling. Perverts, in effect, have a hard time tolerating the fact that a problematic might be living, open, gaping, insoluble. And what they have "chosen" to undertake, faced with these problematics, is to block them, that it is to say, to respond to them in a definitive fashion. One of the questions that appears to occupy them to the highest degree is that of alterity and, among others, the sexual alterity of any face-to-face encounter. And, to escape the very movement that might give rise in them to an avowal of alterity, perverts interpose, between the other and themselves, a reductive and confrontational image of the real, an image that denies any question. A male pervert was about to look at the woman, to see her yawning sex-gap and the absence of a penis and the presence of a vulva. He is held up by a shoe, by a garter. Just before knowing as much, just before going any further. The economy of going further does not take in anyone, not even the pervert. But its comforting answer is sexually satisfying in that at the very least it provisionally appeases, that it seems to choke off a libidinal breach in order to plug it, at least for the moment. Obviously, this movement calls for repetition. But this latter in its own way remains sexually satisfying. Only rarely do perverts enter into analysis, and for a very simple reason: everything, for them, happens as if it were not the place for questions but were rather a permanent system of answers for any question. One speaks of perversion when this kind of behavior addresses itself to the sexual alterity of the other and when it leads to overt disavowal. But perversity also exists in many other sectors of life in the production of results that silence the questions. Here we are at the heart of our subject—the advertising effect.

Perversity/Consumption

Perversion takes its root in the intolerable infinitude of a questioning and in doing so proceeds by way of a disavowal of/answer to this problematic.

Advertising, as we have been saying, solicits desire not with the purpose of obtaining its consent but instead with the intention of hiding from us the yawning gap through the play of an object/answer/disavowal that, from this point of view at least, bears all of the characteristics of the perverse object.

What perverts cannot tolerate is the lack, is difference. So they invent, in its place and instead of this difference, a quasi-delirious image of a nonlack. They set up a controlled scene of the sadomasochistic type or they design an answer that focuses on a sexually coded accessory like a spiked heel or an earring; it does not matter which, since what is important is that they protect themselves from having to go so far as to admit the existence of yawning gaps.

What advertising proposes is no different. Allusions to desire, to the lack, to the yawning gap—in each of the advertisements we analyzed to this point we have been able to demonstrate our hypothesis abundantly. But as soon as this gap is evoked, what advertising—and the ritual of consumption, by the same token— proposes is a stopgap answer. An object, as if it would truly fulfill us. This then to say that we consume in order to avoid what is intolerable about desire, in order to maintain the economy of our yawning gap; in the same way, the necrophiliac avoids the fact that the other, still alive, should possess the power to get away. *And, in that sense, we are all perverse.* Perhaps not sexual perverts in the strict sense of the term, but we are all touched by perversity, and in a certain manner this is in no way radically astonishing: the perverse solution, as seldom as it appears in analysis, clinically reveals itself to be extremely useful and advantageous. By this lure, in effect, from the perverse relational prototype, something of the unfolding of life allows itself a haven, a moment of pause (let us note that the pervert is still sometimes frustrated to remain permanently on this level): something coalesces that otherwise would move and thereby disturb, would reveal a reality the pervert prefers to disavow.

Consumption operates in the same way: it permits desire to not explore itself in its foundations but to take refuge in a fetish object and in this way disavow itself. Just as sadomasochism allows its protagonists in a complex if not a complicated play of controls and of distancing mechanisms to avoid a relation that would more amply take into account the field of difference and alterity, the product-gadget object allows silence concerning desire or the lack, allows pretending that—at least momentarily—it is fulfilled.

The advantage is immense from an *economic* point of view (in the double sense of the term) and we all take pleasure from it—from a pleasure, moreover, that has, for the collective mechanism, infinite lubricating virtues.

No question about it, in this exchange a little death and a little inertia prevail over life. But is it really so simple?

Death/Perversion/Consumption

Premature ejaculation therefore bears its share of perversion. Having encountered the woman-other at the threshold of their own tolerance, having in every way met a representation that for them is adequate, male perverts take their pleasure on the borders of an anticipated abyss. They take sexual pleasure in having come "so close" to what, precisely, they are afraid of one day reaching. This level comforts them. They have, at the threshold of the other, neither to deploy their man-being, nor to understand further what the woman-being means. They conclude there, before the end. They consume before the acknowledgment of its yawning gap.

A perversity without malice, one might say, since it is fundamentally matched by a relative impotency. But is it so clear, since in this game the female other, precisely, is deprived of the additional sexual pleasure she is refused? A man-being who forbids that the woman-being deploy herself shrivels up. The potential relationship is short-circuited in a kind of touristic summary of the other. Something having to do with depth keeps itself from taking place.

And in a sense it is true that premature ejaculation is utterly inoffensive. It is situated more on the side of a lack of the additional-being than from the point of view of an absolute lacuna. It is not on the side of death, since it lives, it moves; it desires, it gets hard and relaxes. Nor is it from the side of confining narcissism, since the other is encountered, touched. This does not prevent that, fundamentally, premature ejaculation belongs to nonprogradiance, to a difficulty in pushing penetration of the other further and the self-understanding that one might encounter as a result.

The logic of the advertiser does not exceed this logic of premature ejaculation. There, the other-desire-yawning gap is touched upon or evoked but is never encountered in depth. As in the case of clinical perversity, one can never be sure that it is a question of a major lacuna or, rather, of a lack of going further, of a lack of going beyond appearances. It lives, it moves, but, simply, it does not go any further.

But any further than what, exactly, since would not absolute nonconsumption also belong to death?

Is it not specific to the very structure of diverse desiring mechanisms to take recourse in these multiple pauses? To these landings where they can catch their breath? To these convenient states of relative rest? Otherwise, wouldn't one quite simply die of starvation or exhaustion?

We know, for example, that compulsion always starts everything over again, never stops talking about an obsession that steers clear of life. And perverts, upon examination, appear precisely to belong to a clinical group where this compulsion to start every problem all over again entirely dominates their existence.

For our part, we believe that on this very theme there exists a fertile field of research. Pauses are not inherently perverse. One could even postulate that, faced with any other, there always exists a greater possible opening and that we are never anywhere but at a very particular point in our evolutions: thus perverse with regard to time to come [*l'a-venir*], closed toward the un-perceived [*l'imperçu*], flattened with respect to a plausible dynamism. The advertising perversion would thus not in itself consist in its proposition of landings. It would originate from its intention to confuse landing and life, defense and desire, pause and progress—in short, in its wish to have us adopt as moving what, upon analysis, appears to be strangely immobilizing.

Advertising, Morality, and Propaganda

The question that suggests itself here is curiously complex. On the one hand, it is easy to have the feeling that life will circulate to the extent that a certain overture/yawning gap will allow for progradiance; on the other hand, we are sure that life cannot inherently be reduced just to this notion of mobility. The landings we evoke are just as necessary to survival as more mobile periods, if only as a way of "catching one's breath," or "taking a step back." Otherwise it is death by exhaustion, by sheer starvation.

What we know about advertisements of things is that they open onto desire, that they let it be glimpsed but just as quickly propose—as a protection against unfurling, as a pause—a *screen* product. We end up wishing, ideally, perhaps naively, for a discourse that sustains and encourages that desire be set to work without denial, without a mask with regard to the yawning gap. But is this ever possible?

What seems clear is that the problematics that live in us—individuation, power, sexualization—represent a quasi-infinite potential for possible developments. For centuries to come, these problematics will continue to ground what is essential about human reflection on the human race. These problematics will thus never, properly speaking, be definitively closed.

On the other hand and at a specific moment in time, as humans we have at our disposal a certain ensemble of what passes for answers to these questions. And, evidently, certain discourses have as their function praising these provisional solutions—interpreting them as adequate. This is the role, for example, of propaganda and of religious morality just as it is for advertisements of things.

Despite all of our science fiction novels, we have no idea what the everyday car will be like in the year 2020 and even less how the general question of transportation will be phrased in the year 3000. We all presume that cars and the question of transportation will have evolved. By the same token, what we are admitting is nothing other than the precariousness of contemporary propositions.

The ideal car belongs to the order of the phantasm. In the meantime, various manufacturers assure us that they are *already* producing it. Their advertising thus works like a safety catch, like a protection against the unfurling of absolute desire. The expression "state-of-the-art technology" here takes on its full meaning. It is a matter of the best there is to offer: the rhetoric thus has, as a consequence, to be extremely shrewd to both open upon a desired "more" and end up with "what is."

The resemblance of this dynamic to that of the reconciliation to the "sufficiently good" mother is all too apparent. In the case of the "correct" mother, one will recognize an important work of mourning in relation to the megamaniacal expectations of the child: here, this work specific to mourning is cleanly eluded. The advertiser wants perfume X or car Y to take the place of the object of desire—leading, finally, to a repression of desire itself.

The logic that presides over the elaboration of a text of ideological propaganda reflects the same type of intentions. The ideological group—and we are all card-carrying members—cuts out of the real a certain number of statements or truths that save the subject from a more adventurous research, from more precarious or mobile statements.

A repertoire of screen statements that will secure the thinker against the wavering back and forth that results from a more relativist position is established there as well.

The play of partially filled yawning gaps—of half-truths that seem intolerable not to perceive as absolute—once again is reproduced.

In the field of the exact sciences, Kuhn has studied a parallel phenomenon by taking up the question of the production of "normal sciences."

Accusing a witch doctor of engendering illness is far preferable to the absence of any theory, Lévi-Strauss reminds us. The proverb says more simply, "Un tien vaut mieux que sûr tu l'auras" ["A bird in the hand is worth two in the bush," "One is better than nothing," and so on—Trans.]. We strongly agree since through this dynamic exchange, it is desire, in its very potential of progradiance, that we abandon to the security of the same. The established order finds in each one of us its psychological match. Propaganda and advertising are effective precisely to the extent that we ardently wish for them to be.

Religious morality operates along vectors of an identical nature. Better to adapt oneself, however heavily, to the yoke of sin and the forbidden than to have to confront the delirious meanderings of the unconscious oneself. This is at least the economical proposition that many subjects adopt. Or, rather, they opt for another morality, whether liberal or right wing, Sartrean or philanthropic; it matters little in that what is basically at work is the search for a coherence that protects from unfurling and that this search should appear sufficiently important to justify the sacrifice one makes for it.

Our inquiry leads back to a second inquiry that would be its inverse: what then, in effect, is this mysterious desire that requires so many ramparts to keep it at bay?

The life/death duality comes to mind almost right away: the rhythm of the pauses (landings) of progradiance; but this duality here seems to us more like a harmonic law than a pair of opposing forces. And, by the same token, the reflection on advertising leads us to the very heart of analytic theory.

The Sacrificial Dimension of the Ritual of Consuming

In *The Violence and the Sacred,* René Girard proposes an interesting hypothesis on the social function of ritual. The sacrificed animal, he says, represents and by this fact avoids the social group, and fratricide takes effect. His thesis has as its object, among others, to oppose itself to Freudian statements according to which any religious or totemic organization would in essence return to a representation-consecration of the immortality/mortality of the original Father. And, to be sure, Girard opens a perspective on the bond of parity that Freud silenced. But what seems even more probing, in light of his text, is that the ritual, the religious gesture, and the public ceremony have as their function to act on a symbolic scene of drives or desires whose dealings, on a more concrete scene, would be prejudgable, in a general way, in terms of the greater good of the group.

Now consumption, like ritual, involves a sacrificial dimension. Contrary to what happens in friendly exchange, in barter, or in certain other forms of commerce, consumption (of products) only takes place on condition of the surrender of one's money—of one's power—for an object that has just sealed the agreement. Beyond its obvious economic function, it seems to us that this surrender of power operates in an extremely significant manner on the symbolic level.

Instead of violently attacking the sensual young girl who poses next to a flaming red Porsche, "I" chooses to buy the Porsche (therefore surrendering its violence, its primal libido) and to make this ritual contract materialize by the—at least provisional—surrender of its buying power. As a result, it thus consents—in more ways than one—to reinforce the social order that holds that it is better to know how to secondarize one's primal desire than it is to act blindly. And the "I" assures itself the respect from its peers that is due to those who master the code.

In this light, advertising acquires a double status. It directs the look toward a particular product, but above all it really becomes a public discourse on the destiny of everyone's drives. For the drives that seek objects for themselves, advertising proposes products that, by the same stroke, it designates as acceptable. It is therefore, in the full sense of this term, a *moral agency*.

The sacrifice, however, is not just a material one. Beyond buying power, what the "I" here sacrifices is equally an important part as much of its object libido as of its narcissistic libido.

The psychoanalytic reflection on the destiny of perverts, their lack of creativity, and the absence, finally, of a libido that is their own, here clarifies the debate in a dramatic way. Joyce McDougall, among others, rightly insists on this permanent renewal by perverts of their stereotyped tableau. For Masud Khan, the formulation will be even more lapidary: perverts, he tells us, agree to deny themselves all by themselves, that is to say, to disavow the forces of their own destiny, to attach themselves to the protective level of the perverse scene as much as to the anguish of the scene of the other, which could, beyond this frozen fiction, be of value were they to let it be. There it is a question, for us, of the principal sacrifice specific both to the perverse ritual and to the act of consuming: here the subject itself turns aside its own desire in favor of the survival of a perverse dyad in the case of perversion, of a collective operation in the case of consumption. In Mahlerian terms, we would say that, in order to avoid the anticipated pangs of separation, the subject here mourns its individuation. Fratricide does not take place. The beautiful girl is not violated. The "I" buys its Porsche or drinks its beer in order to avoid attaining that desire and seals, with this sacrifice of self, just as with its buying power, a ritual contract that maintains the "togetherness" of the group. Such a mourning requires enormous, and constant, pressure. Moreover, the role propaganda, homily, the ceremonial, and national holidays play is taken into account again by an advertisement that, by this simple fact, cannot not be both repetitive and omnipresent—the stake into which it inserts itself being, in effect, too primordial to be relegated to the shadows of discretion or silence.

Paradoxical Advertisements and Perversion

At first glance, certain advertisements or certain advertising elements appear paradoxical. Thus, in the Metropolitan Insurance advertisement we analyzed in chapter 4, one wonders a little what draws the spectator toward a familial landscape as broken up as that of this utterly divided American family. Elsewhere, for example in the Esso advertisement (chapter 4), one asks oneself about the means of a "seduction" of the spectator by way of a system of communications so marked by double binds. Sadism almost in its pure state can be found in a large number of advertisements (Absorbine Jr., for example) and one asks oneself once again about the appeal of these spectacles. On this subject one could even suggest that, in most of the dyads or spoken interactions represented in television advertisements, we are in the presence of pseudomutuality or of a double bind, of out-and-out generalizations or, in a more global manner, of modes of communication at the brink of the morbid and this according to the very terms of the Palo Alto school on various pathologies of communication (Watzlawick, Bateson, and others).

Our astonishment results, however, from a profound mistrust as much with respect to advertising seduction in itself as with respect to seduction in the most global sense of the term.

In a classic conception of the act of seducing, seducers deck themselves out in their finery to induce in the seduced a kind of dream aspiration, a kind of idealized image of the possible relation. This is, we should note, only one possible case of seduction. It is the prototype, for example, of courtly love or of the romantic ballad. Other methods are just as plausible; they even risk, in many cases, showing themselves to be infinitely more effective. It is thus that one discovers, upon analysis, that seduction by interposed idealization imposes an important work of overtaking-sublimation upon the object of seduction, whereas the network of complicities freely offered in the form of a wink seems devoid of any restrictive requirement. This is an immense advantage that advertisements of things readily use to their profit.

Are you feeling weak? Perplexed? Troubled? I thought so. Me too. Can't we still share some good times?

Family a wreck? Communication painful? Don't dwell on it. After all, people aren't going to break their backs offering you a difficult model of perfectly healthy communication!

You are shielding yourself from your desire? You wish for landings on which to rest rather than climb on in pursuit of your questions all the way to their logical conclusion? Fine. We will be accomplices by counting on as much wherever you are.

After all, is the mirror's role to reflect the image of what should be?

In everyday seduction, don't we have recourse, all of us and each one of us, much more to winks in the direction of a complicit ease than to these exhausting ideals of perfection?

The success of advertising indicates, among other things, that we enjoy being seduced in this way.

One will here object, no doubt, that theater is also a representation of what is and that it seduces its spectator thanks to a similar wink. But, undeniably and absolutely contrary to advertising, theater in this regard takes as its purpose to name or envelop, to illustrate or deepen the understanding of a conflict. In a sense, theater and cinema *disturb* their interlocutors, provoke or stimulate them. To the extent that it has as its mission to present objects that are proper for satiating desire in its most diverse of expressions, advertising thus could not both challenge and reassure the subject, that is to say, both open and close a human debate. Concerned with the pause and the desiring dynamic around an object as product, it will fundamentally aim to conclude this debate, indeed any debate. If not, it would be something else: a reflection on life, an essay or a novel, whatever—but it would no longer be an advertising text.

Obviously, here again, there is room to introduce a large number of nuances and avoid idealizing, a priori, a kind of pseudoreality that would itself be a work of art.

Theater and painting, literature and architecture are often complacent, facile, and superficial. It is not obvious—a priori—that they always or necessarily disturb their interlocutor. It is even rather remarkable that works of theater or art that are too disturbing should incubate for a long time in marginal parts of the city before meeting with broad success. The number of artists recognized more after death than during their lifetimes illustrates this sometimes essential marginality of artistic production.

On the other hand, one sees many thoughts, subversive in appearance but finally strongly complacent, catch on by virtue of an analyzable promotional factor. In many regards, Lacan was not always the most profound of contemporary analysts, but without a doubt he knew remarkably well how to ensure his self-advertisement [Norman Mailer is the obvious American equivalent, and not just because of his *Advertisements for Myself*]. In the same way, certain media have known how to find an enviable place in the intellectual world not always in terms of the absolute pertinence of what they have to say but, instead, in view of an entirely different function—in particular that of ensuring for the intellectual community a relative identity of views on primary subjects. This is true of, for example, the *Nouvel observateur,* which has taken as its mission the propagation of intellectual-socialist truth in France, and of *L'Humanité* in the communist camp. In the United States, *The Atlantic* will, in a certain manner, have a similar breviary function for intellectuals. This subject alone would merit an entire study.

What is important to perceive here, on the other hand, is that the function or reassuring homily or of ideic institution knows neither frontier nor class law nor political opinion: it concerns us all in more ways than one. And whether it is a matter of consuming Dali—because art too is consumed—or the most banal *Paris-Match* or *National Enquirer,* the stake is profoundly the same. The hubbub surrounding discourse is identical to the hubbub over the latest American cars. The invitation to reduce oneself, to pervert oneself, or to disarm oneself in order to fit in works in one just as much as in the other.

It is always to the subject and to the subject alone that it falls, in the final analysis, to accept or avoid perversion. Everything one can say about the art used here as a metaphor is that it appears, on the whole, to suggest more about deperversion to more people than ordinary advertising. That is all.

The message that is most like advertising is not always or necessarily to be found on a billboard. Somewhere, we all more or less need propaganda to survive and we all make reference, in a more or less acknowledged way, to the con-

stant homilies that reassure us about belonging and about what will become of
our televisually guided drives.

Alibi and Signifier

At the start of this research, we, like many scholars, adopted a position that was
both naive and, we would say, paranoid. Advertising was, in this regard, the bad
object. It subtly manipulated our desire, drew our attention despite the crowd and
the long list of our preoccupations. The question we were asking then came down
to the "how" of this seduction. We were in a quest for artifice or for shrewdness
that, in the hollow of rhetoric, snatched us up and then diverted us from our
"real" desire.

This was, in fact, to willfully and profoundly misconstrue [*méconnaître*] the
very nature of the process we name desire.

The "real" or "authentic" object that we were attributing to desire does not
exist. But we continued to pursue it, sensing in advance that in the phenomenon
of consumption something had without a doubt been diverted — something that,
originally, had to be directed *elsewhere*.

Bit by bit, what became clear is that this desire in a raw state was profoundly
intolerable. A yawning gap without a specific object, a quest for an object A^3 or
for the absolute, this movement of the libido never found total satiation in the real
world.

We knew this already, of course, since others before us had spoken of this
phenomenon. But at the same time we also did not know this, in our own way
dupes of this advertising diversion that we could not name or put a finger on.
Now is it not here, precisely, at the bottom of this dupery — our own — where the
very essence of the advertising phenomenon resides?

Desire is yawning gap, insupportable, intolerable, absolute thirst, lack of the
object A. Desire calls for defense. It solicits its own diversion. And this is, perhaps, finally what this study will simply have recalled.

We are easily scandalized by propaganda — especially by the propaganda of
others: what a narrow view, we are ready to think to ourselves. Nevertheless,
propaganda operates on a level of which we are all acutely aware. It consolidates
collective discourse, Moscovici tells us, projects on the outside of the group an
area of debate that otherwise will be conflictual. We would add that it claims to
name, in the real, the objects that "matter," the debates "worthy" of our efforts. Perhaps without propaganda we would watch our thoughts start to waver.

Desire is yawning gap and, consequently, the forever unsatisfied search for the
dream object. Some discourses draw profit from this sometimes disquieting mobility in order to propose to us elements of the easy life, stopgaps, objects of
pseudosatisfaction. Otherwise, and this must be repeated, it is the wavering or

the taking over, on another level, of anguish that emerges. In this precise sense, advertisements for products operate like propaganda. The object advertising offers to us is *not the object of desire, but an alibi for no longer desiring the object.* What it projects on the exterior of the group as a "strange phenomenon" is the quest for the phantasmatic object. The place where it consolidates collective thought is the conviction it propagates that this world of free circulation of goods contains all of the objects necessary to satisfy us. Thanks to advertising, therefore, it is no longer necessary to desire.

At the beginning of the present study we were convinced that advertising solicited then redirected desire. What we would now even more tend to assert is that advertising, just like religion, propaganda, or pornography, serves more to strangle or check every form of desire, to encourage repression, than to propose a form of exploration of any sort.

In pornography, everything spreads, everything is on display: everything is verified on the brutal anatomical scale of things. There is no room left for desire. Is desire exploited? It is not obvious, but instead is disavowed: skirted. Pornography is set up as an *alibi* in order to be able to elude desire just as the notion of sin is an *alibi* for not exploring the more anguishing idea of free will or of progradiance.

Why then should we all have to be so afraid of desire and its yawning gap? There, after all, is the real question. In product advertisements, among others, that to which we more or less consent is a displacement of the link or of the relation toward a more punctual circumstance, to avoid intimacy in favor of something that can be touched right now.

So why should we all be so afraid of yawning gaps?

The Maternal Monster and the Elocutionary Act

The object A, the signifier to the first power (S_1), the absolute guard against the yawning gap does not exist, can barely be represented (Aulagnier, *Violence de l'interprétation*). Yet, at the very same time, finally it alone exists, it alone dominates us, truly preoccupies us. Having surged forth from out of nowhere, yet omnipresent, it obsesses us. This is again what one seeks through individuation (the other), power, or sexualization. And this quest would ultimately have no plausible end if a voice did not intervene from somewhere to say, "You are married, you are an owner, you are guilty, are condemned, are a father or a mother"—a voice that, by its elocutionary act, cuts through the real, imposes a date for the event, places a time limit on the level of association. This voice, described by Ducrot, named performative by Austin, is not just the voice of reason or of jurisdiction. It is the statement of the possible shape of desire. Without it, one is forever in search of a partner, always trying to determine one's precise responsibility. The elocutionary or performative cuts through the living, claims to know, has the power to define. Following this, something can be undone or be reconstructed. The voice allows anchoring.

"I have dared," claims Guy Laroche.

"When you're a Quebecer, you're proud of your choice," says Molson.

"Here are the musts" of Cartier.

These are all lies, of course.

Laroche's woman, stretched out on a public bench near the Hudson River in Manhattan, might be wearing the latest creation of the most chic clothing designer; she dares to wear the most plunging neckline imaginable; she remains stereotypical, perfectly in conformity with current images. She has acquired the signs that allow her to say the "I have dared" that she utters publicly. She shows us the current limit, the hem by way of which, in the contemporary real, it is proper to assert that one has acceded to the absolute of audaciousness.

I have dared: "How I have dared, through fashion, to choose my style; how I have dared, instead of banality, to have preferred beauty; how I have dared, despite others, to be myself; I have dared with my perfume. I Have Dared, a new perfume from Guy Laroche." A curious message in which transgression gets confused with total obedience to the normative code. The norm and the unabashed margin are wedded: difference means being a model of what is the exception, audaciousness a model of resembling. Yet, by the same token, it is where one can indicate how it is plausible to take appropriate action concerning one's desire, even while *denying* it to oneself. A rule by which the eccentric being knows the exact potential outcome of its challenge to the social order is stated.

Recuperation, would Marcuse say? Perhaps. We would say: an eagerness to provide desire with a place of execution in the mortal sense of this term — a place to appease so as not to be finished.

"Sensual but not too far from innocence," the Jontue text will say. Everything stays safe. Desire is intact. Untouched. Unviolated.

The mask finally lets the Nice 'n Easy woman be herself: "It lets me be me."

"Emeraude, the liquid emerald."

"Precious. Sensual, slightly dangerous."

The object A is the image of the mother: the representation of the maternal monster capable both of satiating all instincts and of offering to her desiring child the most fulfilling possible bliss. The object A is the overture of nirvana onto death: on the ultimate event of sexual pleasure. In the meantime, one has to convince oneself that the objects in the real world can satisfy something, can check the flow. Speech is elocutionary: "You dare." From this moment on, with this perfume, audacity rules. Here it is. Here is what we predicted, programmed, established. Here are the "musts" of Cartier. Good objects, the goods. Those things it would be good to possess. An avenue is traced, staked out, lit with floodlights for us. The product is presented as the relay by way of which one will have to consider that one's desire has been set to work—so the product can be sold, of course, but also, and this is no less important, so that the desiring flow can stop.

Elsewhere, in the other direction, what one has to assume is desire's confrontation with the yawning gap: the face-to-face meeting with a desire that is not so sure where it is going or what it really wants. But elsewhere is also the possibility of prograpdiance. I dared to prefer beauty to banality; despite others, dared to be myself. Who would not want as much? In the life of castration, still this desire goes through a conflict or a debate, through gentle negotiations or difficult emergences. Here, audacity sells and the disavowal of castration flies away with the exchange of play money.

Will we be masochistic enough to admit to our castration despite such an offer?

Nonetheless, the consuming ritual consigns another sacrifice, that of the narcissistic investment of its own operation of overture to its historical yawning gap.

The "Us" draws its power from all these little investments deposited on the sly. The "Us" is a multi-billion-dollar bank of individual savings accounts of the "I" that one hopes to see mature.

On the side of desire, it is a free-fall toward the yawning gap mother; on the other side, a huge invitation that proposes that we not wallow in desire is addressed to us. The alibi is provided. Is it a crime, after all, not to desire oneself? Precious, sensual, a dangerous little nothing, Coty's Emeraude advertisement specifies where, in a luxurious penumbra, a couple in love embrace tenderly. The accent is placed on this dangerous little nothing that perfume suggests, this dangerous little nothing that lets you flirt with a relation, lets you get close without having to interact.

At its genital limit, at its upper landing, at its most sophisticated echelon, it is to this pleasure at avoiding other pleasure that advertising is content to draw its spectator. Glints and colors, textures and symmetrical curves, shadow and light, refinement in the construction of images, this advertisement, the one from the Sunday paper and from fancy magazines, is dressed in silk and a shirt of hair. You can almost smell it, thanks to the way its forms and magnificent tones spread out. We are in the antechamber of pleasure. But this is only in order to learn that it is dangerous, that it would be better just to avoid it. The abyss vanishes. At the guardrail, a too-helpful hand firmly keeps us from falling. We look down at what could befall us, on the moving side. We have a front-row seat, but along with it the absurd assurance of never setting foot on stage. For you must not take pleasure. If you did, you might not consume. "Sensuous," yes, "but not too far from innocence."

Overture for a Subversion

There is absolutely no interest in wanting to propose a conclusion for a work of this sort; such a conclusion would be far from obvious, and still would be even were we to have something like an aphorism to offer. Nonetheless, a kind of truth emerges for us at the end of these labors, a somewhat unexpected half-truth whose name is intuition and for which we would hope that the historical coincidence of the industrial era and the advertising era does not have its roots just in financial circles. It seems to us, as a matter of fact, that the sole function of advertising is not the sale of consumer products, but that it also targets the free circulation of partial drives. Now, if this intuition is correct, the more human beings are freed from labor and entrust a greater role to machines, the more we have to keep vigilant watch to stay informed of the plausible future of our libidinal energies. In counterpoint to this hypothesis, one notices, in an absolutely parallel way, that the relative collapse of religious morality equally indicates a transfer of the moral burden to the paraindustrial complex: a kind of ultimate secularization of a formerly clerical function, in the primary meaning of the expression. Equally, one also notes, in related fields, that the more scientific mechanisms allow various questions truly to be opened, the more someone is there with a ready-made answer. And everything happens as if, as soon as a more intimate contact with our yawning gap became materially possible, we were to become even more ingenious in countering this movement of eventual progradiance.

Obviously, this is only a hypothesis, and, not being historians, we do not have at our disposal the necessary instruments for demonstrating it.

If it is correct, however, that is to say, if it is true that morality is recently secularized if not to say postindustrialized, one has to wonder what sort of subversive force will be capable of counterbalancing this perverse energy.

Not that we believed that there might be, on the one hand, bad perverts and, on the other, wonderful subversives. This would be too simple and the real seems rather to be made up of a kind of permanent equilibrium of perversion and subversion. But at times we are still dreamers, sometimes even uneasy faced by such a disproportion between rare subversive energies and the institutional giganticism of the mechanisms of perversion.

Such a disproportion is perhaps the effect of a law of human nature — at least this is what observation here once again leads us to observe. But we remain dreamers. All the same . . .

Notes

Chapter 1. The Poster: Desire, Defense

1. [Translator's note] The French — "Un MacKeen, ça coute la peau des fesses" — is idiomatic and cannot be translated directly. The English expression "that's no skin off my back" comes close to the meaning of the French, which reads literally: "MacKeen jeans: that costs the skin off your butt."

2. We will see in chapters 2 and 3 this essential relation with the imaginary, with a supposedly different relation that grounds the advertising act.

Chapter 2. History of a Passage into Sameness

1. The term *béance* ["gash," "gap," "yawning gap," etc.] is here introduced in the guise of pictorial or representational partner of the term *écart* ["distance," "gap"], from which desire originates.

To better identify this notion — which, however, we posit as ultimately ungraspable — it is important to acknowledge that any work refers, beyond all explicit or manifest content, to another, let us say, *"lacking"* content.

Rothko's painting *represents*, granted, but it evokes as well when it does not hide an entirely different painting.

This second work, to the side of the first, interests us in more ways than one.

Desire, we mentioned earlier, originates from the gap [*écart*] separating need and demand — which signifies, in particular, that *every encounter* supposes on the part of any subject an acknowledgment of fact (in reality, Mr. X is bald), but also a period of waiting or anticipation (one necessarily phantasmatic and unnamable). Between this real vision and the period of waiting or the expected object, clearly a gap exists.

When "I" encounters he, I acknowledge he but nevertheless perceive the missing "He."

The same is true for a painting or a novel or a film.

Yet things become complicated when the work in question sends back to the ''I'' the representation of this distance, this yawning gap [*béance*].

Bergman's film *Scenes from a Marriage* is one example of this scenario. The couple represented is both enviable (exemplary to a degree) and blank; their love is both idealized and disappointing. Bergman thus refers us back to the usual desire-wish gap.

In advertising, on the contrary, as we show in the text that follows, it is in particular a question of *covering over* this gap.

2. It is not necessary, under the pretext of establishing art as an absolute, to declare it to be unconditionally subversive. To begin with, subversion is opposed to the idea of perversion and originates from the fact that it spawns desire more than need. Any so-called work of art is far from these criteria, and one will recall, on this issue, the everyday financial concerns of the art world. One can only recall the unspeakable litigation over Rothko's estate.

On the other hand, it is totally false to imagine that all advertising is unconditionally perverse. Sometimes advertising covers over desire less well than certain works of art.

See Lee Seldes, *The Legacy of Mark Rothko* (New York: Penguin Books, 1978).

3. Desire—primal and basic to psychic life—appeals to or nourishes phantasm. Yet we do not have a precise fix on this desire. Most of the time, on the contrary, we are faced with ''fragmentary desires'' or *drives* directed, for their part, toward real objects and that in this way represent, in the psychic apparatus, organic need.

Therefore we take note, in the final analysis, of two series of phenomena: one of psychic representation (desire leading to drive), the other by nature having more to do with the organism (instinct leading to need).

Advertising concerns itself little with desire, and greatly with drives. It therefore has to succeed in masking the first, yet retain its energy and set forward drive, since the latter and the latter alone will be satisfied in the real world.

One can therefore suggest—this is the case for our text—that advertising tries to posit drive in the place of desire, to make of it a kind of substitute for primal desire. The linkage ''sparkling beverage—bubbling brook—earthly paradise'' amply illustrates this strategy: brook and beverage are (the advertiser would have us believe) paradigmatically equivalent. One can be substituted for another.

All that remains, in this schema, is to insert a condition. Desire is reduced to (partial) drive, which can find satisfaction on *condition* of satisfying the (superegoistic) sacrifice of the purchase. It is here a matter of the fundamental appeal of the advertising gesture: the appeal to *specific action*.

4. See, on this subject, Milton Glaser, *Graphic Design* (Woodstock, New York: Overlook Press, 1973). The print advertisements collected in a book classified by bookstores in the art books category, strike us first of all as posters, the style of an author, when we discover that most of them are meant for advertising. The same phenomenon occurs with Folon and Mathieu.

5. For the use of the term *ideology*, from this point on we have sought to adopt the position of François Châtelet (*Histoire des idéologies*, vol. 1 [Paris: Hachette], 10-11). Given the importance of this concept, we believe it useful to cite this position as faithfully as possible. Thus we extract from his introduction these brief passages that we consider to be significant: ''This latter [the term *ideology*] is, today, it is true, overloaded with signification. According to classic sociology, it is collective representations and what binds a society together; for Ludwig Feuerbach, it is a projection in a reassuring imaginary universe of a contradictory and unsupportable real situation; for Karl Marx, an intellectual veil, 'a moral justification and spiritual flavor' broadcast by the dominant class to mask and mark its domination; for Louis Althusser, it is the place of a rhetoric incapable of justifying the production of its concepts and the diverted expression of the interests of a social stratum or class; a grab bag into which are thrown haphazardly all of the errors and stupidities, in other words all the adversary's ideas; according to today's current acceptance, ideology is at the very least a confused notion. . . . Qualified here as ideology is the more or less coherent system of images, ideas, ethical princi-

ples, global representations, and, as well, collective gestures, religious rituals, kinship structures, techniques of survival (and development), expressions that we now call artistic ones, mythic or philosophical discourses, power organizations, institutions, statements and forces that this latter sets into play, a system having as its goal to regulate in the heart of a collectivity, a people, a nation, a state, the relations individuals maintain with their own kind, with foreigners, with nature, with the imaginary, with the symbolic, with gods, hopes, life and death."

If we understand the term *ideology* in this sense, we believe in effect that advertising becomes one of its major lubricators, and particularly on the level of the human symbolic and imaginary orders that it continually tries to influence.

Whenever the term *ideology* is employed in what follows, it will be used in the sense of this note.

6. In the newspapers and periodicals of the end of the nineteenth century, one discovers a large number of advertising slogans that refer to this trilogy of strength, health, and courage: medical advertisements, but also incitive texts about life in the country, in the suburbs, etc.

See Max Gallo, *The Poster in History* (New York: McGraw-Hill, 1974).

7. The expression "twentieth-century man" is of course ambiguous. However, we maintain a parallel ambiguity.

In theory, the one we name "twentieth-century man" is only a very particular type of citizen who revels in speed and electronics, a kind of person who would fit right in with popular science and "the American way of life."

In reality, this person does not exist, or at least hardly exists at all. But don't worry: advertising is there not so much to speak to this person as to *constitute*, to *fabricate* this person.

"Twentieth-century man" does not exist or at least hardly exists at all. Yet, on the television screen, the existence of such a person is assumed and *proposed* on a daily basis, exactly the way Christian morality daily proposes the existence of *saints* or the way Marxist morality proposes the existence of *exemplary proletarians*.

8. The reader will by now have noticed the omission in this text of the term *society*. This term is, in effect, too ambiguous. It refers at once to Jewish Society, to the Society of Nations, to the Society of Horticulture in the canton of Whal. Equal ambiguity, equal polyvalence are of little help.

The idea of society or of a "great society" that we evoke here is, precisely, very blurred, abstract, and conceptual. Better: it is *imaginary*.

The nation that produced *Easy Rider* indeed wants to imagine itself (or be imagined) as one, as coherent, clearly identified, and as a consequence it calls itself (or wants to be called) a society.

Our intention—let there be no mistake—is not specifically anti-American. French society does not "exist," either—except in its own fiction, etc.

Chapter 3. Associative Drift

1. [Translator's note] The term *signifiance*, as opposed to *significance* or *meaning*, would stress the active process of a reader or spectator of an ensemble or sequence of signs whose intelligibility is not fixed but presumes a necessary interpretive participation. In this sense, *signifiance* would be the product of a process of reading whose outcome depends as much on the unnamed, sequential relations between signs encountered by a "subject" as on the logical sum of their combined punctual meanings. In other words, if *signification* could be reduced to the equation "one plus one is two," then *signifiance* would be "one plus one is always at least three." In his introduction to his translation of *Image/Music/Text*, Stephen Heath quotes Roland Barthes's own introduction to the term Julia Kristeva introduced in *Semiotiké: Recherches pour une sémanalyse* (Paris: Seuil, 1969): "when the text is read (or written) as a moving play of signifiers, without any possible reference to one or some fixed signifieds, it becomes necessary to distinguish signification, which belongs to the plane of the product, of the statement, of communication, and the work of the signifier, which belongs to the plane of production, of the process of stating, of symbolization—this work being called *signifiance*.

Signifiance is a *process* in the course of which the 'subject' of the text, escaping the logic of the *ego-cogito* and engaging in other logics (of the signifier, of contradiction), struggles with meaning and is deconstructed ('lost'); *signifiance*—and what immediately distinguishes it from signification is thus precisely a work: not the work by which the (intact and exterior) subject might try to master the language (as, for example, by a work of style), but that radical work (leaving nothing intact) through which the subject explores—entering, not observing—how the language works and undoes him. *Signifiance* is the 'un-end of possible operations in a given field of a language.' Contrary to signification, *signifiance* cannot be reduced, therefore, to communication, representation, expression: it places the heart of the subject (of writer, reader) in the text not as a projection . . . but as a 'loss,' a 'disappearance' '' (*Image/Music/Text*, 10, translation slightly modified).

2. [Translator's note] The term *scotomization* is introduced by Freud in his article "Fetishism" (1927) in order to challenge its use by Laforgue (1926) to account for the infant boy's perception of a woman's lack of a penis; in a footnote added later, Freud changes his mind, retracts his own initial attribution of his colleague's mistake, but nonetheless lets his initial argument stand. "Now a new term [scotomization] is justified when it describes a new fact or brings it into prominence. There is nothing of that kind here; the oldest word in our psychoanalytical terminology, 'repression,' already refers to this pathological process. If we wish to differentiate between what happens to the *idea* as distinct from the *affect*, we can restrict 'repression' to relate to the affect; the correct word for what happens to the idea is then 'denial.' 'Scotomization' seems to me particularly unsuitable, for it suggests that the perception is promptly obliterated, so that the result is the same as when a visual impression falls on the blind spot of the retina. In the case we are discussing, on the contrary, we see that the perception has persisted and that a very energetic action has been exerted to keep up the denial of it. It is not true that the child emerges from his experience of seeing the female parts with an unchanged belief in the woman having a phallus. He retains this belief but he also gives it up; during the conflict between the deadweight of the unwelcome perception and the force of the opposite wish, a compromise is constructed such as is only possible in the realm of unconscious modes of thought—by the primary processes. In the world of psychical reality the woman still has a penis in spite of all, but this penis is no longer the same as it once was. Something else has taken its place, has been appointed its successor, so to speak, and now absorbs all the interest which formerly belonged to the penis." (Sigmund Freud, "Fetishism," *Sexuality and the Psychology of Love*, translated by Joan Riviere [New York: Collier, 1963], 215–16).

Chapter 5. Religion, Perversion, Consumption

1. For Propp, then for Greimas, who once again brings up the issue and elaborates on it, the mythic or fairy tale would be constructed around four stages. *Disjunction:* the prince catches sight of the beauty but she is inaccessible to him. *Contract:* he could have the beauty if . . . *Trial:* he confronts the dragon, brings back the treasure. *Conjunction:* they get married and have many children. It seems to us that, in contrast to this narrative tale, the advertising prototype forgets the trial segment of this sequential construction. The contract is barely sketched where the untried conjunction takes place. This omission clearly reinforces the feeling of an easy life without castration of any kind and avoids the dynamic restatement of a problematic: since there is no trial, everyone can sleep in peace.

2. The notion of progradiance is here introduced on an intuitive level and, thereby, risks taking on unintended moral connotations. In order to open the question more rigorously, we should situate it with respect to two theoretical axes that currently mark a debate at the heart of contemporary psychoanalysis—the way that even theory carries with it its own problematics.

According to the first of these theoretical models, being is ruled by an instinctual life/death duality. And consequently, certain gestures or behaviors (for example, repetition and masochism) move in the direction of inertia whereas others aim for life, for drive and libidinal boost. From this perspective, the concept of progradiance would qualify the whole of those behaviors that drive toward life in opposition to those that lead to libidinal withdrawal, to a certain drive stagnation, and, final metaphor, to the state of inorganic death.

In the frame of the second model of theorization, being is split into narcissistic components and libidinal drive components. The narcissistic components try to reconstitute into existence a beatific state of being—corresponding to fetal well-being—where no effort is justified, where everything is provided by an ambient world. On the other hand, drive components actively seek out objects of investment, accept and manage conflict, in short, sustain the *life of relation*. Progradiance, the way we understand it here, to begin with qualifies this kind of more relational behavior.

Still, we will try to introduce a second notion, namely, progress, since merely looking for answers is not enough to actually progress. And we know all too well that pathology most often originates from answers that are either ready-made, static, or are recursive to problematics that require, fundamentally, more openness. Progradiance also qualifies human behavior moving in the direction of such an opening or, in more classical language, in the direction of *maturity*.

These two axes of theorization (life/death; libido of the object/narcissistic libido) in another way stress an important conceptual difficulty. If progradiance is marked, grossly, by libidinal or relational investments, it is false to declare that any narcissistic investment or any manifestation of the death drive should be intrinsically regradiant. Those who do not invest themselves narcissistically perish. Those who do not advocate an equilibrium's return to a state of rest die of exhaustion. Here psychoanalysis confronts a necessary theorization of the desired norm or vital equilibrium. Such a theorization is far from obvious at this moment of our evolution. And if it is desirable that we have definite ideas in this regard, it has to be recognized that such is not the case and that, to a very great degree, we will rely, normally, on a very instinctive model of human maturation.

3. [Translator's note] The reference here is to Lacan's famous distinction between ''objet A'' and ''objet a.'' See Jacques Lacan, *Ecrits*.

Bibliography

We provide here only principal works consulted for the present study.

Advertising

Barthes, Roland. *Mythologies*. Trans. Annette Lavers. New York: Hill and Wang, 1973.

Bedell, Clyde. *How to Write Advertising That Sells*. New York: McGraw-Hill, 1952.

Bogart, Leo. *Strategy in Advertising*. New York: Harcourt Brace and World, 1967.

Bouchard, Jacques. *Les 36 cordes sensibles des Québécois*. Montreal: Editions Héritage, 1976.

_____. *L'autre publicité: la publicité sociétale*. Montreal: Editions Héritage, 1981.

Brochand, Bernard, and Jacques Lendrevie. *Le publicitor*. Paris: Dalloz, 1983.

Brune, François. *Le bonheur conforme*. Paris: Gallimard, 1981.

Cadet, André, and Bernard Cathelat. *La publicité*. Paris: Payot, 1968.

Chenz. "Marty Evans . . . représentant de la 'grande' photographie publicitaire." *Zoom* 60 (March 1979): 42–56.

Club des directeurs artistiques. *Bilan*. Paris, 1968–81.

Collet, M. *Publicité et arts graphiques*. Geneva, 1969.

Dichter, Ernest. *The Strategy of Desire*. Garden City, N.Y.: Doubleday, 1960.

Durand, Jacques. "Rhétorique et image publicitaire." *L'analyse des images. Communications* 15 (Paris, 1970): 70–95.

Enel, F. *L'affiche, fonctions, langage, rhétorique*. Paris: Mame, 1971.

Galli, G., et al. "Modelli e valori nella pubblicità televisiva." *Quaderni di IKON* 12 (1970).

Glatzer, R. *The New Advertising*. New York: Citadel Press, 1970.

Hirschberg, L. "When You Absolutely, Positively Want the Best." *Esquire,* August 1983: 53–60.

Joannis, H. *Le processus de la création publicitaire*. Paris: Dunod, 1978.

Key, W. S. *Subliminal Seduction*. Englewood Cliffs, N. J.: Prentice-Hall, 1973.

Kluzer, Andrea. "Consumi sociali e pubblicità." *Il millimetro* 33 (February 1972): 4–31.

Lagneau, Gérard. *Le faire-vouloir*. Paris: S.A.B.R.I., 1969.

Lavoisier, Benedicte. *Mon corps, ton corps, leur corps*. Paris: Seghers, 1978.

Leduc, Robert. *How to Launch a New Product*. London: Crosby Lockwood, 1966.

––––––. *La publicité, une force au service de l'entreprise*. Paris: Bordas, 1982.

Longman, Kenneth A. *Advertising*. New York: Harcourt Brace Jovanovich, 1971.

Manescau, J. "Les meilleures campagnes publicitaires de Ben Oynes." *Le photographe* 1367 (January 1980): 39–52.

––––––. "Pub télé: éroticisme en direct." *Il* 49 (March 1983): 48–55.

"Les mythes de la publicité." *Communications* 17 (1971). Texts by Friedmann, Péninou, Lagneau et al.

Ogilvy, David. *Confessions of an Advertising Man*. New York: Atheneum, 1963.

Péninou, G. *Intelligence de la publicité*. Paris: Laffont, 1978.

Porter, M. "That's Why the P. C. Is a Tramp." *P. C. Magazine* 1983: 329–36.

Séguéla, J. *Ne dites pas à ma mère que je suis publicitaire*. Paris: Flammarion, 1979.

––––––. *Hollywood lave plus blanc*. Paris: Flammarion, 1982.

Swinners, J. L., and J. M. Briet. *Les dix campagnes du siècle*. Marello-Veyrace, 1978.

Victoroff, D. *Psychologie de la publicité*. Paris: PUF, 1970.

––––––. *La publicité et l'image*. Paris: Denoël Gonthier, 1978.

Watier, Maurice. *La publicité*. Montreal: Pauline and Médiaspaul, 1983.

Semiotics, History, Sociology

"L'analyse structurale du récit." *Communications* 8 (1966). Articles by Barthes, Eco, Griti, et al.

Arendt, Hannah. *The Life of the Mind: Thinking*. New York: Harcourt Brace Jovanovich, 1978.

––––––. *The Life of the Mind: Willing*. New York: Harcourt Brace Jovanovich, 1978.

Austin, J. L. *How to Do Things with Words*. London: Oxford University Press, 1962.

Barnicoat, John. *A Concise History of Posters*. London: Thames and Hudson, 1972.

Barthes, Roland. *Image/Music/Text*. Essays selected and translated by Stephen Heath. New York: Hill & Wang, 1977.

––––––. *The Fashion System*. Trans. Matthew Ward and Richard Howard. New York: Hill & Wang, 1983.

Baudrillard, Jean. *Le système des objets*. Paris: Seuil, 1967.

––––––. *Seduction*. Trans. Brian Singer. New York: St. Martin's, 1990.

Benveniste, Emile. *Problems in General Linguistics*. Trans. Mary Elizabeth Meek. Coral Gables, Fla.: University of Miami Press, 1971.

Brecht, Bertolt. *Sur le cinéma*. Paris: L'Arche, 1970.

Castoriadis, Cornelius. *The Imaginary Institution of Society*. Trans. Kathleen Blamey. Cambridge, Mass.: MIT Press, 1987.

Châtelet, François. *Histoire des idéologies*. Paris: Hachette, 1978.

"Cinéma." *Revue d'esthétique* (1973), special issue organized by Dominique Noguez.

Collectif. *Sémiologie de la représentation*. Brussels: Complexe, 1975.

Covin, M. "A la recherche du signifiant iconique." *Revue d'esthétique* 1977.

de Saussure, Ferdinand. *Course in General Linguistics*. Trans. and annotated by Roy Harris. London: Duckworth, 1983.

Diel, Paul. *Symbolism in Greek Mythology*. Trans. Vincent Stuart, Micheline Stuart, and Rebecca Folkman. New York: Random House, 1980.

Ducrot, Oswald, and Tzvetan Todorov. *Encyclopedic Dictionary of the Sciences of Language*. Trans. Catherine Porter. Baltimore: The Johns Hopkins University Press, 1979.

Eco, Umberto. *La structure absente*. Paris: Mercure de France, 1972.

––––––. *The Open Work*. Trans. Anna Cancogni. Cambridge, Mass.: Harvard University Press, 1989.

Foucault, Michel. *Madness and Civilization*. Trans. Richard Howard. New York: Pantheon, 1965.
_____. *Discipline and Punish: The Birth of the Prison*. Trans. Alan Sheridan. New York: Pantheon, 1977.
Fresnault-Deruelle, Pierre. *L'image manipulée*. Paris: Edilig, 1983.
Gallo, Max. *The Poster in History*. Trans. Alfred and Bruni Mayor. New York: McGraw-Hill, 1974.
Genette, Gérard. "Essai d'analyse narrative." *Problèmes d'analyse textuelle* 1971: 177–89.
Girard, René. *The Violence and the Sacred*. Trans. Patrick Gregory. Baltimore: The Johns Hopkins University Press, 1977.
Goffman, Erving. *Strategic Interaction*. Philadelphia: University of Pennsylvania Press, 1969.
Greimas, Algirdas Julien. *Structural Semantics*. Trans. Danielle McDowell, Ronald Schleifer, and Alan Velie. Lincoln: University of Nebraska Press, 1983.
_____. *On Meaning*. Trans. Paul J. Perron and Frank Collins. Minneapolis: University of Minnesota Press, 1987.
_____. "Image(s) et culture(s)." *Communications* 29 (1978).
Kracauer, Siegfried. *From Calgari to Hitler*. Princeton, N. J.: Princeton University Press, 1947.
Kristeva, Julia. "Narration et transformation." Paris: *Semiotica,* 1964.
_____. *Recherches pour une sémanalyse*. Paris: Seuil, 1969.
_____. *Polylogue*. Paris: Seuil, 1977.
Kuntzel, Thierry. "The Film-Work." Trans. Larry Crawford. *Enclitic* 2, no. 1 (Spring 1978): 38–61.
Lasch, Christopher. *The Culture of Narcissism*. New York: Norton, 1978.
Lévi-Strauss, Claude. *The Savage Mind*. Trans. Claire Jacobson and Brook Grandfert Schoepf. New York: Basic Books, 1963.
_____. *Anthropologie structurale deux*. Paris: Plon, 1973.
Les sciences humaines et l'oeuvre d'art. Brussels: La Connaissance, 1969. Texts by Marin, Lascault, et al.
Lyotard, Jean-François. *Discours, figure*. Paris: Klincksieck, 1971.
_____. *Economie libidinale*. Paris: Minuit, 1974.
Marin, Louis. *Etudes sémiologiques*. Paris: Klincksieck, 1972.
Martinez, A. *Eléments de linguistique générale*. Paris: Armand Colin, 1970.
Melon, M. *La télévision dans la famille et la société moderne*. Paris: Editions Sociales, 1969.
Metz, Christian. "Remarques sur le mot et le chiffre." *La linguistique* 1967.
_____. "Spécificité des codes et spécificité des langages." *Semiotica* 1969.
_____. "L'étude sémiologique du langage cinématographique." *Revue d'esthétique* (2–3–4), 1973.
_____. *Film Language*. Trans. Michael Taylor. New York: Oxford University Press, 1974.
_____. *Language and Cinema*. Trans. Donna Jean Umiker-Sebeok. The Hague: Mouton, 1974.
_____. *The Imaginary Signifier*. Trans. Celia Brown, Annwyl Williams, Ben Brewster, and Alfred Guzzetti. Bloomington: Indiana University Press, 1982.
Morin, Edgar. *La méthode: La nature de la nature*. Paris: Seuil, 1977.
Nigili, A. *International Poster Annual*. Tefven, 1967.
Propp, Vladimir. *Morphology of the Folk Tale*. Trans. Laurence Scott. Austin: University of Texas Press, 1968.
Ropars-Willeumier, Marie-Claire. *L'écran de la mémoire*. Paris: Seuil, 1970.
_____. *Le texte divisé*. Paris: PUF, 1981.
Searle, John R. *Speech Acts*. London: Cambridge University Press, 1969.
Serres, Michel. *La naissance de la physique dans le texte de Lucrèce*. Paris: Minuit, 1977.
_____. *The Parasite*. Trans. Lawrence R. Schehr. Baltimore: The Johns Hopkins University Press, 1982.
Tchakotine, S. *Le viol des foules par la propagande politique*. Paris: Gallimard, 1952.
Vernet, Marc. *La diffraction paradigmatique et syntagmatique*. Brussels: Degris, 1973.
Waldman, Diane. *Mark Rothko 1903–1970*. New York: Abrams, 1978.

Warner, Rex. *The Stories of the Greeks*. New York: Farrar, Straus & Giroux, 1967.
Yanker, Gary. *Prop Art*. Paris: Planète, 1972.

Psychoanalysis

Abraham, Karl. *Selected Papers*. New York: Basic Books, 1953–55.
Amaldo, G. *Fondements de la psychopathologie*. Paris: PUF, 1982.
Arlow, Jacob A. "Ego Psychology and the Study of Mythology." *Journal of the American Psychoanalytical Association* 9 (1961): 371–93.
———. "Fantasy, Memory and Reality Testing." *Psychoanalytical Quarterly* 38 (1969): 28–51.
Arlow, Jacob A., and C. Brenner. *Psychoanalytic Concepts and the Structural Theory*. New York: International Universities Press [n. d.].
Bettelheim, Bruno. *Symbolic Wounds*. Glencoe, Ill.: Free Press, 1954.
———. *The Uses of Enchantment: The Meaning and Importance of Fairy Tales*. New York: Knopf, 1976.
Bigras, J. *Les images de la mère*. Montreal: Hachette, 1971.
Bion, Wilfred R. *Elements of Psychoanalysis*. New York: Basic Books, 1963.
———. *Learning from Experience*. New York: Basic Books, 1963.
———. *Transformations*. New York: Basic Books, 1965.
Bouvet, M. *Oeuvres psychanalytiques*. Paris: Payot, 1967.
Bowlby, John. *Separation, Anxiety and Anger*. New York: Basic Books, 1973.
"Cinéma et psychanalyse II," *Ça cinéma* 16. Articles by Metz, Bellour, Rose, et al.
De M'Uzan, M. *De l'art à la mort*. Paris: Gallimard, 1977.
Désir et perversion. Paris: Seuil, 1967. Texts by Joyce McDougall, De M'Uzan, et al.
Dufrenne, Roger. *Bibliographie des écrits de Freud*. Paris: Payot, 1973.
Enriquez, E. *De la horde à l'etat*. Paris: Gallimard, 1983.
Entretiens sur l'art et la psychanalyse. (Cerisy-la-Salle, 1962). The Hague: Mouton, 1968. Articles by Clancier, Green, et al.
Fenichel. *The Psychoanalytic Theory of Neurosis*. New York: Vail-Ballou, 1945.
Freud, Sigmund. *Delusion and Dream*. Trans. Helen M. Downey. New York: Moffet, Yard, 1917.
———. *Inhibitions, Symptoms and Anxiety*. Trans. Alix Strachey. London: Hogarth, 1936.
———. *Totem and Taboo*. Trans. James Strachey. New York: Norton, 1952.
———. *Civilization and Its Discontents*. Trans. James Strachey. New York: Norton, 1962.
Green, André. *Narcissism de vie, narcissisme de mort*. Paris: Minuit, 1983.
Greenstadt, M. William. "Heracles: A Hero Figure of the Rapprochement Crisis." *International Review of Psycho-Analysis* 9, no. 1 (1982): 1–23.
Grunberger, B. *Le narcissisme*. Paris: Payot, 1971.
Haineault, Doris-Louise. "L'arrache-désir." *Interprétation* 1979: 255–64.
Haineault, Doris-Louise, and Jean-Yves Roy. "Les dieux que l'on consomme." *Recherches québécoises sur la télévision*. Montreal: Editions Coopératives Albert St.-Martin, 1980.
Jacobson, Edith. *The Self and the Object World*. London: Hogarth, 1965.
Irigaray, Luce. *This Sex Which Is Not One*. Trans. Catherine Porter with Carolyn Burke. Ithaca, N. Y.: Cornell University Press, 1985.
Khan, Masud. *Le soi caché*. Paris: Gallimard, 1976.
Klein, Melanie. *The Writings of Melanie Klein*. London: Hogarth, 1975.
Klein, Melanie, Paula Heimann, and Roger Money-Kyrle. *New Directions in Psychoanalysis*. London: Maresfield Reprints, 1977.
Krys. *Psychanalyse de l'art*. Paris: PUF, 1978.
Kristeva, Julia. *Powers of Horror*. Trans. Leon Roudiez. New York: Columbia University Press, 1982.

_____. *Tales of Love*. Trans. Leon Roudiez. New York: Columbia University Press, 1987.

Lacan, Jacques. *Ecrits. A Selection*. Trans. Alan Sheridan. New York: Norton, 1977.

_____. *The Four Fundamental Concepts of Psychoanalysis*. Trans. Alan Sheridan. New York: Norton, 1979.

Leclaire, Serge. *On tue un enfant*. Paris: Seuil, 1975.

_____. *Rompre les charmes*. Paris: Inter Editions, 1981.

Lussier, A. *Les déviations du désir*. Conference held in Montreal, Sept. 1–4, 1982.

McDougall, J. *Plea for a Measure of Abnormality*. New York: International Universities Press, 1980.

_____. *Theaters of the Mind: Illusion and Truth on the Psychoanalytic Stage*. New York: Basic Books, 1985.

Mahler, Margaret. *Selected Papers V.* New York: J. Aronson, 1979.

Major, René. *Rêver l'autre*. Paris: Aubier-Montaigne, 1977.

_____. *L'agonie du jour*. Paris: Aubier-Montaigne, 1979.

Meltzer, Donald. *Sexual States of Mind*. Ballinluig: Clunie Press, 1973.

_____. *Les structures sexuelles de la vie psychique*. Paris: Payot, 1977.

Montrelay, Michèle. *L'ombre et le nom*. Paris: Minuit, 1977.

Moscovici, Serge. *La psychanalyse, son image et son public*. Paris: PUF, 1961.

_____. *Introduction à la psychologie sociale* 1 and 2. Paris: Larousse, 1972–73.

Olivier, C. *Les infants de Jocaste*. Paris: Dënoel Gonthier, 1980.

Ortony, Andrew, ed. *Metaphor and Thought*. London: Cambridge University Press, 1979.

Pontalis, J. B. *Entre le rêve et la douleur*. Paris: Gallimard, 1977.

Psychanalyse des arts de l'image (Colloque de Cerisy). Paris: Clancier-Guenard, 1981. Texts by Anne Clancier, Henriette Bessis, et al.

"Psychanalyse et cinéma." *Communications* 23 (1975). Texts by Barthes, Bellour, Kristeva, Kuntzel, Metz, et al.

"Psychanalyse et engagement." *Interprétation* 3, no. 3, (July–September, 1969).

Reik, Theodor. *Listening with the Third Ear*. New York: Farrar Straus Giroux, 1983.

Roy, Jean-Yves. *Etre psychiatre*. Montreal: Etincelle, 1977.

Searles, Harold F. *Collected Works on Schizophrenia*. London: Hogarth, 1965.

_____. *Counter Transference and Related Subjects*. New York: International Universities Press, 1979.

Tristiani, J. L. *Le stade du respir*. Paris: Minuit, 1978.

Viderman, Serge. *La construction de l'espace analytique*. Paris: Denoël, 1970.

_____. *Le céleste et le sublunaire*. Paris: PUF, 1977.

Volmatr, Wiart. *Art and Psychopathology*. Amsterdam: Excerta Medica Foundation, 1969.

Winnicott, D. W. *Playing and Reality*. London: Tavistock, 1971.

_____. *Through Paediatricians to Psychoanalysis*. London: Hogarth, 1975.

Index

Compiled by Hassan Melehy

Names and terms

Theory and History of Literature

Doris-Louise Haineault and **Jean-Yves Roy** are both practicing psycho-analysts in Montreal, Quebec.

Kimball Lockhart has taught in the departments of French and Italian and Humanities at the University of Minnesota. He is the editor of *The Film Issue* (*Diacritics* 15, no. 1 [Spring 1985]) and the author of *Foibles,* a forthcoming collection of fiction.

Wlad Godzich is professor of emergent literatures at the University of Geneva.